Praise for Bill Wagner and
The Entrepreneur Next Door

*For anyone who aspires to the challenges of entrepren[eurship]
It is the most comprehensive and useful source on th[e]
actions required to achieve entrepreneu[rship]*

—MARK EDWARDS, PH.D., PROFESSOR, STRATEGIC MARKETING AND ENTREPRENEURSHIP,
ARIZONA STATE UNIVERSITY AND CEO OF TALENTDNA

*Bill Wagner's timing is perfect. Opportunities abound for entrepreneurs today, and
The Entrepreneur Next Door arrives just in time. Whether you're a born
businessperson or what Bill calls a "wantapreneur," this book gives you a
step-by-step blueprint to success. Thank you, Bill, for disproving the adage
that only some people can be great entrepreneurs.*

—RAFAEL PASTOR, CHAIRMAN OF THE BOARD AND CEO, VISTAGE INTERNATIONAL

*I never thought that a book entitled The Entrepreneur Next Door would attract
my attention, let alone keep it. I like the approach of starting with a deep personal
analysis—a sense of self, and then moving on from there. These points of contact
are content hooks that pulled me along in the process of seeing where I fit in.
Especially interesting is the ability to see exactly where you are. Using the tools
in the book make that effect even more powerful. This is a book for doubters
and nay-sayers. It's a conversion experience!*

—MICHAEL T. HILLER, VICE PRESIDENT ADMINISTRATION, STANFORD FEDERAL CREDIT UNION

*Bill Wagner has an uncanny, objective understanding of the dynamics of the
workplace environment and in this engaging and humorous book, he shares
his insights, candor, and ability to take a complex subject such as personality,
bring it to life and make it understandable.*

—MATTHEW SHAY, PRESIDENT 2006, INTERNATIONAL FRANCHISE ASSOCIATION

The Entrepreneur Next Door *is a must read for anyone considering a future in franchising. At It's A Grind Coffee House, we are always looking for an entrepreneur with the ideal personality for our business. They are more successful, achieve greater growth sooner, and certainly are more enjoyable to work with. Bill's five tier Performance Pyramid is one of the best cognitive processes I have seen in managing the growth of our franchisees.* The Entrepreneur Next Door *truly brings it home and the reader with it. It works! Read it, learn and get ready to grow.*

—STEVE OLSON, SENIOR VICE PRESIDENT, IT'S A GRIND COFFEE HOUSE

The information found in The Entrepreneur Next Door *will take any person regardless of their background to new heights in their personal and professional development. From struggling business owners to the salesperson on the street, the useful and practical strategies offered by Bill Wagner should be at the top of everyone's "must read" list, especially if they are serious about being successful. If you and your company want to do more, be more, and have more, then* The Entrepreneur Next Door *will take you to the next level and beyond.*

—CHUCK BAUER, SALES COACH, DALLAS TEXAS

Congratulations on your book, it is a major effort that will certainly cement your reputation in the world of entrepreneurial scholarship! I appreciate having the opportunity to read this great academic work! Best of luck for a blockbuster success!

—GORDON LOGAN, CEO, SPORTS CLIPS, INC.

Bill has an amazing ability to disarm type-A executives. His book helped my colleagues and I learn how to use our natural strengths to become better leaders, better spouses, better parents and better people! I learned how to use my strengths to deliver better service and develop a more profitable company.

—KIM ELLIS, PRESIDENT, BISON ADVERTISING, INC

Just when you think you've seen it all, an entirely different type of profiling emerges which demonstrates the seemingly limitless possibilities in understanding human behavior and its impact on performance and job match. We now have the tool to build an 'awesome' team.

—RONALD L. MCDANIEL, PRESIDENT, POINT MUGU FEDERAL CREDIT UNION

Bill Wagner has unique insights into the characteristics and behaviors of entrepreneurs. Are certain people better 'wired' for succeeding in business than others? Bill Wagner seems to know.

—JOE MATHEWS, FRANCHISE PERFORMANCE GROUP, CO-AUTHOR STREET SMART FRANCHISING

In my opinion, Bill's involvement with The Lloyd Group has been a key factor in our continued growth and success.

—ADAM L. EISEMAN, CEO, THE LLOYD GROUP

In a graduate school of business, we cover an enormous number of topics. I wish we had a class solely to learn and understand the impact of one's personality on their ultimate choice of endeavor and success. Your content is one of the most useful and long-reaching messages my students have had.

—KATE MCKEOWN, PROFESSOR, ENTREPRENEUR, FORDHAM UNIVERSITY

You have contributed greatly to the growth and education of our YEO membership. Rarely have I worked with a company that provides so much. Your presentations at all YEO's International Conferences and universities always receive extremely high ratings and your exceptional knowledge provides our members with valuable take-home value.

—RICHARD BRIGHT, MARKETING AND COMMUNICATIONS DIRECTOR,
YOUNG ENTREPRENEURS' ORGANIZATION (YEO)

In an organization such as ours we both expect and demand the best. You have come through for us again and again. Because of our position in the industry we can often times be very picky as to the vendors and consultants we embrace and our selection of your firm has been one of our better decisions.

—DON J. DEBOLT, PRESIDENT 2004, INTERNATIONAL FRANCHISE ASSOCIATION

Bill has given us great insight into how different characteristics perform and helped us assess what kinds of people are better suited in each kind of unique job-related roles. Embracing Bill's systems is a rock-solid investment.

—JEFF WALKER, CEO, SUPER D/PHANTOM DISTRIBUTION

You helped our members to anticipate company growth issues and look realistically at the future of their businesses. More importantly, you created an understanding how their own behaviors and actions affect their personal growth potential.

—Robert S. Morgan, President, Council of Growing Companies

In a world where everyone seems to be plugging their latest and greatest, Bill Wagner and his team at Accord Management Systems deliver. We now understand what makes our employees and franchise owners tick and are therefore able to create custom-tailored solutions to meet everyone's needs.

—Rick Basch, Vice President, The Little Gym International

Bill Wagner

The
Entrepreneur
Next Door

Discover the Secrets to Financial Independence

EP
Entrepreneur.
Press

Editorial director: Jere L. Calmes
Cover design: Barry T. Kerrigan
Composition and production: Eliot House Productions

This publication is designed to provide accurate and authoritative information in regard to the subject matter covered. It is sold with the understanding that the publisher is not engaged in rendering legal, accounting, or other professional services. If legal advice or other expert assistance is required, the services of a competent professional person should be sought.

Library of Congress Cataloging-in-Publication Data
Wagner, Bill.
The entrepreneur next door/by Bill Wagner.
    p.   cm.
ISBN 1-932531-96-3 (9781932531961 : alk. paper)
1. Entrepreneurship. I. Title.
HB615.W32 2006
658.02'2—dc22   2006004269

Printed in Canada

11 10 09 08 07 06   10 9 8 7 6 5 4 3 2 1

Contents

Acknowledgments _____ xv

Foreword: *Create Your Own Declaration of Independence*
   by Jeffrey Gitomer _____ xvii

Preface _____ xxi

PART I

Who Is the Entrepreneur Next Door?

CHAPTER 1
How to Succeed in Business: The First Time _____ 3

Who IS the Entrepreneur Next Door? _____ 5

Choice and Destiny _____ 6

The Greatest Knowledge Is Self-Knowledge _____ 9

Entrepreneurs vs. Prodigious Savers from *The Millionaire Next Door* _____ 10

Climbing the Performance Pyramid _____ 11

Chapter 1: The Bottom Line _____ 18

CHAPTER 2

**Your Personality Can
Pave the Way to Success** _____ 19

Why Personality? _____ 21

What Determines Success or Failure? _____ 23

Tools, Tests, Surveys, and Assessments _____ 24

The Role EQ Plays in Business _____ 31

Knowledge and Behavior Aspects _____ 32

In Their Own Words: What Entrepreneurs Said about Starting a Business __ 34

Chapter 2: The Bottom Line _____ 40

CHAPTER 3

Are You an Entrepreneur or a Wantapreneur? _____ 41

Putting It Into Perspective _____ 49

Chapter 3: The Bottom Line _____ 61

CHAPTER 4

How the Four Personality Factors Work _____ 63

The Four Factors _____ 64

In Their Own Words: Where Entrepreneurs Got the
   Ideas to Start Their Own Businesses _____ 68

Chapter 4: The Bottom Line _____ 71

CHAPTER 5

Entrepreneurs and Wantapreneurs _____ 73

Trailblazers _____ 74

Go-Getters _____ 75

Managers _____ 77

Motivators _____ 79

Authorities _____ 81

Collaborators _____ 82

Diplomats _____ 84

Personality Factors and Entrepreneurship _____ 85

Chapter 5: The Bottom Line _____ 92

CHAPTER 6

The DNA of Entrepreneurial Success _____ 93

The Benefits of Understanding Personality _____ 94

Short-Term Personality Changes_____ 96

Find the Long-Term Personality _____ 99

Chapter 6: The Bottom Line _____ 100

CHAPTER 7

Triumphs and Tragedies _____ 101

In Their Own Words: What Entrepreneurs Said about

   Their Defining Moments _____ 103

Trailblazers' Strengths and Weaknesses_____ 105

Go-Getters' Strengths and Weaknesses _____ 108

Managers' Strengths and Weaknesses_____ 110

Motivators' Strengths and Weaknesses _____ 112

Authorities' Strengths and Weaknesses _____ 114

Collaborators' Strengths and Weaknesses _____ 118

Diplomats' Strengths and Weaknesses _____ 120

Strength and Weakness Self-Assessment _____ 123

Personal Action Plan _____ 123

Chapter 7: The Bottom Line _____ 130

CHAPTER 8

Entrepreneurs and Wantapreneurs:
What Drives Them_____ 131

Lessons Learned _____ 133

In Their Own Words: What Entrepreneurs Said about

   Defining Moments in Their Personal Lives _____ 133

Trailblazers' Motivation _____ 135

Go-Getters' Motivation _____ 138

Managers' Motivation _____ 139

Motivators' Motivation _____ 142

The Role Self-Awareness Plays _____ 145

Authorities' Motivation _____ 145

Collaborators' Motivation_____ 148

Diplomats' Motivation _____ 150

Motivation Self-Assessment_____ 152

Working Style Self-Assessment _____ 152

Chapter 8: The Bottom Line _____ 153

PART II

How Entrepreneurs and Wantapreneurs Operate

CHAPTER 9

Education and Experience _____ 157

Education _____ 158

Experience _____ 160

Background _____ 162

Job-Fit _____ 163

In Their Own Words: What Entrepreneurs Said

   They've Learned from Their Experience _____ 165

   What Entrepreneurs Said about Surprise Business Challenges _____ 166

Chapter 9: The Bottom Line _____ 167

CHAPTER 10

How Entrepreneurs and Wantapreneurs Learn _____ 169

Trailblazers' Learning Style _____ 170

Go-Getters' Learning Style _____ 171

Managers' Learning Style _____ 172

Motivators' Learning Style _____ 173

Authorities' Learning Style _____ 174

Collaborators' Learning Style _____ 175

Diplomats' Learning Style_____ 176

Learning Style Self-Assessment _____ 177

Chapter 10: The Bottom Line_____ 178

CHAPTER 11

How Entrepreneurs and Wantapreneurs Lead or Manage _____ 179

The People Factors _____ 180

Growing Leadership Skills _ 184

In Their Own Words: The Single Most Important
  Experience/Knowledge that Prepared Entrepreneurs
  to be CEOs or Leaders _ 188

How Specific Personality Styles Lead _ _ _ _ _ _ _ _ _ _ _ _ _ _ _ _ _ _ _ 190

Trailblazers' Leadership Style _ 190

Go-Getters' Leadership Style _ 191

Managers' Leadership Style _ 192

Motivators' Leadership Style _ 194

Authorities' Leadership Style _ 195

Collaborators' Leadership Style _ 196

Diplomats' Leadership Style _ 198

Leadership Style Self-Assessment _ 200

Chapter 11: The Bottom Line _ 201

CHAPTER 12

Knowledge Is the World's Equalizer _ _ _ _ _ _ _ _ _ _ _ _ **203**

Building Consensus _ 205

In Their Own Words: What Entrepreneurs
  Said about Sound Advice _ 207

Personal Development Self-Assessment _ _ _ _ _ _ _ _ _ _ _ _ _ _ _ _ _ _ 209

Chapter 12: The Bottom Line _ 209

CHAPTER 13

How Entrepreneurs and Wantapreneurs Sell _ _ _ _ _ _ _ **211**

Trailblazers' Selling Style _ 214

Go-Getters' Selling Style _ 215

Managers' Selling Style _ 216

Motivators' Selling Style _ 218

Authorities' Selling Style _ 219

Collaborators' Selling Style _ 221

Diplomats' Selling Style _ 222

Selling Style Self-Assessment _ 223

Chapter 13: The Bottom Line _ 224

PART III

Win, Lose, or Draw

CHAPTER 14

What Makes Personalities Tick and What Ticks Them Off _____ 227

Trailblazers' Code of Conduct _____ 228

Go-Getters' Code of Conduct_____ 229

Managers' Code of Conduct _____ 230

Motivators' Code of Conduct_____ 231

Authorities' Code of Conduct _____ 233

Collaborators' Code of Conduct _____ 234

Diplomats' Code of Conduct_____ 235

Code of Conduct Self-Assessment _____ 236

Chapter 14: The Bottom Line_____ 236

CHAPTER 15

Beating the Odds _____ 237

Turning Developmental Considerations into Strengths _____ 238

Goal-Orientation and Motivation _____ 241

Emotional Expression _____ 242

Social Insight and Empathy _____ 243

In Their Own Words: What Entrepreneurs Said about
   Their Biggest Challenges _____ 244

Chapter 15: The Bottom Line_____ 247

CHAPTER 16

How Entrepreneurs and Wantapreneurs Beat the Odds with the Performance Pyramid _____ 249

Trailblazers_____ 250

Go-Getters_____ 250

Managers _____ 251

Motivators _____ 251

Authorities_____ 251

Collaborators _____ 252

Diplomats _____ 252

Personality Style Self-Assessment _ 253

Chapter 16: The Bottom Line _ 254

CHAPTER 17

**The Goldilocks Theory: Creating an
Organization That's Just Right** _ _ _ _ _ _ _ _ _ _ _ _ _ _ _ **255**

Situation and Challenge I _ 256

Situation and Challenge II _ 258

Situation and Challenge III _ 259

Situation and Challenge IV _ 259

Situation and Challenge V _ 262

Situation and Challenge VI _ 263

Now What? _ 263

In Their Own Words: What Entrepreneurs Said about
   the Corporate Environment _ 265

   What Entrepreneurs Said Sets Their Company Apart _ _ _ _ _ _ _ _ _ _ _ 266

   What Entrepreneurs Said about Their Greatest Business Challenges _ _ _ _ 267

   What Entrepreneurs Said They Have to Accomplish Before Retiring _ _ _ _ 269

Bibliography _ **271**

Books _ 271

Article _ 272

About the Author _ **273**

Glossary _ **275**

Index _ **279**

List of Figures

Figure 1.1: Performance Pyramid _ 11

Figure 1.2: Personality Factors _ 13

Figure 1.3: Entrepreneurial Elements _ 14

Figure 2.1: Entrepreneurial Elements Measured by the HBDI _ _ _ _ _ _ _ _ 25

Figure 2.2: The Ideal Entrepreneur _ 26

Figure 2.3: Sample Entrepreneur EQ Survey Result _ _ _ _ _ _ _ _ _ _ _ _ _ _ 32

Figure 3.1: Your Entrepreneurial Profile _ _ _ _ _ _ _ _ _ _ _ _ _ _ _ _ _ _ _ 42

Figure 5.1: Trailblazer Personality Graph _ _ _ _ _ _ _ _ _ _ _ _ _ _ _ _ _ _ 74

Figure 5.2: Go-Getter Personality Graph _ _ _ _ _ _ _ _ _ _ _ _ _ _ _ _ _ _ 76

Figure 5.3: Manager Personality Graph _ _ _ _ _ _ _ _ _ _ _ _ _ _ _ _ _ _ _ 78

Figure 5.4: Motivator Personality Graph _ _ _ _ _ _ _ _ _ _ _ _ _ _ _ _ _ 80

Figure 5.5: Authority Personality Graph _ _ _ _ _ _ _ _ _ _ _ _ _ _ _ _ _ _ 81

Figure 5.6: Collaborator Personality Graph _ _ _ _ _ _ _ _ _ _ _ _ _ _ _ _ _ 83

Figure 5.7: Diplomat Personality Graph _ _ _ _ _ _ _ _ _ _ _ _ _ _ _ _ _ _ _ 85

Figure 5.8: Male & Female Entrepreneurs Are More Alike _ _ _ _ _ _ _ _ _ _ 86

Figure 5.9: Female vs. Male Entrepreneur Graphs _ _ _ _ _ _ _ _ _ _ _ _ _ _ 88

Figure 5.10: Deviation in the McQuaig System™ _ _ _ _ _ _ _ _ _ _ _ _ _ _ 89

Figure 5.11: YEO Chart of Personality Types (N=1,509) _ _ _ _ _ _ _ _ _ _ _ 90

Figure 6.1: Dating or Vacation Personality _ _ _ _ _ _ _ _ _ _ _ _ _ _ _ _ _ 97

Figure 7.1: Personal Action Plan—Strengths _ _ _ _ _ _ _ _ _ _ _ _ _ _ _ _ 124

Figure 7.2: Personal Action Plan—Developmental Areas _ _ _ _ _ _ _ _ _ _ 125

Figure 7.3: Your Personal Action Plan—Strengths _ _ _ _ _ _ _ _ _ _ _ _ _ 127

Figure 7.4: Your Personal Action Plan—Developmental Areas _ _ _ _ _ _ _ _ 128

Figure 9.1: Graduation Rates _ 158

Figure 9.2: Grades* _ 159

Figure 9.3: Age When Started First Business _ _ _ _ _ _ _ _ _ _ _ _ _ _ _ _ 161

Figure 9.4: Occupation of Entrepreneur's Parents _ _ _ _ _ _ _ _ _ _ _ _ _ 163

Figure 9.5: The Best Salespeople _ 164

Figure 11.1: Surprise Business Challenges _ _ _ _ _ _ _ _ _ _ _ _ _ _ _ _ _ 180

Figure 11.2: Top Three People Challenges _ _ _ _ _ _ _ _ _ _ _ _ _ _ _ _ _ 181

Figure 11.3: Effectiveness of Leaders in Your Organization _ _ _ _ _ _ _ _ _ 183

Figure 11.4: Point Easy _ 197

Figure 12.1: Time Spent on Personal Development/Education (Annual) _ _ _ 204

Figure 17.1: Master Franchise Case Study—Employee Job-Fit _ _ _ _ _ _ _ _ 257

Figure 17.2: Master Franchisee Case Study _ _ _ _ _ _ _ _ _ _ _ _ _ _ _ _ _ 258

Figure 17.3: Engagement and Personality Survey of Leading Franchisor _ _ _ 260

Figure 17.4: Personalities Involved with Each Accomplishment _ _ _ _ _ _ _ 260

Acknowledgments

I T WAS THE MCQUAIG SYSTEM™ AND ITS MANAGING DIRECTOR, MAUREEN TOWNSON, that allowed this book to come to life. It was their system that I used to measure the personalities of our entrepreneurs. The McQuaig Institute is a leader in the field of psychometric use and application. I reviewed more than 20 different instruments before choosing The McQuaig System. It's simply the best.

A special thank you to my mother-in-law, Blanche Salick, who some 15-plus years ago made an investment in me, both financial and motivational.

Al Hazan has been my TEC Chair (The Executive Committee) for the past four years. It has been his mission to teach me how to be a better leader. I have fought him every step of the way. It is largely through his efforts that I am succeeding. I have learned that it is easier to listen than deal with his wrath.

Joseph Mancuso, President of the CEO Club Inc., allowed us to reprint his entrepreneur quiz in Chapter 3. He is a leading resource and is the founder of the CEO Club, the largest nonprofit CEO peer organization.

The co-founders of Plumeus, Vratislav Jerabek and Ilona Jerabek, are two of the most brilliant entrepreneurs I have been fortunate enough to work with. They are the creators and providers of more than 100 online assessments. When you take one of our online tests at www.theentrepreneurnextdoor.com, it will be their handywork that you are enjoying.

The Young Entrepreneurs Organization (YEO) allowed me the access to its members and was instrumental in the research for this project. For those of you who haven't figured it out yet, YEO is the premier learning organization for young entrepreneurs.

Ann Herrmann-Nehdi, CEO of Herrmann International, graciously allowed us to use the HBDL tool in our survey work. There are a number of ways of looking at entrepreneurship; understanding how an entrepreneur thinks is an essential element.

TEC 511 is my TEC group that Al Hazan has chaired. Its members have been instrumental in my growth and development. They are: Chris Brown, Steve Clodfelter, Howard Davis, Bob Ferra, John Hasenauer, Beverly Kaye, Wendell Keith, Paul Revlin, Frank Spaeth, Rosa Warschaw, and Rudi Weinberg.

My book agent, Jeff Herman, of the Jeff Herman Literary Agency, LLC.

Jere Calmes, editor *extraordinaire* at Entrepreneur Press, and Karen Billipp of Eliot House Productions.

Susan Ingram, my Project Manager, whose diligence allowed the details of this work to take on a whole new meaning.

Last, but not certainly least, is my writing coach and mentor, Toni Robino, and her senior editor, Doug Wagner, at With Flying Colours. I was determined to write this book myself, and through Toni's holding me accountable, with patience and coaching, she allowed me the opportunity to fulfill one of my entrepreneurial aspirations. With any luck, she will have been my harshest critic, which means, of course, that you, the reader, can't be.

I have omitted e-mail addresses, phone numbers, and contact information because in this world things change too fast. You will find contact information on the book's web site, www. theentrepreneurnextdoor.com.

Create Your Own Declaration of Independence

by Jeffrey Gitomer

LOOKING FOR REAL INCOME?

What are you doing about it?

I started selling candy bars door to door when I was seven years old. I thought it would be a good idea to raise money for charity—buying candy bars for a nickel and selling them for a dime. I raised about $15 and gave all the money to charity, not realizing I was supposed to keep my costs so I could do it again. Entrepreneurial success and failure at the same time.

Everyone remembers their first entrepreneurial experience. It might have been a school fundraiser, Junior Achievement, or working at an early age in your family's business. Chances are, that's when the questions, "Do I like this? Is this for me? Is it fun?" started drifting through your mind. If you have an entrepreneurial spirit, those questions stay with you as you enter the working world. And so do the choices—working for someone else or working for yourself.

I had the entrepreneurial urge at an early age and it stayed with me my whole life. When did it hit you? What have you done about it so far?

Some people have the entrepreneurial spirit in their blood. Others try to acquire it once they find out that working class America is not for them, or they get laid off or downsized, or they hate their bosses, or they're not making the kind of money they'd like to (or need to) make.

The American Dream is available for anyone who decides to reach for the brass ring. Most people have short arms. They may think about it. They may look at others who do it. They may even harbor a secret desire to do it. But they keep their hands in their pockets. The American Dream is only achieved when someone has a strong desire, decides to take a risk, and believes he has the wherewithal to make it happen.

How about you? Are you looking for more? Are you looking to be your own boss? Are you looking to achieve greater wealth? Do you have enough desire and fortitude to turn the dream into a reality?

Hey, the guy next door has done it. So can you!

If you have a spark of entrepreneurial spirit in your soul, this book will not only help you uncover it—it will show you how to use it. Not in a general way, but in a way that is specifically tailored to your personality, which means it gives you the best chance to succeed.

Words of Caution

This is not a book you can read quickly. It's definitely not a "one-size-fits-all." Rather, this is a book that interacts with your thought process, helps you capture and understand your personality and skill set, and then provides working guidance so that you can start a business, build a business, and succeed based on the proven methods and results of others.

Words of Reality

Everyone who succeeds in business seeks guidance. Bill Wagner's book is a built-in mentor. Bill knows entrepreneurs the way I know salespeople—top to bottom, inside and out. Having known Bill personally for years, I can attest to his expertise, his thoroughness, and his firm grip on reality. He is not just a voice of experience, but also a voice of wisdom.

Words of Encouragement

Becoming a successful entrepreneur doesn't have to take as long or be as hard as you think. If you find out how to succeed based on *your own* personality, and you learn how to hire and manage people based on *their* personalities, you can achieve your goals in half the time, with half the headaches.

The Entrepreneur Next Door is not just a book. It's a blue print that shows you the step-by-step process for building your own business and creating independence, financial independence, for yourself and those you love.

—Jeffrey Gitomer, author of
The Sales Bible and *The Little Red Book of Selling*

Preface

The Entrepreneur Next Door is based on research and empirical evidence that prove personality is the most important variable in how and why you will succeed or fail as an entrepreneur.

First and foremost, your personality and how well you manage it will have a greater impact on your overall business success than will your skills, education, knowledge, and experience.

Second, but equally important, hiring the right person for the right job—based on personality—is one of the most effective ways to ensure your business success. When someone has the right personality for a particular job, the chances of him doing the job well are dramatically increased.

If you don't have the right personality for a particular position, it doesn't preclude your success. But it does make it more challenging and often more stressful. The question to ask is, "Since I have a choice, what am I most passionate about and what do I most want to do?"

As many very successful entrepreneurs have demonstrated, it's less important to be an expert in the type of business you're running than it is to be an expert at running your business.

By learning how your particular personality type is most likely to succeed, you can take the fast track to entrepreneurial success. By learning how to hire and manage your employees based on their personality types, you're on your way to greater freedom and financial independence.

The Research Study

Over the course of five years, my company, Accord Management Systems Inc., surveyed 1,509 entrepreneurs who were under the age of 40 and had annual business revenues exceeding $1 million each. The vast majority of my research participants were members of the Young Entrepreneurs Organization (YEO). Our study group had an average age of 31 and a net worth of $3.1 million.

Each entrepreneur completed a personality survey, an emotional intelligence test, and a brain dominance test. They also completed a 160-question survey regarding their backgrounds, experience, education, beliefs, strengths, and challenges. (Some of their answers can be found in the book under: "In Their Own Words.")

When Hackett and Associates (HRCX Inc.) completed its analysis of the research data, and I began to review the results, I was intrigued by the grouping of similar traits. I had never anticipated so much strength, power, raw dominance, and ego in one segment of the population. That moment was the beginning of my path to document entrepreneurs' secrets and frustrations—rich and colorful information about my favorite topic, entrepreneurs, and most importantly, how anyone can become one.

If you can truly get to know yourself and the innate tendencies of the people who work for you, you can follow the Five-Tier Performance Pyramid that I share with my clients and achieve the results you desire. Understanding your personality and your employees' unique personalities is paramount to your success because Personality is Tier I of the Performance Pyramid. It forms the foundation for Tier II: Job Behaviors, Tier III: Actions, Tier IV: Metrics, and Tier V: Results. (I explain the Performance Pyramid and each tier in detail in Chapter 1.)

Accuracy

I have made every attempt to ensure that the information, data, quotations, and results included in this book are completely accurate. If you find a mistake or what you believe is an inaccuracy of any kind, please call Oprah immediately. Actually, if Oprah invites me to appear on her show, I won't be apologizing for inaccuracies. I'll be there to share some of the most profound information that entrepreneurs need in order to succeed, and in their understanding, can provide motivating work situations for their employees.

Throughout the course of the book I talk about the Young Entrepreneurs Organization (YEO), which changed its name to Entrepreneurs' Organization and The Executive Committee (TEC) and is now Vistage International. I refer to them as YEO and TEC because those were their names during the time I was conducting my research and writing this book.

Value

My business and career is based on providing strong take-home value. The vast majority of my clients are entrepreneurs and the only thing they are interested in is results. If you're not convinced by the end of Chapter 1 that your entrepreneurial success can be greatly enhanced by this book, then I hope you borrowed the book from the library; I wouldn't want you to say you didn't get your money's worth. But if you are convinced, and you accept the concepts found within my book, then put these ideas into action—now. You're in for the ride of your life!

Note: The use of the pronoun "he," is in no way an inference that this book is for, or about, men alone. "He" is representational of both "he" and "she" and is used simply to avoid the cumbersome "he/she" "him/her," which tends to distract from the content of the material.

Who Is
the Entrepreneur
Next Door?

How to Succeed in Business

The First Time

AMERICA IS IN THE MIDST OF AN ENTREPRENEURIAL REVOLUTION. EVERY 45 SECONDS a new business is born. Tragically, two out of three perish before their third birthdays. Yet, despite this stark reality, half the U.S. population entertains the idea of self-employment; 700,000 Americans take the leap every year. Today, there are more than 16 million small businesses operating within the United States.

Through extensive research and testing, my wife, Renee, and I, co-founders of Accord Management Systems Inc., now know how and why some entrepreneurs become multimillionaires, others do moderately well, some barely survive and most don't. *The Entrepreneur Next Door* describes the natural entrepreneurial personality types (born leaders), the corporate leaders often referred to as intrapreneurs, and those who would like to be in business but have not had the opportunity, the wherewithal, or perhaps the inclination. I will refer to this last group as "wantapreneurs." Wantapreneurs are often successful business owners but not necessarily founders or born leaders. They are able to leverage their strengths and compensate for their limitations.

You'll also find out what happens when entrepreneurs become their own worst enemies. Most entrepreneurs don't achieve the level of success, financial or otherwise, that they dream or scheme about, and not surprisingly, these entrepreneurs have some personality traits in common. This book discusses the pitfalls and potential land mines that go hand in hand with the various entrepreneurial personalities and offers insights for solving these challenges.

For example, consider some very successful, and very different, entrepreneurs:

- Bill Gates of Microsoft displayed the big-picture thinking necessary for success even though he may have initially lacked the education or experience to accomplish his goals.
- Conrad Hilton knew little of the lodging and service industry when he decided to build his first hotel. He had unwavering determination, self-confidence, and a strong belief in himself.
- Wayne Huizenga of Waste Management and Blockbuster Video fame seems to have the Midas touch when it comes to starting companies. His string of successes has spanned the trash-removal business, video rental, music sales, professional sports, and most recently, automobile sales.
- Herb Kelleher of Southwest Airlines solidified his initial idea by writing it on a napkin. For 30-plus years his company has maintained profitability.

These examples are simply a few who made the headlines. There are millions of other successful business leaders and owners that have several things in common: an entrepreneurial or wantapreneurial personality and enough self-awareness to choose or manage a compatible business and hire those who possess the traits to maximize business growth and success.

The American marketplace abounds with more opportunities than ever. Potential entrepreneurs have a broad spectrum of options to choose from. They can become founders of their own enterprises, buy franchises or distributorships, buy existing businesses, or create their own brands of products or services. Success on each of these entrepreneurial paths requires a slightly different personality, and matching the personality to the opportunity increases the chances of success.

Because of the uncertain economy, lack of corporate security, economic layoffs, and downsizing, the motivation for people to go into their own businesses is greater than ever. Even with the current employment climate, people have greater motivation and sometimes greater flexibility to move among jobs. The abundance of possible business ventures makes the dream of owning a business attainable for more people.

Nevertheless, even with the entrepreneurial revolution in full swing, there's a critical shortage of insight into the mind and personality of an entrepreneur. America's television stations, bookstores, radio stations, and newsstands are filled with innumerable "experts" offering basically the same sound-bite information about what entrepreneurship is and how one can succeed as an entrepreneur. Unfortunately, the commonly accepted plan for entrepreneurial success works primarily for people who possess an entrepreneurial or a leader personality. The experts profess a singular solution that works best with that singular personality. That's great if you happen to be among the small percentage of the population that has an innate leadership personality, but if you don't, the chance that those how-to-succeed-in-business books will work for you is minuscule at best.

Who IS the Entrepreneur Next Door?

The genesis of this book began nine years ago when Thomas Stanley and William Danko's book *The Millionaire Next Door* (Pocket, 1998) was first published. I was one of more than two million readers fascinated with this glimpse into the saving and spending habits of millionaires. Actually, I believe most readers bought it because they wanted to gain insights into how they could also become millionaires. Their book surveyed 400 households with a net worth of $1 million or more. What was interesting to me was that more than 70 percent of the respondents were not entrepreneurs. They were schoolteachers, bus drivers, and professionals such as doctors, attorneys, and CPAs. Only 30 percent of those surveyed were actually entrepreneurs.

It was then that my curiosity got the best of me, and I set about comparing Accord Management Systems' survey group with their survey group. The members of our survey group, for the most part, belonged to the Young Entrepreneurs Organization, were under the age of 40 when they completed the survey, and had annual business revenues in excess of $1 million each.

Here's the essence of our findings: The survey group for *The Millionaire Next Door* had an average age of 57 and a net worth of $3.7 million: our study group had an average age of 31 and a net worth of $3.4 million. How was it that the members of our group, relatively speaking, were still kids but had amassed similar net worth in 25 fewer years? They didn't have the advantage of compound interest, but they did have the advantage of having very strong entrepreneurial personalities, and more important, they were enjoying opportunities that were very well suited to who they were.

Simply put, we're able to measure one's personality and predict success for a given role. The world's best bookkeeper has a great bookkeeper personality, a great salesperson has a great salesperson's personality, and a successful entrepreneur has a great entrepreneur's personality. But a great bookkeeper will rarely become a great financial controller or a CFO.

Unlike most books, this one has been written with messages specifically designed for people with a range of different personalities. Remember the story about Goldilocks? Some personalities are too big, some are too small, and some are just right. There's no such thing as a good or bad personality. The rightness of someone's personality is more determined by the requirements of the opportunity. Basically, you want to get the right people on the bus and into the right seats. And, you definitely want to be on the right bus and in the right seat yourself!

Some opportunities require a lot of personality, and some require very little. Each reader has a different personality, and it's typically much different from the author's. As an example, if you read a book on leadership by former General Electric chairman Jack Welsh and you don't have his strong personality, the stories that he shares are good stories, but they may not be ones that will help you learn how to be a great leader. In *this* book, however, there are elements and stories that have been written about and for each one of us.

Choice and Destiny

Given my family history, it was surely destined that I would become an entrepreneur. My grandmother, born in the late 1800s, was a wily businesswoman. Possessing both a real estate license and a law degree, Grandma was the first entrepreneur in my life. I have fond memories of a two-story house on Main Street that she sold "on contract for deed" at least a dozen times. We called it the yo-yo house. People would make payments for a couple of years and then leave, and she'd sell it again. Each time, I was the official painter and maintenance person. I was also the guy who got something of greater value than the cash. I got the experience.

I also got the education. I graduated with a degree in business from Bradley University, in Peoria, Illinois. There's an interesting story here. I originally attended Arizona State University from 1969 to 1972. I finished my degree in Peoria, but not in the '70s or the '80s or the '90s. It was just several years ago. I can remember finishing my senior year at Bradley back in 1973. I was three semester hours short of my degree requirements, and Dean Bausch said, "Bill, it's summer school, it's one class, and it will be behind you forever." Like many of you, I have difficulty being told what to do. So it wasn't until almost 30 years later that I went back. I was 48 years young, and I was setting my goals. I said that I wanted to have a book written by the time I was 50 and that I wanted to have my college degree. I went back to Peoria and met with the current dean of the School of Business. We petitioned the school to change the residency requirements. I took two classes, passed, and now have my college degree. I also achieved my second goal, which was to have a book written by my 50th birthday. And after celebrating that goal, I learned a valuable lesson. There's a huge difference between having a book written and having a book published. Now it has been published.

As much as I appreciate my education and the opportunity to learn new skills, it's clear that my personality has the greatest impact on my behavior and my choices. Consequently, with the exception of a short three-year sentence with Xerox and Frito-Lay, I've worked for myself for most of my life. I'm a risk-taker, sometimes much to my wife Renee's dismay. We have very different personalities, and while our strengths often complement one another, we tend to approach life from opposite angles. Yet, as co-founders of Accord Management Systems Inc., we're both fascinated with the predictable behavior of entrepreneurs—their strengths and their weaknesses—which we call "developmental considerations" because it sounds nicer.

This next statement is for the record. I wouldn't be enjoying the same level of success if it weren't for Renee. She's the balance that I require in my life. Unfortunately, I think I sometimes benefit more from her than she does from me. Renee has a calming influence on many, where I'm more like Captain Chaos.

Over the course of eight years, the employees of my company, Accord Management Systems Inc., and I have interviewed and studied the behaviors of more than 1,500 fearless business founders and leaders. Most were under 40 years old, and many were in their 20s and 30s. They all had sales of more than $1 million a year. What we discovered from our study is that, different as these entrepreneurs appeared, they share a number of common personality traits, and these traits were the predominant indicators of their success, outweighing education, family ties, skills, and experience.

In fact, of the entrepreneurs we studied, more than 80 percent have very similar personality traits. There's a great deal of truth to the notion that entrepreneurs are born, not made. Although upbringing, belief system, education, training, and development affect our ultimate behaviors, our core personality remains relatively constant throughout our lives. In other words, if you start out as a lion, you're not going to turn into a lamb, regardless of what you do or don't do. There may be times when you can act like a lamb, but it's difficult to maintain that behavior for an extended period of time.

It's also believed that our personalities are developed after we're born, as opposed to something we are born with. Do you know of a set of identical twins? They may have precisely the same DNA, but their personalities can be very different. There was a recent case in which one of two identical twins was accused of a heinous crime. The authorities had DNA evidence but couldn't tell which of the twins was the culprit. They looked at more than 100,000 DNA markers and still couldn't tell the difference. Did I mention that one of the twins has been in and out of the prison system for most of his life and the other is an upstanding citizen? Go figure.

To experience the greatest level of success and fulfillment, entrepreneurs should choose business ventures that are in sync with their true personalities. Those who choose well tend to prosper. Those who don't find a fit for their personalities would make great material for TV dramas and sitcoms. Can you imagine a receptionist who acts like Rambo or a professional wrestler who acts more like Mr. Rogers? How about a used-car salesman who's quiet and introverted, and doesn't like talking to or interacting with people? You get the idea.

The Entrepreneur Next Door reveals:

- There are hundreds of personality combinations, but they can be pretty much divided into seven basic types. Of these, four are entrepreneurial types and three are wantapreneurial.
- The characteristics that make up the four entrepreneurial generalist personalities and the three wantapreneurial specialist personalities.
- The critical differences among the seven personality types and how they can all achieve success in business.
- What your "Stupid Switch" is and how to turn it off.
- Prospective business areas and opportunities that are compatible with your personality. These are found at www.theentrepreneurnextdoor.com.

- The concept of emotional intelligence and why it's often more important than intellect when managing others and yourself.
- The role of self-awareness in the life of an entrepreneur and how it can enhance your life's balance.
- How to create an absolutely awesome company with the right people in the right positions.

The Greatest Knowledge Is Self-Knowledge

The most important factors that divide entrepreneurs who barely make it from those who make millions are personality and, sometimes more importantly, the awareness to harness it, use it, and learn from it. The most successful entrepreneurs know that the greatest knowledge is self-knowledge. They're not necessarily blessed with a higher intellect or more charisma than others, but they understand how to make the best of their talents and how to manage or compensate for their weaknesses, what are called *developmental considerations* or *potential limitations.*

The Entrepreneur Next Door offers an in-depth character study of the seven archetypes that move and shake our world. Our research shows that most entrepreneurs who reach and surpass their lofty goals are natural leaders, are strong problem solvers, and work well under pressure. But we've also learned that people who don't have these innate abilities can become very successful if they choose the right businesses for their personality types and surround themselves with the right people in the right positions. *This is a major point.*

Through research data, survey results, true stories, and hypothetical scenarios, you will discover how every personality type can grow a lucrative business. The information in this book, coupled with the results of the behavioral assessments provided, will give you priceless insights into your own personality and heighten your self-awareness. You'll find out what makes each of the seven personality types tick and what business might be best suited to your type. The behavioral assessment we used to determine the personalities of our 1,500-plus entrepreneurs was provided by The McQuaig System™ of Toronto, Ontario, Canada.

Are You Taking a Risk?

An entrepreneur was discussing the topic of risk with the host of a radio call-in show. The host said that being in business for oneself was risky. The entrepreneur's definition of risk was living paycheck to paycheck, working for an employer in an "at will" state where you can be laid off or fired without notice. Or worse, your company could shut down. "That," he said, "is taking a risk."

We discovered that people with natural entrepreneurial personalities have a high level of dominance, are independent self-starters, and believe in themselves and their abilities. They don't depend on the opinions of others and often believe that others don't understand them or what they're trying to achieve. People with wantapreneurial personalities are more accepting, accommodating, and agreeable; tend to be more compliant; want to do things the right way; are more relaxed, and sometimes have higher sociability than those with classic entrepreneurial personalities.

Entrepreneurs vs. Prodigious Savers from *The Millionaire Next Door*

Aside from the difference in average age between the entrepreneurs we studied and the millionaires described in *The Millionaire Next Door*, we discovered a number of other differences. Three of the big differences are what kinds of cars they drive, net worth, and work ethic. Consider the car difference.

Is your car foreign or American made?

	Entrepreneurs	*The Millionaire Next Door*
Foreign manufactured	65 percent	42.3 percent
American manufactured	35 percent	57.7 percent

With regard to the make of car, BMWs were the preferred auto of entrepreneurs. The popular autos that followed were Ford Explorer, Infiniti, Mercedes, Chevy Tahoe, and the Lexus LS400. Not one participant of this survey group drove a Saturn. The age of cars driven by these entrepreneurs matches very closely the statistics put forth by Stanley and Danko in *The Millionaire Next Door*. The differences were that *The Entrepreneur Next Door* respondents rarely purchased used vehicles and leased their vehicles 33.3 percent of the time. This makes sense because they were then better able to claim the monthly lease payment as a company expense.

The entrepreneurs in our survey vacation on the average 17.7 days per year, which is almost four work weeks. The longer the older entrepreneurs are in business, the more days of vacation they take. When vacationing, they enjoy getting out of town. They splurge and stay at four- and five-star facilities; 75 percent conduct business while they travel. Our study group is more affluent, more dedicated, and perhaps has a stronger work ethic than the general population. They are willing to work hard, but they want to reward themselves as well, as the question we asked on vacation facilities indicates.

Where do you prefer to stay while on vacation?

Facility	Percent
Resort environment five stars	41.0 percent
Three- and four-star facilities	30.5 percent
Bed and breakfast	3.8 percent
Whatever is convenient	21.0 percent
Rough it in tents or like facilities	3.8 percent

Essentially, we found more differences than similarities between the millionaires next door and the entrepreneurs next door, and it appears that many of these differences can be attributed more to personality than to anything else. Throughout the book, you will learn more about how the entrepreneurs and wantapreneurs in our research responded and hear many of their thoughts and insights. (To read the research survey in its entirety, visit www.theentrepreneurnextdoor.com.)

Climbing the Performance Pyramid

The Performance Pyramid (Figure 1.1) represents a cognitive process for determining who you need to be in a particular role or on a particular project, in order to achieve the results you're looking for. Although entrepreneurs can have seven different

FIGURE 1.1: **Performance Pyramid**

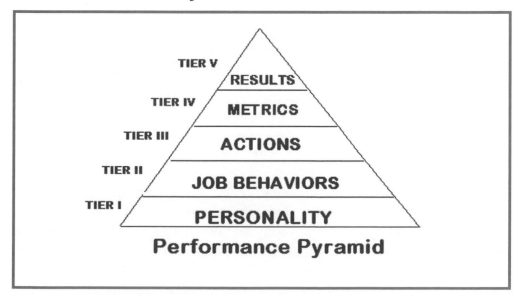

personality types, the job behaviors that are needed to succeed as an entrepreneur are fairly similar.

These behaviors typically require that you demonstrate higher than average dominance and above average sociability. To behave in a way that is most beneficial for the business, you might have to override your emotions or natural tendencies, which usually means stretching your comfort zones.

However, if you know that embracing the actions detailed in Tier III will get the job done, and that you will be rewarded with good results, it will be easier for you to make taking those actions a habit, even if they initially feel uncomfortable.

How well you do this is measured by the metrics that you set up for Tier IV and your results are the ultimate outcome in Tier V.

Tier I: Personality

Personality is defined here as a manifestation of a person's core. It is who people are when they are alone. It is the essence of the person who looks back when that person looks into a mirror. Personality is the stable, least changing aspect of a person's natural style. It develops early in life and remains largely unchanged.

To their benefit, people are able to measure the different aspects of their personalities. I refer to these aspects as factors. It is also possible to measure the level or amount of each of these factors. The bigger these factors are in an individual, the stronger and less changeable they are. Conversely, the smaller a factor is, the more flexible it tends to be.

The personality test I used for the research measures four sets of opposing factors. (These factors will be covered in depth in Chapter 4.) See Figure 1.2 for a diagram of these sets of factors.

1. Dominant versus accepting
2. Sociable versus analytical
3. Relaxed versus driving
4. Compliant versus independent

The two strongest factors in personality are dominance and compliance. When people have more dominance than compliance, they have a more entrepreneurial personality, characterized by strategic and big picture thinking. I refer to these people as Generalists. When people have more compliance than dominance, they have more of a wantapreneurial personality, which is more tactical and detailed or expert-oriented. I refer to these people as Specialists.

FIGURE 1.2: **Personality Factors**

High Dominance DOMINANT	High Sociability SOCIABLE	High Relaxation RELAXED	High Compliance COMPLIANT
Low Dominance ACCEPTING	Low Sociability ANALYTICAL	Low Relaxation DRIVING	Low Compliance INDEPENDENT

Source: The McQuaig Institute®. Reprinted with permission.

The ability to modify or mitigate people's personalities depends on the strength of each factor and the degree of change they are trying to make. For example, I have learned that it's easier for someone with a dominant personality to behave in an accepting manner than it is for an accepting individual to be more dominant. It is also easier for a sociable person to think more analytically than it is for someone who's analytical to be more sociable. People who are driving can appear to be relaxed more easily than relaxed people can be driving. And it's easier for an independent person to learn to handle details than it is for a compliant person to let go of the details. See Figure 1.3 for the traits that are typically associated with various personality factors.

I have discovered and witnessed that if people know and understand the behavioral requirements of a particular position, they have a better chance of manifesting or maintaining those behaviors. It is never easy to do this for an extended period of time, but it *is* possible. Not surprisingly, people's mindsets often determine how likely they are to succeed at making changes or how likely they are to fail. Some people believe that no matter what, they can win, whereas others resign themselves to losing before they even begin. Most people are somewhere in between. Regardless of where people are along that range, however, the way they think and how they choose to behave are motivated by their personalities. Thankfully, people also possess the power and the freedom to change their thoughts and actions—at least to some degree.

Research studies indicate that if you have the right personality to do a particular job, your chances of success are five times greater than if you have the wrong personality. There is another side of these studies, and that is that there is always a small percentage of

FIGURE 1.3: **Entrepreneurial Elements**

High Dominance DOMINANT	High Sociability SOCIABLE	High Relaxation RELAXED	High Compliance COMPLIANT
Generalist	Outgoing	Patient	Specialist
Competitive	Friendly	Steady	Conscientious
Goal-oriented	Persuasive	Methodical	Detail-oriented
Risk taker	Collaborative	Loyal	Thorough
Resuts-oriented	Consensus builder	Prefers a predictable work environment	Prefers a well-defined structure
Self-confident	Enjoys interacting with others	Wants to think things through	Risk adverse
Cautious	Work-oriented	Strong sense of urgency	Strong minded
Deliberate	Logical	Multitasks	Determined
Likes to specialize	Deals with facts	Works well under pressure	Likes freedom of action
Accommodating	Analytical	Prefers a varied and active work environment	Strong willed
Agreeable	Problem solver	Impatient, driving	Independent
Low Dominance ACCEPTING	Low Sociability ANALYTICAL	Low Relaxation DRIVING	Low Compliance INDEPENDENT

Source: The McQuaig Institute®. Reprinted with permission.

people with the wrong personality for a job who are successful. It appears that these individuals use a cognitive approach to determine the right behaviors for the job, take the corresponding actions, and therefore achieve the desired results. Read on for how this works.

Tier II: Job Behaviors

The consulting our company has been involved with these past ten years has taught us one thing. With awareness, a cognitive understanding and the right information, we can:

1. Determine the BEHAVIORS required for a task or position.
2. Determine and demonstrate the right ACTIONS necessary to accomplish our goals.
3. Determine the correct METRICS to gauge our change or growth.
4. When we accomplish these things, we typically achieve our RESULTS.

The process is actually simple and intuitive. For example, look at the qualities of a successful storeowner or store manager. An ideal store manager should possess the following qualities:

- Flexibility in moving from one project to another
- Ability to hold others accountable
- Good listener
- Effective communicator
- Convincing
- Independent
- Good with numbers
- Friendly
- Team player
- Visionary

Which of the above qualities are skills (things you can learn to do or get better at), and which are determined more by personality? They are all based on personality. Now, what if people don't have those qualities? Does that mean they can't do the job? NO, NO, NO, it doesn't. What it *does* mean is that if they can display or adopt these qualities or behaviors, then they will have a better alignment with the position's requirements and ultimately can achieve better results.

Tier III: Actions

Actions are influenced by people's personalities and the required job behaviors, or expectations, for a particular role or position. Take a look at the actions that would demonstrate the qualities of a successful store owner or manager in Tier II. Imagine I am discussing the required actions for an owner or manager of a hair salon.

FLEXIBILITY. Multi-tasking—easily moving from one aspect of the business to another, including managing staff and process, interacting with customers, marketing, and selling products or services.

ABILITY TO HOLD OTHERS ACCOUNTABLE.   Hiring and firing employees, taking corrective action in a timely manner, and confronting people when necessary.

GOOD LISTENER.   Letting the speaker express his entire point without interrupting, repeating or paraphrasing what the speaker has said to ensure understanding, writing or recording important points so that no details are missed, and most importantly, making sure the speaker feels that he has been listened to.

EFFECTIVE COMMUNICATOR.   Clearly expressing ideas, giving directions, and describing goals and plans. Saying what you mean and meaning what you say, but doing so in a way that isn't offensive or defensive.

CONVINCING.   Expressing a level of warmth and self-confidence that leads others to believe that your way of thinking is correct and should be followed.

INDEPENDENT.   Operating without strong rules, policies, procedures, or guidelines.

GOOD WITH NUMBERS.   Understanding and using the metrics of your business in order to be a better manager or leader. Using these numbers in a timely way to speed up response time and accountability.

FRIENDLY.   Working well with others, asking for their opinions, and valuing their contributions. Collaborating with and building consensus with others. Coming out of your office; walking the four corners and interacting with your staff and clients.

VISIONARY.   Working on the business, as opposed to in the business. Marketing your product, service, or location. Maintaining a big picture perspective and working toward long-term goals.

Tier IV: Metrics

Actions (Tier III) without metrics (Tier IV) could be nothing more than misdirected efforts. It is absolutely essential to measure the accomplishments of our actions. Without doing so, how do we know we are progressing, moving, or achieving? When you think about it, metrics are everywhere. At an early age we have our allowance and consider what we can buy with it or save for. We measure almost everything. Today's Dow Jones is 11,204. Seventy-one is today's high temperature. The approximate ROI, return on your investment, from your purchase of this book could be as much as $82,759. If you can't measure it . . . you can't manage it.

Tier V: Results

As you have seen, there's a difference between the behaviors that I have listed and the actions that naturally stem from those behaviors. If you were to attach metrics to each action, you could measure the levels of accountability and accomplishment that ultimately provide the desired results. By creating a cognitive approach to succeeding in a role, people both with and without the preferred personality for this position can accomplish similar results.

It's interesting to note that personality becomes more important as a person moves up the corporate ladder. Sure, skills are important, but almost every CEO I've worked with has commented that their company's most important asset is having the right people in the right positions. Not every successful CEO has the perfect personality for the job, but the ones who excel understand that certain behaviors and actions are required to generate the results they are seeking.

Leadership

A number of authors have espoused the virtues of leadership, but in my opinion, many have missed the mark. These books presume that if one leader can accomplish his goals, then all other leaders should be able to duplicate those efforts and therefore get the same results. NO. It doesn't work that way. It only works that way for a select few; it works for those with similar personalities and situations. If the author or leader possesses the Tier I capability, understands the Tier II requirements, and has been able to make things a reality because of his Tier III commitments then it works. Unfortunately most authors are missing the "how to." In *The Entrepreneur Next Door* web site, we look at models from various authors, including Jim Collin's *Good to Great* and discuss the necessary "how to" from a personality perspective.

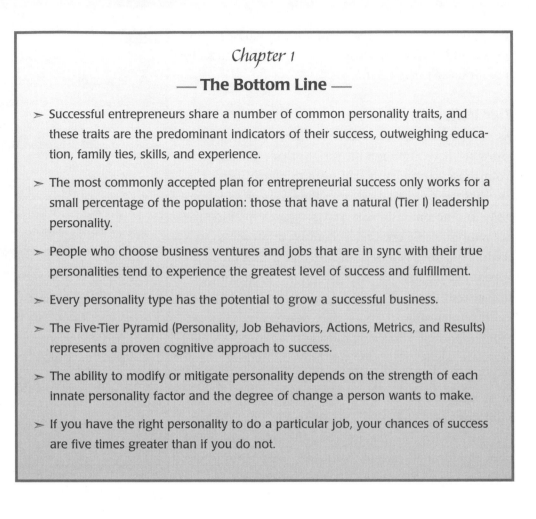

Chapter 1

— The Bottom Line —

➤ Successful entrepreneurs share a number of common personality traits, and these traits are the predominant indicators of their success, outweighing education, family ties, skills, and experience.

➤ The most commonly accepted plan for entrepreneurial success only works for a small percentage of the population: those that have a natural (Tier I) leadership personality.

➤ People who choose business ventures and jobs that are in sync with their true personalities tend to experience the greatest level of success and fulfillment.

➤ Every personality type has the potential to grow a successful business.

➤ The Five-Tier Pyramid (Personality, Job Behaviors, Actions, Metrics, and Results) represents a proven cognitive approach to success.

➤ The ability to modify or mitigate personality depends on the strength of each innate personality factor and the degree of change a person wants to make.

➤ If you have the right personality to do a particular job, your chances of success are five times greater than if you do not.

2

Your Personality Can Pave the Way to Success

PERSONALITY IS UNDOUBTEDLY THE MOST SIGNIFICANT FACTOR IN UNDERSTANDING WHY some people can do certain jobs easily while others struggle with the same tasks. Based on my experience and countless interviews, it seems that our personalities are pretty much ingrained by the time we are in our late teens. Individuals can, however, have adaptive personalities.

Recent best-selling books, such as *Good to Great* by Jim Collins (Collins, 2001) champion the virtues of "Level Five Leadership" and "getting the right people on the bus." *Now, Discover Your Strengths* by Marcus Buckingham (Free Press, 2001) suggests placing employees in positions compatible with their strengths. *Follow This Path* by Curt Coffman (Warner Business Books, 2002) may be the first nonacademic book that provides the how-to in managing the developmental side of a business. These books have one common thread: their conclusions are based on substantial objective research.

The missing link in their research is that they measured *organizations,* not the people who founded, managed, or led these organizations. This is critical because they are looking at a level of organizational health or potential dysfunction without considering the strengths of those who create and run these organizations. It's the leaders of organizations who provide direction and formulate values, mission, and vision. It's the personalities of these leaders and the personalities of their employees that determine how successful an endeavor will be.

The research that my company, Accord Management Systems Inc., has collected clearly demonstrates that assessing an entrepreneur's core personality is a highly accurate way of predicting his potential, the types of businesses he's likely to enjoy, and the challenges he may experience.

For the past several decades, entrepreneurship has been viewed as a one-size-fits-all process for starting businesses. Only recently have those of us who study this phenomenon concluded that being a successful entrepreneur is about much more. Today, systems of organizational measurement can accurately predict the success or failure of an enterprise based on the personality of the individual who is starting or buying the business. The results of these assessments also indicate in which types of businesses each entrepreneurial personality type is likely to excel. That's significant because it means that everyone, even those who aren't natural-born leaders, can succeed in business ventures by understanding themselves and hiring those with the necessary traits that they themselves may not possess.

I've discovered that there's an even greater benefit to knowing and understanding the personalities and tendencies of the people you manage, work for, and work with: increased awareness of others and yourself, you have the knowledge and power to make more intelligent decisions and to choose the most appropriate entrepreneurial path.

The research findings that my company has amassed on business success show that four entrepreneurial personality types—Trailblazers, Go-Getters, Managers, and Motivators—own and run the majority of successful businesses. A smaller but impressive number of strong businesses are run by people who possess one of the three Wantapreneurial, or Specialist, personality types—Authorities, Collaborators, and Diplomats. (Chapter 5 provides a general description of these personality types.)

The key is for people to be aware of the traits they *do* have and to develop or hire the essential success traits they need to bridge the gap.

Why Personality?

The formulation and study of personality from an objective perspective began over 70 years ago. In the early 1930s, Louie Thurstone wrote the book *Vectors of the Mind* that documented studies that found there was a high level of consistency between a person's choice of descriptive words and his personality. If I felt that terms such as *strong-willed* and *confident* described me, chances were good that I had a more dominant personality. There are literally hundreds of words or descriptors that are used in scientifically determining one's personality.

During World War II, an actuary who worked for the U.S. Army Air Corps was asked to create an assessment that would help the Air Corps determine who would make the best fighter pilots and who would make the best bomber pilots. The behavioral requirements of a bomber pilot are being careful, precise, matter-of-fact, by-the-book, methodical, calm, introspective, and accommodating. The fighter pilot, on the other hand, is seen as more aggressive, self-confident, outgoing, driving, somewhat casual in his thinking, independent, and strong-willed. The two pilots' personality types are almost opposite. The bomber pilot would look at himself in the mirror before a day's mission and say something to the effect of, "Grant me the ability to drop my payload exactly where it needs to be, allow me the ability to safely return my ship and crew, and above all keep me from screwing up." Meanwhile, his fighter-pilot brethren might say, "Grant me the ability to splash a few of those suckers, and if those bomber pilots don't get out of my way . . ." Well, you get the picture. This was one of the first real job-fit applications that was determined by assessing the position as well as the applicant.

> **Tools**
>
> My sample group was asked, "Regarding the people side of your business, what tools, technology, or systems do you utilize?" The number-one answer was reference checking (78.9 percent) and the number-two answer was personality testing—51.6 percent were using these instruments to select the right employee and also to determine how to work with them. This number is much greater for this study group because they are more comfortable embracing technological accelerators than larger corporations tend to be. The other reason is that in this study group the decisions are made by the CEO, not the human resources department.

Entrepreneurs Share Their Favorite Business Mottoes

"We suck less." —Anonymous

"A World that Works Because Business Works." —Frances Fujii

"Find a way." —Shelby Russ

"If it's worth doing, it's worth doing right." —Drew Clancy

"Persist until you succeed." —Doug Evans

"NETWORK exists to make its clients look good." —Linda Tessar

"Have fun and make the kids smile, biz and personal." —Shep Hyken

"With experience comes mistakes, from mistakes comes wisdom. And right makes might." —Anonymous

"Bliss in action." —Vince Poscente

"Prosperity through quality." —Wolf Bielas

"Deliver top quality work and have fun doing it." —Ashley Postlewaite

"You cannot do business by remote control." —Karen Caplan

"We are not planning the future, we are inventing it." —Skip Viragh

(Authors note: Skip was the founder of Rydex funds located in Maryland. Skip was a leader extraordinare. Sadly, he passed away.)

"There's no bigger word in the dictionary than 'if.'" —Jo-Anne Dressendofer

"Put your head down and get it done!" —Jim Frey

"Poverty sucks!" —Anonymous

"Never give up—'can't' is not in the dictionary." —Jay Sweet

Today, personality testing has become a widely used tool to help companies get the people side of their businesses right. The key to using these tools for selection is measuring the behavioral requirements of the position and comparing them with an applicant's personality. You can't measure an applicant in the abstract; you must measure the applicant against the requirements of a position.

Behavioral studies conducted over the past 30 years affirm that personality can be accurately measured and that this valuable insight—when put to good use—can significantly improve our effectiveness and level of success. It's important to point out that *combinations* of behavioral traits define everyone's personality. Two people who share roughly the same traits aren't carbon copies of each other because their experience, education, and skills must be factored into the formula. With the assessment tools we use at Accord Management Systems, four basic scales measure an individual's natural style of behavior to determine his personality type. Based on these measurements, we compare and contrast an individual's levels of dominance and acceptance; sociability and analytical abilities; relaxation and drive; and compliance and independence. The scientific studies that set us on the path to accurately measuring personality came from the works of Gordon Allport, Louie Thurstone, and other behaviorists.

For the purposes of our behavioral research, we used several proven and reliable assessments. One of the systems we used for personality testing was The McQuaig System™ of Toronto, Ontario, Canada. This 30-year-old system indicates that there are seven personality types that make up a broad spectrum. The personalities that we've termed Trailblazers, Go-Getters, Managers, and Motivators possess the strongest innate entrepreneurial personalities, whereas the Authorities, Collaborators, and Diplomats are the wantapreneurial personalities. You'll be introduced to each of these personality types, and as you make your way through the book, you'll gain a greater understanding of what makes them tick and what ticks them off. You'll develop an appreciation for what works for you and for them and what doesn't.

What Determines Success or Failure?

Remember when the Human Genome Project was big news? It seemed like almost every day there was another discovery. On my way from Washington, DC, to a presentation in Minneapolis, I was reading about the Genome Project, and as I do with most books, I turned to the index to see whether there was anything written about personality. There was. The authors had surmised that descendants from Scandinavian countries have a tendency to be tall, thin, introverted, and fair in color of both their hair and eyes. I thought, "Cool!" Remember, I was on my way to Minnesota, the home of the Vikings. And the Vikings are from where? My point, exactly. The next morning, I prepared for my presentation to the 15 CEOs who belonged to a local

When I present, I usually ask the participants when they first noticed they were different from others and what those differences were. In a presentation in New Jersey, an attendee had an extremely high level of dominance, a very low level of sociability, and was highly driven and somewhat independent. He was comfortable being by himself. I refer to his personality type as a Trailblazer. He first noticed he was different from others in high school. He was on the wrestling team and was under the mistaken impression that wrestling is a team sport. He was aggressive and assertive and had a tremendous desire to win. Today as a CEO, he has the exact same motivations. He wants to win all of the time. He knows that his employees represent his corporate team, but in the final analysis, he feels that he is often doing the heavy lifting himself . . . just the way he likes it.

TEC group. My topic was leadership, and in preparation for this workshop, I surveyed the personalities of the 15 members. As they began to arrive, I noticed that almost all of them were tall, thin, blond or bald, and had light-colored eyes and complexion, and as I looked at their personality graphs, I found that they were—you guessed it—introverts.

Tools, Tests, Surveys, and Assessments

So that our research would be well-rounded, Accord Management System used a number of different assessments that added richness, depth, and robustness to this work. We measured the survey group's personality, brain dominance, and emotional intelligence. There is a tremendous body of knowledge on all three topics, so I am telling this story using as much of the data as I can logically put into about 70,000 words. I invite you to go to the web site www.theentrepreneurnextdoor.com for the additional research that was compiled on brain dominance and emotional intelligence.

Brain Dominance

My company worked with the Herrmann Brain Dominance Institute of Lake Lure, North Carolina, and used its assessment because they are the leaders in this area. The HBDI™ is the world's leading thinking styles assessment tool. It identifies one's preferred approach to emotional, analytical, structural and strategic thinking.

The HBDI measures a person's tendencies toward right- or left-brain thinking, which gives a sense of whether they're more conceptual or experiential in their thinking. These tendencies often correspond to specific professions. Engineers, for example, consistently describe themselves as analytical, mathematical, and logical—traits based in the left hemisphere of the brain.

Artists, in contrast, describe themselves as emotional, spatial, and aesthetic—right-brain traits. If a person's tendency toward right- or left-brain thinking can be determined, it gives insight into thought processes. This, in turn, allows us to plan for success in organizations by matching the strengths of an individual within a team and or a position.

Thinking styles are so fundamental that it's easy to overlook their profound influence on teamwork, innovation, market awareness, organizational learning, communication, persuasion, and virtually every other key determinant of business. Some people are markedly analytical, creative or conservative, and these traits often dictate their success or failure. Consider the entrepreneurial elements, listed in order of their importance, in Figure 2.1.

FIGURE 2.1: **Entrepreneurial Elements Measured by the HBDI**

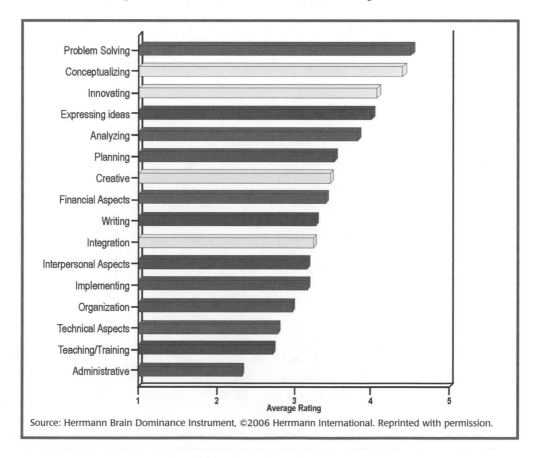

Source: Herrmann Brain Dominance Instrument, ©2006 Herrmann International. Reprinted with permission.

The illustration in Figure 2.2 represents the ideal entrepreneur, someone who has a relatively high level of each mode. Each of four quadrants represents a different thinking mode and thus a different way of looking at the business. The quadrants also have their specific strengths in a buisness environment.

- The A-quadrant *Problem Solver* (upper left). Builds a business on a sound foundation using logical thinking, analysis of facts, processing numbers, focus on the bottom line, or technical and financial activities.
- The B-quadrant *Implementer* (lower left). Tactical in nature, this mode is good at following up on every opportunity, planning approaches, organizing facts, providing detailed reviews and reports, finding overlooked flaws, and staying on task, on time, and within budget.
- The C-quadrant *Communicator* (lower right). Builds human capital, warmly engaging with a strong focus on people, relationships, selling and engaging others. This mode is charismatic in style, in touch with both customers and the team, intuitive, expressive, and often service-oriented.
- The D-quadrant *Risk Taker* (upper right). Gets people on board through the excitement of the vision and going for the dream. This visionary, entrepreneurial,

FIGURE 2.2: **The Ideal Entrepreneur**

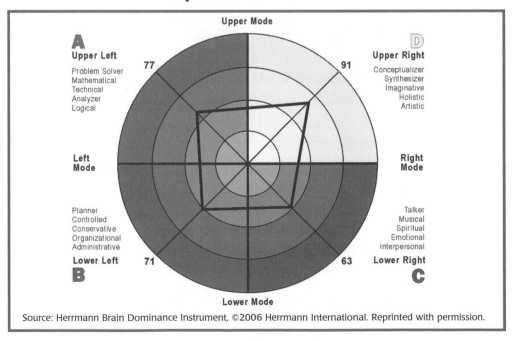

Source: Herrmann Brain Dominance Instrument, ©2006 Herrmann International. Reprinted with permission.

imaginative "starter" looks at the big picture, seeks opportunity, conceptualizes, and is often impatient to move forward.

How does all this tie in? Understanding brain dominance is another filter in understanding entrepreneurs. What your brain dominance is, or isn't, is nearly as important as understanding what you can do with it. Only about 3 percent of our population is evenly balanced in all four quadrants. They can understand issues and people involved with all four quadrants. A drawback, though, is that they may find it difficult to make decisions, as they may be torn by equally strong areas of thought.

> If you can't measure it, you can't manage it. It's essential to embrace and understand how you think and how you process in order to fully take advantage of your capabilities. This knowledge is a blueprint, and when you know how to read it, you can reach your full potential. Otherwise, you run the risk of sabotaging yourself.

Emotional Intelligence

The company Accord Management Systems chose to work with in the area of emotional intelligence is Plumeus Inc., in Montreal, Quebec, Canada. It is an established high-tech company specializing in psychological test development and related products and services. Plumeus is a leader in online psychological testing and has a reputation for quality, flexibility, professionalism, and innovation. The owners are the husband-and-wife team of Vratislav Jerabek and Ilona Jerabek. The goal of their company is to combine deep insight into the human mind with state-of-the-art technology. They do this through large-scale validation studies in order to create a battery of complex self-scoring assessment tools.

Plumeus tests are heavily researched using available multidisciplinary scientific literature and validated using samples of tens of thousands of subjects. Not only are the tests enjoyable, but also the reliability and validity meet the standards set forth by the American Psychological Association (APA). As any expert will tell you, possessing reliability and validity is what makes or breaks a psychological test.

The assessments are scored using complex algorithms that draw on artificial intelligence and system-expert principles, allowing exceptional precision and ensuring scientific accuracy. These algorithms allow us to create computer programs that find solutions to complex problems by approximating human thought processes and mapping the intricacies of human behavior. The Plumeus people know how to do it better than most.

Dr. Thomas J. Stanley, author of *The Millionaire Mind*, devotes a chapter in his book to the success factors related to becoming a millionaire. He identifies seven common areas related to that success:

1. Social skills
2. Orientation toward critics
3. Integrity and moral values
4. Creative intelligence
5. Investing in the stock market or one's own business
6. Luck vs. discipline
7. Intellectual orientation.

Of these seven, four are related to emotional intelligence, or EQ. They are social skills, orientation toward critics, integrity and moral values, and luck vs. discipline. It's important to note that intellectual orientation is ranked the lowest—the least significant—of all the factors, while social skills are ranked the highest.

Emotional intelligence is a learned ability to understand, use, and express human emotions in a healthy and skilled manner—all important to the entrepreneur. Emotional experience and expression are unique to each person. No two people behave, think, express feelings, and act in the exact same way.

Strengthening emotional intelligence supports success:

1. Emotional intelligence is the most important factor in achieving excellence.
2. High levels of achievement, success, and happiness are self-defined and self-directed.
3. The effects of negative and unchecked emotional stress, ineffective and poor relationships, and personal stagnation are financially costly.
4. A personal and emotional accountability system is essential for positive human development.
5. Honest self-assessment is a requisite to positive and intentional personal change.
6. People can develop and change themselves.
7. Learners learn best and teachers teach best in environments that are physically and emotionally safe.
8. Personal meaning is more relevant and powerful than external meaning.
9. Education and learning require the perspective of balance between academic achievement and becoming emotionally intelligent.
10. Healthy and effective relationships, personal leadership, self-management, intrapersonal growth and development, and recognition of potential problems are essential elements for creating a positive and healthy learning climate.

It's critical to identify, experience, understand, and express human emotions in healthy and productive ways. Emotional-intelligence skills are primary factors of motivation and the gateway to lifelong learning and high levels of achievement. Worldwide research indicates that emotional-intelligence skills are essential to all learning. Everyone knows people with high IQs who haven't met with success and others with modest IQs who have succeeded far beyond anyone's expectations. Why? Because these people possess emotional intelligence.

Unlike IQ and personality, EQ can be learned and developed, strengthened, and enhanced throughout your lifetime. When EQ is improved, it benefits your health, relationships, and work.

Many components of EQ correlate with Tier II Behaviors on the Performance Pyramid (Figure 1.1). They include:

- *Self-esteem.* A self-perceived level of personal worth. It is one of the most fundamental of skills and relates to major aspects of both mental health and a healthy personality.
- *Interpersonal assertion.* How effectively an individual uses direct, honest, and appropriate expression of thoughts, feelings, and behaviors in dealings with others. It indicates an ability to be direct and honest in communicating without violating the rights of others.
- *Empathy.* An indication of an individual's ability to sense, understand, and accept another person's thoughts, feelings, and behaviors. Empathy is a primary characteristic of a skilled communicator. People with naturally strong empathy tend to be sociable and outgoing.
- *Drive strength/motivation.* The ability to marshal energy and motivation toward the accomplishment of personal goals.
- *Decision-making.* A perceived skill in formulating and initiating effective problem-solving procedures. The ability to make decisions is a key ingredient of self-acceptance and positive self-regard.
- *Interpersonal awareness.* An individual's ability to evaluate appropriate social, emotional, and physical distance in verbal and nonverbal interactions with others.
- *Time management.* The ability to organize and use time to further individual and career goals. The ability to manage time is an ingredient of self-regard, sensitivity to needs, and perseverance in completing tasks.
- *Leadership.* A perceived skill in positively affecting and influencing the actions of others.

- *Commitment ethic.* A perceived skill in completing projects and job assignments dependably and successfully. People with a strong commitment ethic are usually perceived by others to be dependable and committed, are inner-directed, and persevere in completing projects regardless of difficulties encountered.

- *Stress management.* A perceived skill in managing stress and anxiety. People with skills in managing stress positively are competent managers of time and are flexible, self-assured, stable, and self-reliant.

- *Physical wellness.* The extent to which healthy attitudes and living patterns, which are important to physical health and well-being, have been established. Physical wellness is strongly correlated to positive stress management and high self-esteem. People with high scores have developed high levels of self-control against potentially harmful behavior patterns.

- *Interpersonal aggression.* The violation, overpowering, domination, or discrediting of another person's rights, thoughts, feelings, or behaviors by a particular communication style. High interpersonal aggression is related to the personality characteristics of rebelliousness, resentment, and oversensitive response to real or imagined affronts.

- *Interpersonal deference.* A communication style's indirect, self-inhibiting, self-denying, and ineffectual expression of thoughts, feelings, and behaviors. High interpersonal deference is related to the personality characteristics of apprehensiveness, shyness, and oversensitivity to threat or conflict.

Entrepreneurs with high levels of emotional intelligence would be characterized by:

- High level of acceptance of their personal worth as people or positive self-concepts (self-esteem)

- High level of skill in interpersonal communication characterized by a predominantly assertive position in stress situations (interpersonal assertion)

- High level of skill in judging appropriate social, emotional, and physical distance in verbal and nonverbal interaction with others and in affecting others in a positive way (interpersonal awareness)

- Responsiveness to others from an internal frame of reference and understanding and accepting the behaviors of others (empathy)

- High level of skill in selecting and directing personal energy to accomplish meaningful goals (drive strength/motivation)

- High level of skill in thinking, feeling, and behaving in an autonomous fashion for effective decision making (decision making)

- High level of skill in managing time in order to control responsibilities rather than being controlled by them (time management)
- Ability to comfortably move toward people and affect them in positive ways (sales orientation/leadership)
- Ability to commit oneself to chosen tasks and follow through to completion (commitment ethic)
- High level of skill in managing personal stress and anxiety, resulting in control of self-destructive behavioral patterns (stress management)
- Learned ability to develop healthy attitudes and living patterns that are important to physical health and well-being (physical wellness)

The Role EQ Plays in Business

So that you can better understand the role that emotional intelligence plays in business, Plumeus has provided a sample of an entrepreneur's EQ results. Figure 2.3 and corresponding information are being offered so that you can see what each aspect of emotional intelligence is and why each one is important.

The sample scores that are shown in the results table and listed under various aspects of EQ are those of a fictitious entrepreneur. The scores were purposely pushed toward the high end so I could illustrate the EQ aspects of the ideal entrepreneur.

Figure 2.3 is an example of an ideal entrepreneurial emotional intelligence, one that is outstanding—much higher than average. This person expresses his feelings directly and with good timing. He's optimistic and positive and adapts well to changed circumstances. He deals effectively with stress and interacts and communicates adequately. He's comfortable with himself and knows and appreciates his talents and strong points as well as his weaknesses. He's able to motivate himself and to find the energy and the strength necessary to complete what he wants or needs to get done. He's a resilient person who bounces back after major drawbacks, survives hardship without bitterness, and still manages to give to others. Amazing!

This person seems to have mastered much of the theoretical knowledge necessary to the full development of emotional intellect. Unless a score is perfect, however, there's always room for improvement. You *can* always improve your EQ, whether you scored 10 or 149.

FIGURE 2.3: **Sample Entrepreneur EQ Survey Result**

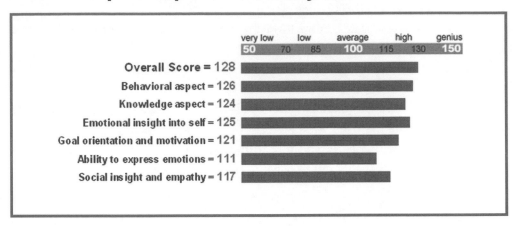

Knowledge and Behavior Aspects

The Knowledge aspect of the scale assesses an individual's ability to recognize or iden-tify the responses—emotional, cognitive, and behavioral—that in the given situation present the most effective way of achieving the desired outcome, whether it is dissi-pating an explosive situation, getting others to go along with what you want, or soothing yourself or others. This scale also assesses how well you can read a situation from overt behaviors of others. A high score means that you know what works, and you know—theoretically—how to do it.

The Behavioral aspect of the scale shows the degree to which you actually apply this knowledge in your everyday life.

EMOTIONAL INSIGHT INTO SELF. This example has quite a high score on emotional insight. (The ideal entrepreneur score is 125.) People with such a score are typically in touch with their emotions and are able to recognize their true feelings. They under-stand their reactions in most situations, and this self-insight prevents miscommuni-cation with others. The fact that they can pinpoint the reason that something is bothering them gives them a sense of self-control. In fact, they can usually console themselves rather than unleashing a flood of uncensored emotions. Having such insight into their emotional "weather" generally means they have high self-esteem and are able to bounce back quite well from life's difficulties.

GOAL ORIENTATION AND MOTIVATION. This example shows a level of motivation and goal orientation that's quite a bit above average. (The sample score is 121.) People with such a score possess a high level of intrinsic motivation and plenty of self-discipline to work toward their goals. They can handle most obstacles effectively and cope with setbacks. In addition, they're able to delay gratification in order to work toward long-term goals and don't depend on external reinforcement (like praise or frequent encouragement) to keep them going. People with high levels of inner drive generally have what it takes to achieve personal goals, which probably stems from self-confidence and a proactive approach to life.

ABILITY TO EXPRESS EMOTIONS. This example shows a high score on emotional expression. (The sample score is 111.) People with such a score have strong skills in expressing feelings and handling the communication of emotions from others. They're able to express their emotions in almost all situations and can typically deal effectively with people who are highly emotional. People who possess the ability to express and recognize emotions are typically communicative, assertive, and self-confident. Because of their ability to share their feelings, they also are generally well-equipped to form mature, intimate relationships. The better able people are to handle emotions, no matter how powerful, the better they can effectively communicate what they need and understand where others are coming from.

SOCIAL INSIGHT AND EMPATHY. This example shows a high level of social insight and empathy. (The sample score is 117.) People in this range are typically able to recognize the emotions of others and understand the motivation behind their actions. They can also put themselves in other people's shoes and empathize, which is obviously an important skill for satisfying and meaningful human interaction.

Overall, this example had both strengths (elements with a high score) and potential strengths (elements with a midrange score) and no significant limitations (elements with a low score). Strengths were:

- Overall high emotional intelligence
- Behaves in an emotionally intelligent way
- Recognizes and controls emotions well
- High intrinsic motivation and goal orientation
- Strong ability to express emotions and deal with emotional people
- Recognizes emotions in others, has insight into motivation behind others' actions, and is empathetic

How to Increase Emotional Intelligence

There are a number of ways to improve your ability to gain insight into your own emotions:

- Stay in touch with your feelings; pay attention to what triggers them and how you react.
- Question your beliefs. Do you think ignoring your emotions will make them go away? While this may be true for minor issues, strong feelings will manifest themselves in other ways (health problems, bitterness, etc.).
- Pay attention to your body when you're upset, sad, or angry. What are the signs?
- Be honest with yourself. Everyone feels things, and it's nothing to hide or be nervous about. Emotions are important signals that you need to listen to.
- Boost your coping skills: Build a supportive social network, learn how to relieve stress, etc.
- If you're prone to losing control of your emotions, try taking a step back from heated situations. Give yourself some time to gain control rather than reacting immediately.
- Practice keeping your feelings under control (without suppressing them), and it will become more natural.
- Build your self-esteem.
- Remember that emotion is just a whirlwind of activity passing through your body and mind. You help create it and feed it; how you react is important to its outcome.
- Get to know yourself better. For example, make a list of your strengths and developmental considerations. The more in touch you are with who you are, the better you can understand and handle your emotions.

In Their Own Words
What Entrepreneurs Said about Starting a Business

Q: *At what age did you first know that you were driven to succeed?*
Eighty percent of this survey group knew they were driven to succeed before they reached the age of 21. Past performance is the greatest predictor of future performance, and these entrepreneurs began their quest at a very early age. They believe in themselves and are willing to be put to the test time and time again.

At what age did you first know that you were driven to succeed?

Age	Percent
11 years old	25%
11 to 15	40%
16 to 20	15%
21 to 25	12%
26 to 30	6%
31 to 35	2%
36 to 45	0%

"I remember getting up very early and searching all over the place to find people who had tickets to a sporting event that I wasn't interested in. My only interest was to find the tickets and sell them."

"Working for a department store as a salesman, going to B-school at night, I already realized how much incompetence there was in management ranks and that I could easily outperform these losers. I always had an entrepreneurial spirit (bought and sold bicycles at age 12), but that didn't really turn into my own business until I had spent four years in retail management and nine years in production management."

"When I was in my early teens, I was constantly devising ways to make money. From selling fireworks (which are illegal in MN) at a very high profit margin, to fixing BMX bikes in my parents' garage, you name it. Also did a lot of buying stuff and 'fixin' it up,' then selling it for profit."

"Peewee football. I never knew I was a good player. I was small but always had a big heart and a strong work ethic. When I tried out for the team, I was one of the last players chosen. I became the MVP of the team and led our team to the championship game. Once I knew I could compete at a high level, I never wanted to leave that place."

"I had my first business at four selling "Shrinky Dinks" door to door in the neighborhood. I loved selling even then and knew I was good at it. I just always knew I would pull it off and make it in the world."

"I used to host dance recitals in my neighborhood that were a great success, and it was my idea and I was in charge. I knew then I could do anything."

"I came to America and even in first grade was clearly an entrepreneur."

"Paying for my own way in college. Working two jobs, 40+ hours a week to pay my tuition bills."

"I have always owned my own business (paper route boy, painting contractor, consulting engineer)."

"I was running three paper routes, pool and lawn service, painted houses and was involved in a choir and developed Temple Youth Group."

"Owned a firewood company, could not find any workers (friends) to work the hours and at the intensity level that I did. All were lazy and not driven at all. I was very driven by money and freedom that it created."

"Grandfather died at age of ten, watched my grandmother liquidate the jewelry business, etc., and decided I wanted to be just like her!!!"

"Would dry cars at the corner car wash for tips, would take packages to cars at the supermarket for tips. Always wanted to sell the most church boosters. Shined shoes going from bar to bar at age ten."

Q: *What were the first steps you took to get your business started?*
They may have written their business plan on a paper napkin. It may have been an afterthought, or possibly, the genesis was an MBA program at Fordham University. Most have niche businesses. They found a business in an economic environment, or in a geographic location that did not have a tremendous degree of competition. They created a niche, and exploited it.

Most started their business with revenues in sight. They stole a client, or one came to them. They had an innovative idea or way of competing. They rarely began their businesses without knowing where their first dollar of revenue was coming from.

"Stole a client from previous employer, started working!"

"Researched the industry. Who were the leaders? Where were they located? How big was the industry? Was it a growing industry? How did technology affect the industry? Then I wrote my first business plan and developed a plan of attack."

"Worked as an employee in the business for 13 years before purchasing it."

"Contacted a large corporation as a potential partner."

"Looked for first customers while employed with previous employer (on my own time)."

"I went to the magazine store and bought business magazines. I ripped the full page ads out and said if they had a full page ad in the magazine, they were big enough to have meetings and hire a person like me to speak at those meetings!"

"Stayed on Daddy's good side! I worked very hard, many late nights, and many, many Saturdays. Proved to him that I would be a worthy partner. Led company for ten years in sales."

"Letting the employees know I knew everything (It was complete bull) was the first step in any of my businesses. You have to let your people know you're leading them the right way."

"No business plan. Just opened the doors and started soliciting clients."

"Asked suppliers to give me credit."

"Found a partner (another fool willing to throw his life away on a whim)."

"Looked in the local classified to find a dry-cleaner for sale."

"Discovered a need, found a profitable solution, and then convinced our client that I was the best resource available. I then flew to Chicago to convince the manufacturer of the same about me."

Q: *What personal attribute or events have led most to your success?* (Personality traits are in italics.)

"*Flexibility, creativeness, persistence,* being able to see and do things in a different way, being a *nonconformist.*"

"*Perseverance*! More than anything, more than intelligence or skills or emotional stability, is *perseverance* (you can't fail if you don't give up)."

"My education and *drive* to build my own business, high-tech growth trends, great economy, networking, and internet acceptance."

"*Vision, focus, perseverance, drive, follow-through,* and the ability to inspire trust and loyalty."

"*Driven. Persistent. Excellent Communicator/Motivator.*"

"I won't accept that it can't be done. I try to only fight battles that I think I can win. I save for a rainy day. I *don't give up,* even when I probably should."

"My *gift of gab* and *persistence.*"

"*Perseverance* and *communication* skills."

"Attributes: intelligence, *opportunistic, communication skills, people skills, willingness to work hard and put in long hours, good sense of humor.* Events: a long history of good luck beginning with God's great gifts enumerated above."

"*Commitment. Vision.*"

"I have been blessed with *technical aptitude* and *selling skills.*"

"*Refusal to fail.*"

"Sheer *drive, determination,* a *positive attitude, cleverness.*"

"I am very *competitive.*"

"I always see the *big picture* first, high level of values. I am commerce-minded. I am *highly impatient* and very tenacious. I see how to connect the dots. I am a good leader and teacher. I have *strong convictions.*"

"*Stubbornness, competitiveness,* strong internal *desire to succeed.*"

"Intelligence, *desire to succeed, desire to continuously learn.*"

"I am extremely *goal-oriented* and *driven. I hate to lose.*"

"*Calm under fire.* Put out fires. Can light fires. Can *get fired up.*"

"*Drive, discipline, common sense, motivator,* and *persuader of people.*"

"Guts!! *Sales skill!! Drive!!*"

"*Courage, belief in myself, confidence, taking action.*"

"*Never quit* and very *fast learner.*"

"*Creativity, tenacity, no-fear attitude,* incredible *relationship skills,* ability to sell anything to anyone, public speaking skills."

"I am a HUGE believer in the pursuit of an activity that resonates with who you are. If you love creating, create. If you love sales, sell."

The responses of the entrepreneurs on the preceding pages represent all five tiers of the Performance Pyramid.

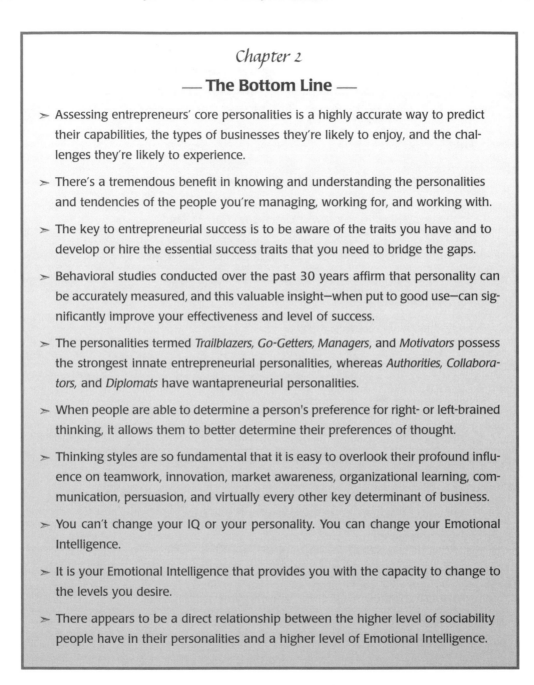

Chapter 2

—— The Bottom Line ——

➤ Assessing entrepreneurs' core personalities is a highly accurate way to predict their capabilities, the types of businesses they're likely to enjoy, and the challenges they're likely to experience.

➤ There's a tremendous benefit in knowing and understanding the personalities and tendencies of the people you're managing, working for, and working with.

➤ The key to entrepreneurial success is to be aware of the traits you have and to develop or hire the essential success traits that you need to bridge the gaps.

➤ Behavioral studies conducted over the past 30 years affirm that personality can be accurately measured, and this valuable insight—when put to good use—can significantly improve your effectiveness and level of success.

➤ The personalities termed *Trailblazers, Go-Getters, Managers*, and *Motivators* possess the strongest innate entrepreneurial personalities, whereas *Authorities, Collaborators*, and *Diplomats* have wantapreneurial personalities.

➤ When people are able to determine a person's preference for right- or left-brained thinking, it allows them to better determine their preferences of thought.

➤ Thinking styles are so fundamental that it is easy to overlook their profound influence on teamwork, innovation, market awareness, organizational learning, communication, persuasion, and virtually every other key determinant of business.

➤ You can't change your IQ or your personality. You can change your Emotional Intelligence.

➤ It is your Emotional Intelligence that provides you with the capacity to change to the levels you desire.

➤ There appears to be a direct relationship between the higher level of sociability people have in their personalities and a higher level of Emotional Intelligence.

CHAPTER

3

Are You an Entrepreneur or a Wantapreneur?

Who is the entrepreneur? What molds and motivates him? How does he differ from the nine-to-fiver, and where are those differences most telling? Why will one brother set out to build a business while another aspires to promotions and perks? Why does one sister stay up nights working on a business plan while the other brags about her pension plan? Is it brains? Luck? Hard work? Or something else all together?

When most people think of entrepreneurs, such well-known names as Henry Ford, Edwin Land, or Apple Computer's Steven Jobs come to mind. But in fact, American entrepreneurs number in the millions. Of the 16 million

41

businesses in this country, more than 12 million are operated as sole proprietorships. And while not all these businesses can be labeled "entrepreneurial ventures," *Webster's Dictionary* defines an entrepreneur as "one who manages, organizes, and assumes the risk of a business or enterprise."

Why, then, is the entrepreneur sometimes thought of in almost mythical terms? The answer is easy. Like cowboys of the Old West, the entrepreneur represents freedom: freedom from the boss, freedom from the time clock, and with a lot of hard work and more than a little luck, financial freedom.

So who is the entrepreneur? Anyone who has ever looked at a problem and seen it as an opportunity is a likely prospect. The same goes for anyone who feels as if his ambition is held in check by corporate red tape. But it takes more than just cleverness and frustration with the status quo to get an entrepreneurial venture off the ground.

While there's no single entrepreneurial archetype, certain character traits indicate an entrepreneurial personality. In the following quiz developed by the Center for Entrepreneurial Management, I have concentrated on those indicators. If you've ever wondered whether you have what it takes to own or manage your own business, here's your chance to find out whether you're an entrepreneur, an intrapreneur, or a wantapreneur.

What follows is a diagnostic tool to help determine your entrepreneurial profile as compared with the 3,000 members of the Center for Entrepreneurial Management. The Entrepreneur Quiz (Figure 3.1), first developed in the late 1960s, is updated every four years. It has appeared in publications as diverse as *Penthouse* and the *Harvard Business Review*.

FIGURE 3.1: **Your Entrepreneurial Profile**

Circle one answer for each question. If you already believe you're an entrepreneur, follow these directions: Circle one answer for each question. (That's a little joke. Entrepreneurs aren't great at following directions. They're much better at giving them.)

1. How were your parents employed?

  a. Both worked and were self-employed for most of their working lives.

  b. Both worked and were self-employed for some part of their working lives.

FIGURE 3.1: **Your Entrepreneurial Profile, continued**

---

   c. One parent was self-employed for most of his working life.

   d. One parent was self-employed at some point in his working life.

   e. Neither parent was ever self-employed.

2. Have you ever been fired from a job?

   a. Yes, more than once.

   b. Yes, once.

   c. No.

3. Are you an immigrant, or were your parents or grandparents immigrants?

   a. I was born outside the United States.

   b. One or both of my parents were born outside the United States.

   c. At least one of my grandparents was born outside the United States.

   d. Does not apply.

4. Your work career has been:

   a. Primarily in small business (fewer than 100 employees).

   b. Primarily in medium-size business (101 to 500 employees).

   c. Primarily in big business (more than 500 employees).

5. How many businesses did you operate before you were 20?

   a. Many.

   b. A few.

   c. None.

6. What is your age?

   a. 21–30.

   b. 31–40.

   c. 41–50.

   d. 51 or over.

FIGURE 3.1: **Your Entrepreneurial Profile,** continued

7. You are the _____ child in the family.

   a. Oldest.

   b. Middle.

   c. Youngest.

   d. Other.

8. What is your marital status?

   a. Married.

   b. Divorced.

   c. Single.

9. Your highest level of formal education is:

   a. Some high school.

   b. High school diploma.

   c. Bachelor's degree.

   d. Master's degree.

   e. Doctorate.

10. What is your primary motivation in starting a business?

    a. To make money.

    b. I don't like working for someone else.

    c. To be famous.

    d. To have an outlet for excess energy.

11. Your relationship with the parent who provided most of the family's income was:

    a. Strained.

    b. Comfortable.

    c. Competitive

    d. Nonexistent.

FIGURE 3.1: **Your Entrepreneurial Profile,** continued

12. If you could choose between working hard and working smart, you would:

   a. Work hard.

   b. Work smart.

   c. Both.

13. On whom do you rely for critical management advice?

   a. Internal management teams.

   b. External management professionals.

   c. External financial professionals.

   d. Only myself.

14. If you were at the racetrack, on which of these would you bet?

   a. The daily double—a chance to make a killing.

   b. A 10-to-one shot.

   c. A three-to-one shot.

   d. The two-to-one favorite.

15. The only ingredient that is both necessary and sufficient for starting a business is:

   a. Money.

   b. Customers.

   c. An idea or product.

   d. Motivation and hard work.

16. If you were an advanced tennis player and had a chance to play a top pro, you would:

   a. Turn it down because he could easily beat you.

   b. Accept the challenge but not bet any money on it.

   c. Bet a week's pay that you would win.

   d. Get odds, bet a fortune, and try for an upset.

FIGURE 3.1: **Your Entrepreneurial Profile,** continued

17. You tend to "fall in love" too quickly with:

    a. New product ideas.

    b. New employees.

    c. New manufacturing ideas.

    d. New financial plans.

    e. All the above.

18. Which of the following personality types is best-suited to be your right-hand person?

    a. Bright and energetic.

    b. Bright and lazy.

    c. Dumb and energetic.

19. You accomplish tasks better because:

    a. You are always on time.

    b. You are super-organized.

    c. You keep good records.

20. You hate to discuss:

    a. Problems involving employees.

    b. Signing expense accounts.

    c. New management practices.

    d. The future of the business.

21. Given a choice, you would prefer:

    a. Rolling dice with a one-in-three chance of winning.

    b. Working on a problem with a one-in-three chance of solving it in the allotted time.

FIGURE 3.1: **Your Entrepreneurial Profile,** continued

22. If you could choose from among the following competitive professions, your choice would be:

    a. Professional golf.

    b. Sales.

    c. Personnel counseling.

    d. Teaching.

23. If you had to choose between working with a partner who is a close friend and working with a stranger who is an expert in your field, your choice would be:

    a. The close friend.

    b. The expert.

24. You enjoy being with people:

    a. When you have something meaningful to do.

    b. When you can do something new and different.

    c. Even when you have nothing planned.

25. In business situations that demand action, will clarifying who is in charge help to produce results?

    a. Yes.

    b. Yes, with reservations.

    c. No.

26. In playing a competitive game, you are concerned with:

    a. How well you play.

    b. Winning or losing.

    c. Both of the above.

    d. Neither of the above.

FIGURE 3.1: **Your Entrepreneurial Profile**, continued

Add your totals and find out whether you have the personality of an entrepreneur or a wantapreneur.

Scoring: The scoring is weighted to determine your Entrepreneurial Profile. The rating guide appears after the analysis of the questions.

1) a = 10	2) a = 10	3) a = 5
b = 5	b = 7	b = 4
c = 5	c = 0	c = 3
d = 2		d = 0
e = 0		

4) a = 10	5) a = 10	6) a = 8
b = 5	b = 7	b = 10
c = 0	c = 0	c = 5
		d = 2

7) a = 15	8) a = 10	9) a = 2
b = 2	b = 2	b = 3
c = 0	c = 2	c = 10
d = 0		d = 8
		e = 4

10) a = 0	11) a = 10	12) a = 0
b = 15	b = 5	b = 5
c = 0	c = 10	c = 10
d = 0	d = 5	

13) a = 0	14) a = 0	15) a = 0
b = 10	b = 2	b = 10
c = 0	c = 10	c = 0
d = 5	d = 3	d = 0

FIGURE 3.1: **Your Entrepreneurial Profile**, continued

16) a = 0	17) a = 5	18) a = 2
b = 10	b = 5	b = 10
c = 3	c = 5	c = 0
d = 0	d = 5	
	e = 15	
19) a = 5	20) a = 8	21) a = 0
b = 15	b = 10	b = 15
c = 5	c = 0	
	d = 0	
22) a = 3	23) a = 0	24) a = 3
b = 10	b = 10	b = 3
c = 0		c = 10
d = 0		
25) a = 10	26) a = 8	
b = 2	b = 10	
c = 0	c = 15	
	d = 0	

Total Points = _____

Putting It Into Perspective

The following percentages are based on a survey given to the 2,500 members of the Center for Entrepreneurial Management.

1. How were your parents employed?

   a. Both worked and were self-employed for most of their working lives.   4%

   b. Both worked and were self-employed for some part of their working lives. 10%

c. One parent was self-employed for most of his working life.	36%
d. One parent was self-employed at some point in his working life.	16%
e. Neither parent was ever self-employed.	34%

The independent way of life is not so much genetic as it is learned, and the first school for any entrepreneur is his home. It's only natural that a child who has grown up in a home where at least one parent is self-employed is more likely to try his own hand at owning a business than a child whose parents were in, say, civil service. Research has shown that to be the case more than two-thirds of the time.

2. Have you ever been fired from a job?

a. Yes, more than once.	17%
b. Yes, once.	34%
c. No.	49%

This question is tricky because the independent-thinking entrepreneur will often quit a job rather than waiting around to get fired. The dynamics of this situation are the same, however. The results from the entrepreneur's brashness and reactivity fuel his almost compulsive need to be right. Steven Jobs and Steven Wozniak went ahead with what would become Apple Computer when their respective employers, Atari and Hewlett-Packard, rejected their project. And after National Cash Register fired Thomas Watson in 1913, he joined the Computer-Tabulating-Recording Co. and ran it until a month before his death in 1956. He also changed the company's name to International Business Machines, now IBM. The need to be right very often turns rejection into opportunity.

3. Are you an immigrant, or were your parents or grandparents immigrants?

a. I was born outside the United States.	7%
b. One or both of my parents were born outside the United States.	10%
c. At least one of my grandparents was born outside the United States.	36%
d. Does not apply.	47%

America is still the land of opportunity and a hotbed of entrepreneurship. The displaced people who arrive here every day—be they Cuban, Korean, or Vietnamese—can still turn hard work and enthusiasm into successful business enterprises.

4. Your work career has been:

    a. Primarily in small business (fewer than 100 employees).   62%

    b. Primarily in medium-size businesses (101-500 employees).   15%

    c. Primarily in big business (more than 500 employees).   23%

It's been said that "inside every corporate body, there's an entrepreneur struggling to escape." However, small-business management is more than just a scaled-down version of big-business management. The skills needed to run a big business are altogether different from those needed to orchestrate an entrepreneurial venture. While the professional manager is skilled at protecting resources, the entrepreneurial manager is skilled at creating them.

5. Did you operate any businesses before you were 20?

    a. Many.   24%

    b. A few.   49%

    c. None.   27%

The enterprising adult first appears as the enterprising child. Mowing lawns, shoveling snow, and promoting rock concerts are all common examples of early business ventures. And while every kid who runs a lemonade stand won't necessarily grow up to be an entrepreneur, a kid who runs a chain of lemonade stands is a good bet.

6. What is your age?

    a. 21–30.   18%

    b. 31–40.   38%

    c. 41–50.   26%

    d. 51 or over.   18%

The average age of entrepreneurs has been steadily falling since the late '50s, when it was found to be between 40 and 45. Our most recent research puts the highest concentration of entrepreneurs in their 30s, but such people as Jobs and Wozniak, Ed DeCastro and Herb Richman of Data General, and Frederick Smith of Federal Express all got their businesses off the ground while still very young. Although we look for this start-up age to stabilize right around 30, there are always exceptions that leave us wondering. Computer whiz Jonathan Rotenberg is just such an exception. He presides over the 10,000-member Boston Computer Society, publishes the slick magazine *Computer*

Update, and earned up to $1,500 a day as a consultant. In 1978, the promoter of an upcoming public computer show solicited his advice. After conferring with him several times on the phone, the promoter suggested they meet for a drink to continue their discussion. "I can't," Rotenberg replied. When asked, "Why not?" he answered, "Because I'm only 15."

7. You are the _____ child in the family:

a. Oldest.	59%
b. Middle.	19%
c. Youngest.	19%
d. Other.	3%

Entrepreneurs are most commonly the oldest children in their families. With an average of 2.5 children per American family, the chance of being the first child is about 40 percent. Entrepreneurs tend to be the oldest children about 60 percent of the time.

8. What is your marital status?

a. Married.	76%
b. Divorced.	14%
c. Single.	10%

Our research concluded that the vast majority of male entrepreneurs are married. But then, most men in their 30s are married, so that alone isn't a significant finding. However, follow-up studies have shown that most successful entrepreneurs have exceptionally supportive spouses. (While our results didn't provide conclusive results on female entrepreneurs, we suspect that their husbands would have to be doubly supportive.) A supportive mate provides the love and stability necessary to balancing the insecurity and stress of the job. A divorce or a strained marriage or love life can simply add too much pressure to an already-strained business life.

It's also interesting to note that bankers and venture capitalists look a lot more favorably on entrepreneurs who are married than on those living with their mates without the benefit of legality. As one venture capitalist told us, "If an entrepreneur isn't willing to make a commitment to the person he or she loves, then I'll be damned if I'm going to make any financial commitment to them."

9. Your highest level of formal education is:

    a. Some high school.   1%

    b. High school diploma.   17%

    c. Bachelor's degree.   43%

    d. Master's degree.   30%

    e. Doctorate.   9%

The question of formal education among entrepreneurs has always been controversial. Studies conducted in the 1950s and '60s showed that many entrepreneurs, like W. Clement Stone, failed to finish high school, not to mention college. And Polaroid's founder, Edwin Land, has long been held up as an example of an "entrepreneur in a hurry" because he dropped out of Harvard in his freshman year to get his business off the ground.

Our data concludes that the highest educational level most commonly achieved by entrepreneurs is a bachelor's degree, and the trend seems to be headed toward an MBA (Few entrepreneurs have the time or patience to think about a doctorate.) You will, however, find more and more entrepreneurs writing books as opposed to theses. This work is such an example.

10. What is your primary motivation in starting a business?

    a. To make money.   34%

    b. I don't like working for someone else.   56%

    c. To be famous.   4%

    d. As an outlet for excess energy.   6%

Entrepreneurs don't like working for anyone but themselves. While money is always a consideration, there are easier ways to make money than by going it alone. More often than not, money is a byproduct of an entrepreneur's motivation rather than the motivation itself.

11. Your relationship with the parent who provided most of the family's income was:

    a. Strained.   29%

    b. Comfortable.   53%

    c. Competitive.   9%

    d. Nonexistent.   9%

The results here really surprised me because past studies, including my company's own, had always emphasized the strained or competitive relationship between the entrepreneur and the income-producing parent (usually the father). However, our latest study showed that a surprising percentage of the entrepreneurs questioned had what they considered to be a comfortable relationship with that parent. I think that's largely related to the ages and educational backgrounds of entrepreneurs who are children of the '50s and '60s rather than children of the Depression. In most cases, they've been afforded the luxury of a college education, not forced to drop out of high school to help support the family. So the entrepreneur's innate independence hasn't come into such dramatic conflict with the father as it might have in the past. We still see a strained or competitive relationship often fits the entrepreneurial profile, but the nature of that relationship is no longer black and white.

12. If you could choose between working hard and working smart, you would:

    a. Work hard.   0%

    b. Work smart.   47%

    c. Both.   53%

The difference between the hard worker and the smart worker is the difference between the hired hand and the boss. What's more, entrepreneurs usually enjoy what they're doing so much that they rarely notice how hard they're working.

13. On whom do you rely for critical management advice?

    a. Internal management.   13%

    b. External management professionals.   43%

    c. External financial professionals.   15%

    d. Only myself.   29%

Entrepreneurs seldom rely on internal people for major policy decisions, because employees often have pet projects to protect or personal axes to grind, or the entrepreneur may be worried about asking his employees for help—isn't he, after all, supposed to have all the answers? And outside financial sources lack the imagination that characterizes many entrepreneurs—the noblest ambition of most bankers and accountants is to maintain the status quo. When it comes to critical decisions, entrepreneurs most often rely on themselves, outside management consultants, and other entrepreneurs, in that order. There are a number of CEO or entrepreneurial organizations designed to support the owner or manager. A complete list can be found on my web site, www.theentrepreneurnextdoor.com.

14. If you were at the racetrack, which of these would you bet on?

    a. The daily double—a chance to make a killing.   22%

    b. A 10-to-one shot.   23%

    c. A three-to-one shot.   40%

    d. The two-to-one favorite.   15%

Contrary to popular belief, entrepreneurs aren't high-risk takers when they can't affect the outcome. They tend to set realistic and achievable goals, and when they *do* take risks, they're usually calculated ones. Entrepreneurs are confident in their own skills and much more likely to bet on their tennis or golf games than they are to buy lottery tickets or bet on spectator sports.

15. The only ingredient that is both necessary and sufficient for starting a business is:

    a. Money.   13%

    b. Customers.   55%

    c. An idea or product.   20%

    d. Motivation and hard work.   12%

All business begins with orders. And orders come from customers. You may think you're in business when you've developed a prototype or after you've raised capital, but bankers and venture capitalists are only buying potential. It takes customers to buy a product.

16. If you were an advanced tennis player and had a chance to play a top pro, you would:

    a. Turn it down because he could easily beat you.   4%

    b. Accept the challenge but not bet any money on it.   78%

    c. Bet a week's pay that you would win.   14%

    d. Get odds, bet a fortune, and try for an upset.   4%

The question narrows the focus on the risk-taking concept, and the results emphasize what's already been stated: Most entrepreneurs are not high rollers. What's interesting is that more than three-quarters of our respondents would accept the challenge, not so much on the off-chance of winning as for the experience and perhaps the bragging rights. And experience is what entrepreneurs parlay into success.

17. You tend to "fall in love" too quickly with:

a.	New product ideas.	40%
b.	New employees.	10%
c.	New manufacturing ideas.	4%
d.	New financial plans.	13%
e.	All the above.	33%

One of entrepreneurs' biggest weaknesses is their tendency to "fall in love" too easily. As much as they can resolutely focus on results, they can just as easily have trouble focusing on the right concepts. They, therefore, can sometimes be easily swayed as they enjoy the newest in products, suppliers, machines, methods, and financial plans. Anything new excites them. But those love affairs usually don't last long; many of them are over almost as suddenly as they begin. The problem is that while they're going on, entrepreneurs can quite easily alienate their staff, become stubborn about listening to opposing views, and lose their objectivity. Remember, entrepreneurs hate to be sold, but they love to buy.

18. Which of the following personality types is best-suited to be your right-hand person?

a.	Bright and energetic.	81%
b.	Bright and lazy.	19%
c.	Dumb and energetic.	0%

This sounds counterintuitive, but we don't typically hire those who are like us. Instead, we typically hire people who will accept direction and be good followers. We actually need someone more like us for many of our leadership or sales positions, and the reason we don't like that personality type is that it's too much like ours. The answer to this question is easy: "Bright and energetic," right? I'm not so sure. That describes a personality like your own. But stop and think a minute. You're the boss. Would you be happy—or, for that matter, efficient—as someone else's right-hand man or woman? Probably not. And you don't want to hire an entrepreneur to do a hired hand's job.

That's why the "bright and lazy" personality often makes the best assistant. He's not out to prove himself, so he won't be butting heads with the entrepreneur at every turn. And while he's relieved at not having to make critical decisions, his delegating ability makes him a whiz when it comes to implementing them.

19. You accomplish tasks better because:

   a. You are always on time.   24%

   b. You are super-organized.   46%

   c. You keep good records.   30%

There's an answer that's missing. See it? "You are controlling." The correct answer, given the options, was "You are super-organized," as it's the key to an entrepreneur's success. It's the fundamental principle on which all entrepreneurial ventures are based. Without it, no other principles matter. Some entrepreneurs keep lists on their desks, always crossing things off the top and adding to the bottom. Others use note cards, keeping a file in their jacket pockets. Organizational systems may differ, but you'll never find an entrepreneur without one.

> Salvador Dali, the artist, believed that his greatest period of creativity was just as he was falling asleep or upon waking. In order to summon this level of creativity, he used to take afternoon naps sitting upright in a rocking chair. He would place a plate on the floor and hold a set of keys in his hand above the plate. When he was about to fall asleep, he would drop the keys, and he had instant creativity. Whatever works for you, works.

20. You hate to discuss:

   a. Problems involving employees.   37%

   b. Signing expense accounts.   52%

   c. New management practices.   8%

   d. The future of the business.   3%

The only thing an entrepreneur likes less than discussing employee problems is discussing petty-cash slips and expense accounts. Solving problems is what an entrepreneur does best. But problems involving employees seldom motivates him, so discussing them is just an irritating distraction. Expense accounts are even worse. What an entrepreneur wants to know is how much his salespeople are selling, not how much they're padding their expense accounts. This answer also speaks to details, and that's one thing that most successful entrepreneurs are good at delegating but struggle with controlling.

21. Given a choice, you would prefer:

    a. Rolling dice with a one-in-three chance of winning.   8%

    b. Working on a problem with a one-in-three chance of solving it in the allocated time.   92%

Entrepreneurs are participants, not observers; players, not fans. And to be an entrepreneur is to be an optimist, to believe that with the right amount of time and money you can do anything. Of course, luck—being in the right place at the right time—plays a part in anyone's career, but entrepreneurs have a tendency to make their own luck. There's an old story about a shoe manufacturer in the 1800s who sent his two sons to the Mediterranean to scout out new markets. One wired back: "No point in staying, coming home. No one here is wearing shoes." The second son wired back: "Terrific opportunities. No one here is wearing shoes." Who do you think inherited the business?

22. If you could choose from among the following competitive professions, your choice would be:

    a. Professional golf.   15%

    b. Sales.   56%

    c. Personnel counseling.   8%

    d. Teaching.   21%

Sales provide instant feedback on one's performance; it's the easiest job of all for measuring success. How does a personnel counselor or teacher ever know whether he's winning or losing? Entrepreneurs need immediate feedback and are always capable of adjusting their strategies in order to win. Some entrepreneurs brag that they play by the rules when they're winning and change the rules when they're losing. Although I don't endorse that, when it works, it's known as the win-win strategy.

23. If you had to choose between working with a partner who is a close friend and working with a stranger who is an expert in your field, your choose would be:

    a. The close friend.   13%

    b. The expert.   85%

While friends are important, solving problems is clearly more important in business. Often the best thing an entrepreneur can do for a friendship is to spare it the extra strain of a working relationship.

24. You enjoy being with people:

    a. When you have something meaningful to do.   32%

    b. When you can do something new and different.   25%

    c. Even when you have nothing planned.   43%

Like billionaire Daniel Ludwig, many entrepreneurs will state categorically that they have no hobbies. But that doesn't mean they have no social life. In fact, some entrepreneurs can be very social people and, more often than not, very charming. (Remember, an entrepreneur is someone who gets things done, and getting things done often involves charming the right banker or supplier.) And while they'll often have difficulty talking about things other than themselves or their businesses, their enthusiasm is such that whatever they talk about sounds interesting.

25. In business decisions that demand action, clarifying who is in charge will help produce results:

    a. Yes.   66%

    b. Yes, with reservations.   27%

    c. No.   7%

As the saying goes, a camel is a horse that was designed by a committee, and unless it's clear that one person is in charge, decisions are bound to suffer from a committee mentality. Entrepreneurs can be good at collaborating, team-building, or building consensus, but make no mistake, they do so to further their agendas.

26. In playing a competitive game, you are concerned with:

    a. How well you play.   19%

    b. Winning or losing.   10%

    c. Both of the above.   66%

    d. None of the above.   5%

Vince Lombardi, the great football coach, was famous for saying, "Winning isn't everything; it's the only thing," but a lesser-known quote is closer to the entrepreneur's philosophy. Looking back at a season, Lombardi remarked, "We didn't lose two games; we just ran out of time twice." Being in business for oneself is a competitive game, and an entrepreneur has to be prepared to occasionally run out of time. Lombardi knew the value of metrics and getting results!

Your Entrepreneurial Profile

235–285	Successful entrepreneur*
200–234	Entrepreneur
185–199	Latent entrepreneur
170–184	Potential entrepreneur
155–169	Borderline entrepreneur
154 and below	Wantapreneur

*The CEM-member profile is 239

Review your answers, and see which answers received higher scores. Do you understand why one answer may reflect greater entrepreneurial capability than others? Can you imagine yourself thinking or behaving in that manner? If so, what would you have to do differently? If not, how might that limit your success? These are Tier II and Tier III questions because you can see the entrepreneurial behaviors necessary for success and those are coupled with the requisite actions.

If you scored at the high end of the spectrum (200-plus), you already know you're driven to succeed. If you aren't working for yourself, why not? If you are, congratulations!

If you scored at the lower end of the range, it doesn't necessarily mean you're destined to slave for someone else. What it does mean is that you might benefit from professional coaching, developing a mentor relationship, and reading about your areas of interest. You would also benefit from completing a behavioral assessment so that you can better determine your strengths as well as your potential challenges and limitations. You will be able to take a similar assessment by going to www.theentrepreneurnextdoor.com.

Chapter 3
— The Bottom Line —

➤ While there's no single entrepreneurial archetype, certain character traits indicate an entrepreneurial personality.

➤ Although it's far from a necessary ingredient for entrepreneurship, the need to succeed is often greater among those whose backgrounds contain an extra struggle to fit into society.

➤ The skills and personality needed to run a big business are altogether different from those needed to orchestrate an entrepreneurial venture. The professional manager is skilled at protecting resources. The entrepreneurial manager is skilled at creating resources. You may see ten comparisons by going to www.theentrepreneurnextdoor.com

➤ The enterprising adult first appears as the enterprising child.

➤ More often than not, money is a byproduct of an entrepreneur's motivation rather than the motivation itself.

➤ Entrepreneurs seldom rely on internal people for major policy decisions.

➤ Contrary to popular belief, entrepreneurs aren't high-risk takers when they can't affect the outcome. They tend to set realistic and achievable goals, and when they do take risks, they're usually calculated ones.

➤ Entrepreneurs are participants, not observers; players, not fans. And to be an entrepreneur is to be an optimist, to believe that with the right amount of time and money, you can do anything.

➤ The five-tier performance pyramid is alive and well as it provides a behavioral roadmap that contains unlimited opportunity and direction to the entrepreneur.

4

How the Four Personality Factors Work

*I*T WAS IMPOSSIBLE TO GET A STRAIGHT ANSWER FROM MY GRANDMOTHER UNTIL AT LEAST my 17th birthday. I can remember asking her, "So Grandma, how are you feeling?" She would say, "How do you think I should be feeling? I'm 78 years old." Ah, the joys of growing up in a Jewish family. Why is this significant? Much of our success is built on the art of the question, and natural-born entrepreneurs have a tendency to ask specific questions, oftentimes determined by their personalities. They have a tremendous natural sense of curiosity.

The favorite question of the Trailblazers, Managers, and Go-Getters is, "Why?" "Why did you do it that way? Why can't I? Why shouldn't I?" They have a natural curiosity and are always questioning themselves and others. Those who are more compliant, such as the Authorities, Collaborators, and Diplomats, are usually the How people. They always want to know how a project or a task should be done. They are the true experts and need to do things right because when they do things right, they avoid blame. Those with higher levels of sociability are usually our Who people, like Motivators, Collaborators, Go-Getters, and Diplomats. They are usually concerned with whom they need to talk to and whom they need to involve, and they are often strong consensus-builders. The When people make up one of two types: those who are calm, methodical, and patient and those who are more driving and intense and have a high sense of urgency. Having this understanding makes it easier to identify behavioral styles.

The Four Factors

There are four measurable personality factors: dominance, sociability, relaxation, and complicance. See Figure 1.2 on page 13. Each has two separate, opposite traits. On one side of dominance, for example, people have their competitive side, and the opposite side is accepting or accommodating. Particular combinations of factors produce the seven personality types and behavioral styles.

Dominance

Those with a high level of dominance are competitive and goal-oriented people who can be aggressive in resolving uncertainties. Winning is very important to them, and they seek to lead the way in facing new challenges. They aim high and work hard to achieve their aspirations. They face troublesome issues, resistance, and obstacles willingly, and despite them, or maybe because of them, they are determined to attain their goals. They thrive on difficult assignments and tough competition and are usually people of action who make things happen. They tackle problematic situations vigorously, want to enhance performance and results, and don't want to be controlled. They usually display a wide variety of interests and will seek opportunities to handle many projects simultaneously. Ambitious, needing to succeed, they not only welcome but often expect authority over and responsibility for others. Exceptionally assertive and success-oriented, they show up for one reason: to win.

They're results-driven and goal-oriented, seek the big picture, are strategic planners, need opportunities for leadership, and require autonomy, authority, and power. A high level of dominance is necessary in most sales positions, on the executive team, and in marketing and business development. Dominance is often an essential element for those entrepreneurs who are founders of their endeavors. It's important to note that there are varying degrees of dominance.

Those with a low level of dominance are very cautious and deliberate, going out of their way to get along with others. They know how to be a part of a team and work for the good of the group rather than seeking out individual recognition. They enjoy working with good people and will take direction from others, as in a franchise environment. They're careful about making decisions and will typically reserve their decisions until they have thoroughly examined all the facts surrounding the case. They consolidate their efforts and specialize in one area or field of endeavor, wanting to concentrate on that area of expertise. Preferring a conflict-free working environment, they often try to mediate quietly, one on one, especially if co-workers are having problems with one another. They are very accepting and cautious; need encouragement, reassurance, and harmony in relationships; seek accord; avoid confrontation; require freedom from competition; are good followers; and prefer to be supportive of others.

Those who have lower levels of dominance are usually more comfortable working in environments where their success is determined mainly by their ability to follow policies and procedures. Examples would be a franchise, a distributorship, and opportunities that have a strong brand or a great location. Within a corporate environment, they do best in most support, manufacturing, customer-service, financial, and administrative positions. They find confrontational and competitive situations to be difficult.

For extreme examples of dominance levels, think about Rambo and Mr. Rogers; Rambo is the one who's highly dominant, and Mr. Rogers is more accommodating. Which more accurately reflects your Tier I, natural style? Are you more of a Rambo or a Mr. Rogers, or perhaps somewhere in between?

Sociability

Sociability is defined largely by styles of communication. Do you use a lot of words to tell your story, or are you more comfortable using fewer words? Do you have more of a selling style of communication or a telling style? Do you have a preference for working with people, or are you more comfortable working with systems, concepts, and numbers?

People who are highly sociable enjoy receiving recognition, need pats on the back, and want to be part of—or perhaps lead—a well-run team. They need to interact with others and want to be part of a respected group, to seek and build consensus. A highly sociable person tends to be outgoing and extroverted, gregarious, stimulating, socially poised, friendly, and talkative. Higher levels of sociability are typically a requirement in positions that involve selling, customer service, and public relations. However, it's important to point out that too much sociability can have the opposite effect; it becomes difficult to close sales if one has too much sociability, as it can also be difficult holding others accountable.

People with lower levels of sociability tend to be more analytical, self-conscious, serious, and introspective. They can even be secretive and remote. Their style of communication can be more matter-of-fact, strictly business, sometimes sparse or terse. People with lower sociability need the opportunity to think and analyze and prefer private recognition based on their expert status.

Lower levels of sociability are usually found in the back end of the business—financial, production, research and development, information technology, engineering, and other positions that require less interaction with others. An extreme example of a low sociability job would be a toll-taker where people are by themselves all day. From a leadership or entrepreneurial position, he would be most comfortable working behind the scenes.

A good example of sociability opposites would be Bill Clinton and Bill Gates. Clinton, the more sociable, uses his words to communicate from an empathetic perspective, whereas Gates, the more analytical and introverted, thinks more and talks less. Highly sociable entrepreneurs—a company's chief officer, rainmaker, and chaos creator, for example—can enjoy ventures in which they are constantly meeting and dealing with people, such as in retail, public relations, marketing, and selling. Entrepreneurs with lower levels of sociability might find greater enjoyment in franchising or companies where the customer comes to the store based on advertising, location, or brand awareness. In this environment, the more introverted entrepreneur is excellent at dealing with people because the entrepreneur isn't required to sell. The brand, product, or location does the selling.

Which more accurately reflects your Tier I, natural style? Are you more highly sociable, more analytical, or perhaps a combination of both?

Relaxation

The relaxation factor determines a person's pace of work or sense of urgency, the speed at which one is comfortable working. Is a person more comfortable dealing with pressure or would he rather have a more stable, steady work environment?

People with higher levels of relaxation prefer stability and long-term, family-like relationships. They enjoy being rewarded for loyalty, are adaptable to change—with advance notice—and enjoy "familiar" surroundings and activities. A highly relaxed person tends to be more methodical, calm, and patient. He does best in jobs that are repetitive in nature. More than 70 percent of our population has a higher than average level of relaxation, and more than 80 percent of the jobs in our society require a higher-than-average level of patience because they require the worker to handle repetitive tasks on an ongoing basis. Those with a higher level of relaxation are the backbone of our society. They're the loyal workers who make everything run—and run on time.

> ### Creatures of Habit
>
> Those with higher levels of relaxation are often strong creatures of habit. An example would be the highly relaxed technician. Jim travels the country constantly and given his penchant for a lack of surprises his favorite restaurant is Denny's. He always knows what to expect because each one has very consistent quality, including the same menus.

People with lower levels of relaxation enjoy freedom from repetition and need a varied pace. They thrive in a changing environment, want fewer controls, and are good at multitasking. A person with a lower level of relaxation tends to be more intense, driving, and sometimes high strung. They work well under pressure and are typically comfortable sharing that pressure with others. They're good in leadership or entrepreneurial roles that are fast-changing and allow for multiple areas of focus.

Think of the tortoise and the hare. The tortoise is the more relaxed entrepreneur who does well in businesses that are stable and have predictable levels of pressure. A retail environment is a great fit (except on the days after Thanksgiving and Christmas). Tortoises are the backbone of our society. They work well in operations that offer consistent processes such as restaurants, where the pace, although hectic, is always hectic and therefore predictable. Oil-change facilities, laundries, and photocopy shops are other examples.

The hare is the entrepreneur with a lower level of relaxation (and therefore a higher level of drive) who doesn't find enough challenge in these types of opportunities unless they have multiple locations and are constantly looking at and incorporating ways to improve. It is important to remember who finished the race. One of the challenges that those with *driven* personalities have is they think that everyone should be like them . . . and that just doesn't work.

Which more accurately reflects your Tier I, natural style? Are you more relaxed like a tortoise or more driven like the hare, or a combination of both?

Compliance

In essence, the compliance factor is all about the details. Are you good at following procedures and policies, or are you better at working in an environment that's relatively free of structure?

People with higher levels of compliance prefer security, stability, and an understanding of exactly what the rules are. They also deal better with day-to-day responsibilities, tactical applications, strong direction and leadership, opportunities for advanced training, and a job for life. A highly compliant person tends to be precise, cautious, self-disciplined, structured, and sometimes a perfectionist. The more highly compliant entrepreneurs had better be in a business where they're comfortable with rules and structure, which can be found in many successful franchises. They are somewhat risk-adverse. They don't mind taking a risk as long as it is within their area of expertise.

People with a lower level of compliance are more independent and enjoy freedom from structure, freedom from micromanagement, and opportunities to prove their own ideas in a work environment. A less compliant person tends to be more rebellious, unstructured, strong-minded, and sometimes obstinate and self-directed. These more independent people need to do it their own way and will be more comfortable making it up as they go along. A book to go by is the last thing they want or are willing to embrace. They are able to work in those environments where they must figure things out for themselves.

The TV show *The Odd Couple* provides a good example of the compliance extremes. Felix Unger, the professional photographer, is the compliant one, and Oscar Madison, the sportswriter, is less compliant and therefore more independent. Oscar was able to figure it out as he went along. This made Felix absolutely nuts. They both get the job done; they just do it differently.

Which more accurately reflects your Tier I, natural style? Are you more of a Felix who wants structure or an Oscar who wants independence, or perhaps a combination of both? To reaquaint yourself with the four factors, refer to Figure 1.3 on page 14.

In Their Own Words
Where Entrepreneurs Got the Ideas to Start Their Own Businesses

Q: *Where did you get the idea to start your own business?*

"Worked as a consultant for another firm, figured if they could do it, we could do it."

"My husband and I started with a blank slate and invented it based on what we love to do, what we excel at, and what we felt the world needed."

"Had to write a business plan for an entrepreneurial management class at UM evening MBA program. Was watching market trends in my market and saw the technology I could put together to change the industry."

"I was employed in the business and purchased it from my father."

"Looking at what was going on in the world and thinking about an approach that would build a successful company."

"Other industry professionals asked me to start and manage a consortium (membership-based) linking a variety of owner-operated independent companies to provide a national service—almost like a broker."

"My biz is an extension of my hobby. I saw a couple of motivational speakers when I was 23. I said, 'I could do that.' And, I did."

"Saw others doing it, felt I could do better."

"The business I was in at the time."

"Competing product."

"It's a version of what I've been doing for the last eight years."

"I was in the temporary staffing company for several years—liked the staffing part but wanted to make higher margins—saw a need for IT professional consultants as I was making sales calls for the temp business."

"I spoke to a networking breakfast, and it built from there."

"Developing a business plan for an advertising company that I was consulting with."

"I did research to find a company that could provide these services to my customers and could not find one."

"I'd worked in the industry for years, and starting this business was a natural extension of my career."

"Always wanted to own my own staffing company since starting in the field at 24."

"I wanted to sell something small that I did not need to inventory, which had a high value and with which I could identify. Watches met all of those criteria."

"Idea was given to me—the chance to bid on an RFP."

"Customers made me start."

"My father had a developer write a program for his medical practice and I was introduced to the developer and thought there was a viable market. I then set up the company."

"Saw a competing product and knew I could do it better."

"Only one company was dominating the market. No one had enough chutzpa to go against them."

"Worked for a large corporation who thought they knew their market and customer base. They didn't have a clue."

"I needed a place to get a good facial and massage."

"Prior company was eliminating a portion of their business."

Chapter 4
— The Bottom Line —

➤ The four primary factors of our personality are dominance, sociability, relaxation, and compliance.

➤ Those with a high level of dominance are competitive, goal-oriented people who can be aggressive in resolving uncertainties. Those with lower levels of dominance are more accepting, agreeable, and accommodating.

➤ A highly sociable person tends to be outgoing and extroverted, gregarious, stimulating, socially poised, friendly, and talkative. Those who are more introverted are more analytical and reserved.

➤ People with higher levels of relaxation prefer stability, enjoy being rewarded for loyalty, are adaptable to change—with advance notice—and tend to be more methodical, calm, and patient. Their more driving opposites are more flexible and work better under pressure.

➤ A highly compliant person tends to be precise, cautious, self-disciplined, structured, and sometimes, a perfectionist. Those with lower levels of compliance tend to be more independent. They can also be strong willed as they want to do things their own way.

➤ The favorite question of the Trailblazers, Managers, and Go-Getters is, "Why?"

➤ Authorities, Collaborators, and Diplomats usually ask, "How?"

➤ Motivators, Collaborators, Go-Getters, and Diplomats are looking to involve others, so they often ask, "Who?"

➤ Tier I is represented by your natural style of personality. Your success is determined by the relationship between your Tier I personality and your Tier II Job Behaviors. The difference between these two represents a gap. The size of this gap determines the amount of stretching necessary to accomplish the job.

5

Entrepreneurs and Wantapreneurs

ENERALISTS TEND TO HAVE HIGHER THAN AVERAGE LEVELS OF DOMINANCE AND lower than average levels of compliance. For the most part, Specialists are just the opposite, except that Collaborators and Diplomats also tend to have a higher than average level of sociability.

These levels mean that Generalists tend to be natural entrepreneurs. They also mean that Generalists can step on a lot of toes and spend plenty of time in hot water.

Trailblazers

As you can see from the Trailblazer personality graph in Figure 5.1, Trailblazers typically have a high level of dominance, are very driven, and have above-average levels of independence and analytical thought processes. Although these Generalists are the type of people who often come to mind when you think about entrepreneurs, their challenge is building and maintaining lucrative businesses because they are more process-oriented than people-oriented.

FIGURE 5.1: **Trailblazer Personality Graph**

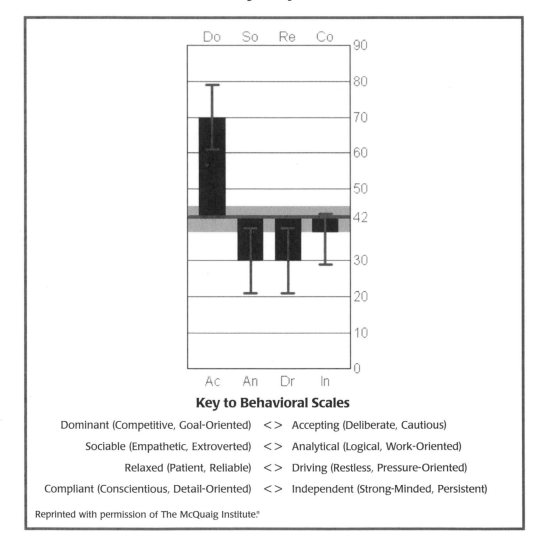

Key to Behavioral Scales

Dominant (Competitive, Goal-Oriented) <> Accepting (Deliberate, Cautious)

Sociable (Empathetic, Extroverted) <> Analytical (Logical, Work-Oriented)

Relaxed (Patient, Reliable) <> Driving (Restless, Pressure-Oriented)

Compliant (Conscientious, Detail-Oriented) <> Independent (Strong-Minded, Persistent)

Reprinted with permission of The McQuaig Institute.®

By nature, Trailblazers are very competitive, ambitious, and goal-oriented—so much so that they have a tendency to be aggressive and sometimes take a steamroller approach. Restless and energetic, Trailblazers have a strong drive and display a sense of urgency, regardless of the task at hand. They tend to have two speeds: fast and faster. Independent, persistent, and decisive, Trailblazers aren't happy unless they're in charge. Most Trailblazers are logical, analytical, practical, and realistic, and they usually base decisions on facts rather than feelings.

Warning: Do not attempt to sway Trailblazers with an emotional argument, because you won't get what you want. Instead, ask them whether they're open to a suggestion. It gives them the opportunity to turn off their stupid switch. That's the little switch located deep within our reptilian brain. It's almost always in the "on" position, but if you ask them if they're open to a suggestion and they say "yes," they will listen and be more responsive than reactive, increasing your chances of getting what you want.

Trailblazers are known for stepping on others' toes because of their intense need to achieve their goals and their tendency to focus more on ideas and methods than on people. Although they may be good at routine and details, they often abhor both, seeking challenges and new opportunities instead. They resent close supervision and are likely to be abrasive, so they tend to experience more people problems than other entrepreneurial types.

> **Stupid Switch**
>
> The stupid switch is that little part of our reptilian brains that causes us to be more reactive than responsive. It causes us to say NO at the flip of a switch. The default setting is usually in the "on" position.

Go-Getters

Go-Getters have a higher-than-average level of both dominance and sociability and are also very driven and independent. See Figure 5.2. Go-getters naturally work by, with, and through others. Generalists are competitive, but their drive to succeed is sometimes tempered by their interest in and concern for others. Ambitious goalsetters by nature, they welcome responsibility and authority but can share some of the spotlight. They are more interested in working with others than in being isolated.

> A Go-Getter I recently interviewed said he makes his wife crazy when they attend the Philharmonic because the music stimulates his creativity and he constantly is writing his ideas on a pad of paper that he always carries with him.

FIGURE 5.2: **Go-Getter Personality Graph**

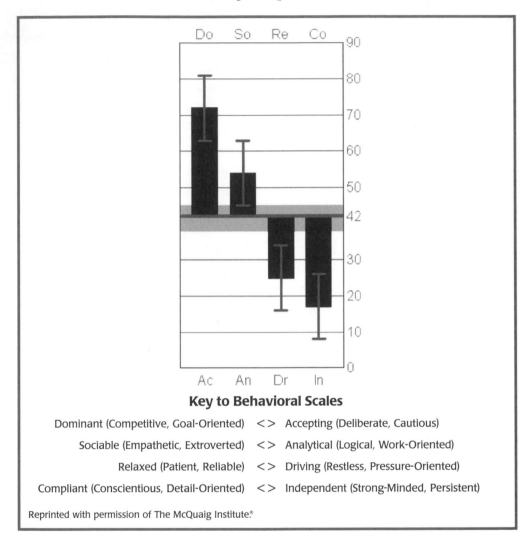

Key to Behavioral Scales

Dominant (Competitive, Goal-Oriented)	<>	Accepting (Deliberate, Cautious)
Sociable (Empathetic, Extroverted)	<>	Analytical (Logical, Work-Oriented)
Relaxed (Patient, Reliable)	<>	Driving (Restless, Pressure-Oriented)
Compliant (Conscientious, Detail-Oriented)	<>	Independent (Strong-Minded, Persistent)

Reprinted with permission of The McQuaig Institute.®

Go-Getters tend to have a high level of energy and often find it difficult to relax. Even when they say they're doing "nothing," chances are they're actually doing *something*. They show a great deal of personal initiative coupled with a compelling sense of urgency to get things done. For Go-Getters, variety really is the spice of life, and they quickly become bored and restless with too much routine: They can handle the routine and details when required, but they'd rather not. They relish their independence, work well under pressure, and tend to be persistent and decisive. Go-Getters enjoy motivating others and are usually good at delegating details but usually not as good at delegating authority. Sociable and outgoing, most Go-Getters are effective communicators, can be very persuasive, genuinely like people, and may even display a Clintonesque quality of empathy and understanding. The Clintonesque Go-Getters are great at reading others.

Go-Getters thrive on challenge and new opportunities and can become surly if they're not achieving their goals. They have a distaste for close supervision and balk at most forms of micromanagement. They're more interested in working with others than with ideas, systems, and methods. They're not happy if the work they do isolates them from other people because they need social stimulation.

> ### Clintonesque Defined
>
> A natural ability similar to that of President William Jefferson Clinton. In his first presidential campaign, he was able to walk into a town hall meeting with total strangers and sense their issues. You find this quality in many of the greatest leaders and salespeople. Ronald Reagan also had this quality. In Transactional Analysis, such qualities are referred to as the *Little Professor*.

Managers

Managers are dominant and independent. In their case, these two characteristics feed each other so that they can appear to be more dominant or independent than they actually are. See Figure 5.3. Managers are also very goal-oriented and can be quite analytical, focusing more on the process and outcomes than on others. These Generalists have a tendency to look at people as vehicles for helping them accomplish their goals. Consequently, they sometimes disregard or overlook the people part of the equation or inadvertently offend people with their straightforward style of communication.

Unlike the two previous entrepreneurial types, who are also Generalists but with a greater sense of drive about getting things done quickly, Managers have a higher level of relaxation and know that some projects simply take more time to complete and some goals take longer to achieve than others. A Manager may want something to be done by tomorrow but will rarely say he wants it done yesterday (a typical comment for Go-Getters, Trailblazers, and Motivators). One of Managers' strengths is that they like to think things through before responding. They're loyal, sometimes to a fault, as they look at their employees as an extension of their families, and as you know, it's difficult firing your family.

Although Managers have a higher level of relaxation, that doesn't mean they're any less competitive or goal-oriented than their counterparts. They love to win and

FIGURE 5.3: **Manager Personality Graph**

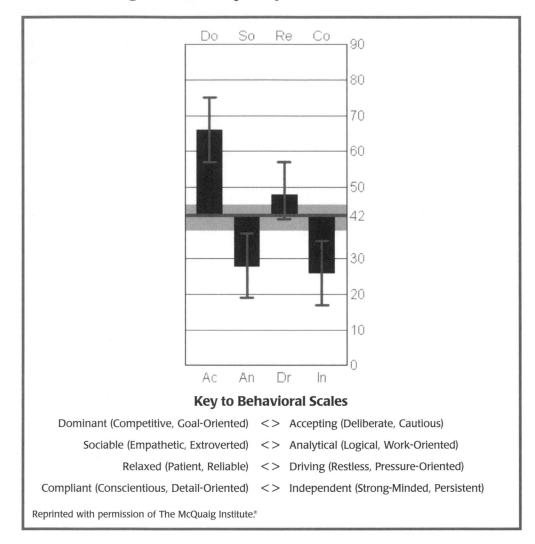

Key to Behavioral Scales

Dominant (Competitive, Goal-Oriented)	<>	Accepting (Deliberate, Cautious)
Sociable (Empathetic, Extroverted)	<>	Analytical (Logical, Work-Oriented)
Relaxed (Patient, Reliable)	<>	Driving (Restless, Pressure-Oriented)
Compliant (Conscientious, Detail-Oriented)	<>	Independent (Strong-Minded, Persistent)

Reprinted with permission of The McQuaig Institute.®

don't hesitate to take chances. They view conflict, resistance, and roadblocks as par for the course and can often use challenges and difficulties as stepping stones or ways to motivate themselves and others. The problem is that sometimes their strong wills coupled with their low level of sociability and high relaxation can be seen as stubbornness or rudeness.

They prosper in environments where they can freely use their sense of initiative and often fight to get their own way—which they firmly believe is the best way or the right way. They make decisions based on facts and are rarely concerned with the opinions or reactions of others. They do not, however, enjoy working with difficult people and will attempt to sidestep personnel problems or steamroll these people, rather than finding a way to work things out.

Because Managers are so reliable and patient, they work well with systems and methods and might be described as calm, cool, and collected—even when the pressure is intense and the stakes are high.

Motivators

Motivators, who also fit the Generalist pattern, have a high level of sociability, an above-average level of dominance, and low levels of compliance and relaxation—meaning they are independent and driven. See Figure 5.4.

Typically friendly and outgoing, Motivators work best when they're interacting with others. They're congenial, optimistic, and more likely to focus on the positive aspects of business and messages rather than on negatives. They believe in others and are supportive and encouraging. Motivators are enthusiastic about sharing their ideas. They work well within a team environment and often enjoy healthy competition with others. A team win is more important to them than a personal win.

Motivators are independent, think autonomously, and are capable of acting on their own. They tend to believe their ideas are right and are often determined to get their own way but will do so by working with and through others. They're persistent, have a strong ability to follow through, and stay on track to get the results they're seeking. Although they don't *have* to be in charge, they prefer leadership roles and enjoy using their initiative. Motivators tend to be restless, so they want to get things done quickly. They set goals that they think are attainable and don't involve too much unnecessary risk.

Motivators prefer to avoid friction with others, but they'll face up to a problem if and when it can't be avoided. Even so, their high level of sociability can lead them to steer clear of confrontation in an effort to be well-liked and popular with others. They're usually

> My writing mentor and coach, Toni Robino, is a Motivator. The name of her firm is With Flying Colours. Motivators are one of the best personalities to work with because they are always upbeat and positive, and have that marvelous can-do attitude. She works phenomenally well under pressure and makes last-minute deadlines look like an art form.

FIGURE 5.4: **Motivator Personality Graph**

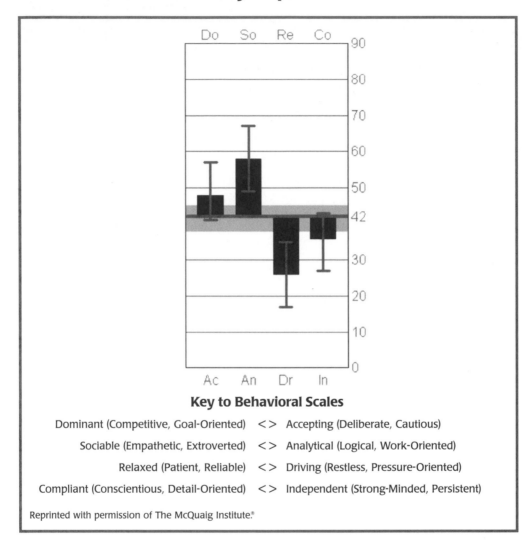

Key to Behavioral Scales

Dominant (Competitive, Goal-Oriented) <> Accepting (Deliberate, Cautious)

Sociable (Empathetic, Extroverted) <> Analytical (Logical, Work-Oriented)

Relaxed (Patient, Reliable) <> Driving (Restless, Pressure-Oriented)

Compliant (Conscientious, Detail-Oriented) <> Independent (Strong-Minded, Persistent)

Reprinted with permission of The McQuaig Institute.®

good communicators but not always as good at listening as they are at talking. They aren't happy in situations that require working alone for long periods of time, and although they can take charge on occasion, they don't respond well to having authority over others in difficult or confrontational situations. They would be better served having the sales manager report to them rather than the whole sales team.

Although Authorities, Collaborators, and Diplomats do not have the most innate entrepreneurial traits, if they have the desire and the will to learn, they can be successful.

The achievements and failures of Specialists in the entrepreneurial arena are typically determined by how well they can expand their comfort zones and increase their skill sets.

Authorities

Those who have this personality are the backbone of our society. They are the loyal workers who make our world work. See Figure 5.5. They're the ones who make our products, service our systems, and always do it right. They are rarely the founders of

FIGURE 5.5: **Authority Personality Graph**

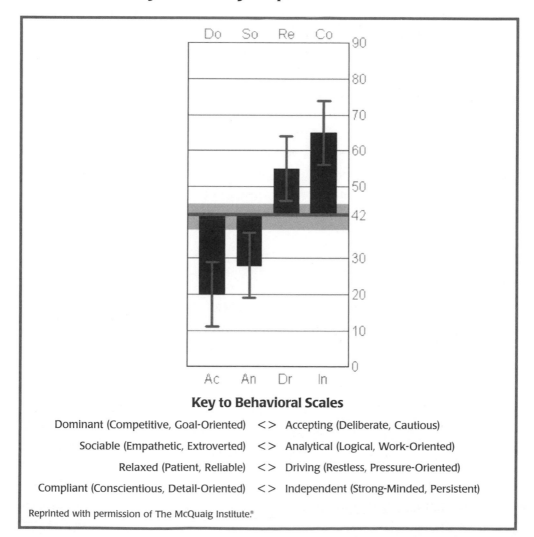

Key to Behavioral Scales

Dominant (Competitive, Goal-Oriented) < > Accepting (Deliberate, Cautious)

Sociable (Empathetic, Extroverted) < > Analytical (Logical, Work-Oriented)

Relaxed (Patient, Reliable) < > Driving (Restless, Pressure-Oriented)

Compliant (Conscientious, Detail-Oriented) < > Independent (Strong-Minded, Persistent)

Reprinted with permission of The McQuaig Institute.®

entrepreneurial enterprises, but these Specialists *can* be excellent distributors or franchisees. They also can do very well when they purchase an ongoing operation.

Authorities are detail- and tactically-oriented and are motivated by doing things one way—the right way. They are very conscientious and cooperative, and follow rules, procedures, and policies carefully. Very thorough with details, they're cautious, deliberate, logical, and analytical, and they make decisions based on facts and figures, rather than on emotions or gut reactions. Relaxed, patient, and peaceful by nature, they're great team players and tend to avoid confrontation.

Steady and reliable, Authorities are comfortable with and can enjoy routine. They aren't necessarily competitive, strong-willed, or highly independent and probably won't want responsibility for difficult people or for difficult decisions outside their areas of expertise. Within their areas of expertise, however, they make quick decisions and can appear to be as strong as most Generalists; their strength just comes from another source—their experience and skills. Their relaxed and easygoing nature isn't usually compatible with pressure and deadlines. That's not to say they can't deal with pressure; as with any pattern or behavior that requires change, they just need an understanding of the actions necessary.

Once the Authority understands the how-to, they then need to take those actions and get the energy to accomplish their goals. I sometimes refer to their personalities as falling into the drill sergeant pattern because they're relatively nonconfrontational as long as others are doing things right but can become confrontational when others fail to follow the rules.

Collaborators

Collaborators have a Specialist, or expert, personality. The primary difference between them and Authorities is that Collaborators have a personality gift called sociability. See Figure 5.6. It's this characteristic that allows Specialists to use their influence to get what they want. They're good at working in customer-service roles, retail sales, or any environment where being convincing is an important aspect of getting the job done and done right. There is a difference between selling cold and having a warm market. Generalist personalities are typically better selling in a cold market whereas Collaborators can be great sales people because they use their sociability to sell their expertise.

Typically thoughtful, considerate, and easy going, Collaborators work well within a society of rules, policies, and procedures. Great as a part of a team, they're sociable

FIGURE 5.6: **Collaborator Personality Graph**

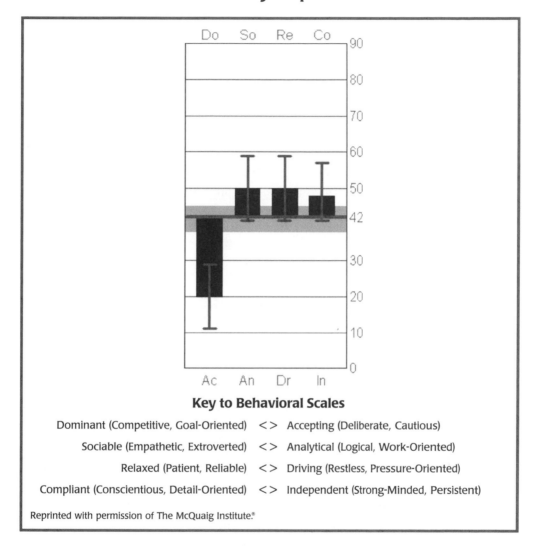

Key to Behavioral Scales

Dominant (Competitive, Goal-Oriented) < > Accepting (Deliberate, Cautious)

Sociable (Empathetic, Extroverted) < > Analytical (Logical, Work-Oriented)

Relaxed (Patient, Reliable) < > Driving (Restless, Pressure-Oriented)

Compliant (Conscientious, Detail-Oriented) < > Independent (Strong-Minded, Persistent)

Reprinted with permission of The McQuaig Institute.®

and outgoing, understand people, and like being helpful. Collaborators, being conscientious and cooperative, follow company rules and directions well. Having a higher-than-average level of patience, they like to think things through before responding, especially to new situations or when faced with new information. They're good at handling details and will produce high-quality work.

From an entrepreneurial perspective, the Collaborator will do well within structured environments where a people element is part of the success. He's good at delegating authority as long as he can hire people who will be loyal to him and follow the rules.

Collaborators aren't necessarily confrontational or even overly strong-willed (independent) and usually won't want responsibility for supervising others or making difficult decisions outside their areas of specialization. If they find themselves in that situation, however, they can still get the job done because of their high level of compliance. They can be rather forceful as long as they know what they're talking about. Take them to areas outside their expertise and they'll want to *become* experts in those areas before they're comfortable with those decisions. More comfortable working with people than with systems, they run the risk of wanting to be liked at the expense of getting results. Provided that they're supported in the organization by a "hit man"—someone to do their bidding and hold others accountable—they can reach their entrepreneurial desires.

Diplomats

Diplomats are restless and driving people who enjoy working with a certain degree of pressure. These Specialists get things done quickly and work well with deadlines. They find that artificial deadlines can serve them well. They're adjustable to change and deal well with new situations. They have a high sense of urgency and like variety, and because of their compliance and their need to do things right, they work at their full capacity. They multitask and keep a variety of jobs going at once. Active and energetic, they vigorously attack the parts of their jobs that they enjoy. See Figure 5.7.

Diplomats are conscientious, sincere, and serious when it comes to their jobs. Good planners who like to prepare for contingencies, they follow directions carefully and are thorough with details. They are good team members and can also lead in certain situations. They have a need to become true authorities within their areas of expertise. They can experience difficulty in delegating details but do a great job when they can do the work themselves.

Diplomats are sociable and outgoing. They genuinely like people and enjoy working with and through others. Empathetic and possessing a chameleon-like quality, they're excellent in most customer-service environments. They're able to see others' points of view and allow them to speak their minds. In general, they get along well with others. They're also optimistic and tend to see the positive side of things.

As leaders, Diplomats are naturals at working with teams and building consensus in dealings with others. A careful approach to decision-making is their natural style.

FIGURE 5.7: **Diplomat Personality Graph**

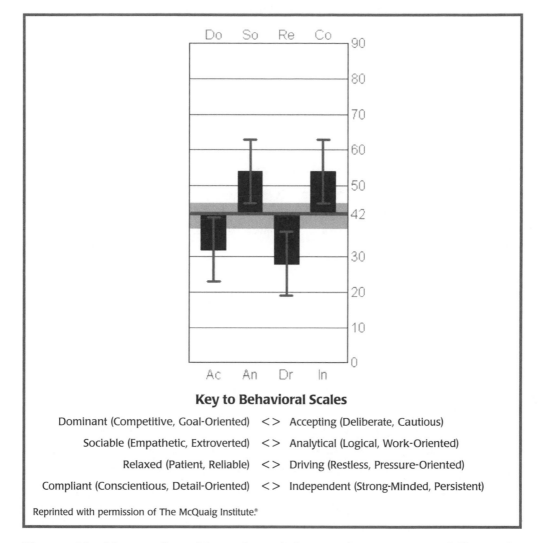

Key to Behavioral Scales

Dominant (Competitive, Goal-Oriented)   < >   Accepting (Deliberate, Cautious)

Sociable (Empathetic, Extroverted)   < >   Analytical (Logical, Work-Oriented)

Relaxed (Patient, Reliable)   < >   Driving (Restless, Pressure-Oriented)

Compliant (Conscientious, Detail-Oriented)   < >   Independent (Strong-Minded, Persistent)

Reprinted with permission of The McQuaig Institute.®

They avoid taking needless risks and use their natural consensus capability as the linchpin of their decision making. They will almost always examine all available options before moving forward.

Personality Factors and Entrepreneurship

According to our research, personality basically comes in three broad classifications. They are the Generalists, who have much greater dominance than compliance and tend to be more strategic and big picture in their thinking. They are also more results-oriented in terms of being able to work well in an environment relatively free of structure.

The second classification is the Specialists. I also refer to these as the Wantapreneurs. The Wantapreneurs have higher levels of compliance than dominance, which means they are more risk adverse, as opposed to Generalists who are willing to take risks. The Specialists prefer doing things within a structure, one way, the right way. They are more tactically oriented and more detail-oriented.

The third classification, which was a relatively small percentage, were neither Generalists nor Specialists. These were individuals who had almost the same amount of dominance as compliance and therefore we refer to them as those in transition. Most people are in transition for a relatively short period of time. When these people are surveyed again six months or a year later, their results often show them to be either a Generalist or a Specialist.

Success or failure is usually due to personal characteristics, such as attitude, motivation, and temperament (personality), according to industrial psychologist Jack H. McQuaig, founder of The McQuaig Institute®. To measure these key personal characteristics, more than 40 years ago McQuaig developed the assessments that today comprise The McQuaig System™. The Accord Management Systems' survey of the personalities of the entrepreneur, the Generalist, emerged using The McQuaig Institute's Word Survey on more than 1,500 men and women, all members of the Young Entrepreneurs' Organization.

Hackett & Associates (HRC Inc.) completed its analysis as a part of this study of 1,509 YEO members (1,270 males and 239 females). Entrepreneurs (Generalists) represented 78.7 percent of the group, 12.3 percent were wantapreneurs, (Specialists), and 9 percent were in transition. The predominance of the entrepreneurial personality among YEO members is evident among both males (80.2 percent) and females (70.7 percent).

In Figure 5.8, the mean scores show the levels of the four factors out of 168 possible points. That makes a score of 42 average. For example, if someone scores a 56 in dominance, she has a higher than average level of dominance.

The men and women in the study had very similar personalities (see Figure 5.9). They are both Generalists. Both have more dominance than any other factor, and both have dominance that is greater than their sociability, although the men have a bigger spread between dominance and sociability. Both the men and the women are very driving and both are relatively independent.

FIGURE 5.8: **Male & Female Entrepreneurs Are More Alike**

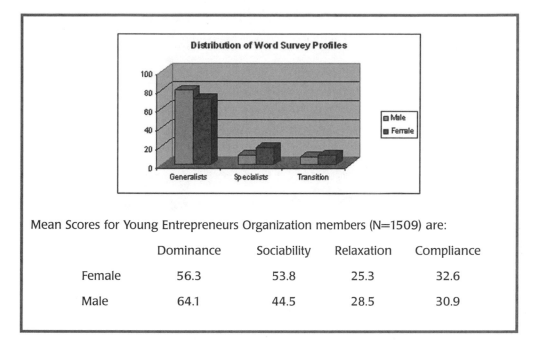

Mean Scores for Young Entrepreneurs Organization members (N=1509) are:

	Dominance	Sociability	Relaxation	Compliance
Female	56.3	53.8	25.3	32.6
Male	64.1	44.5	28.5	30.9

The men have a low of 28.5 to a high of 64.1, so they have a 35.6 point spread. The women, on the other hand, range between 25.3 and 56.3, for a 31 point spread. So the men actually have a slighter bigger personality. What that means is that the male personality will have a greater ability to have an impact on an environment that may be slightly larger, but with the difference of only 4.6 points, I don't know that to be significant. What becomes more significant is the edge that the men will have because their dominance is so much higher than their sociability. That also means the men will have the ability to anger more people more often.

The differences are that male respondents had a greater level of dominance and a 20-point spread, or difference, between their sociability and their dominance. Because of this spread, men have a pronounced edge (not necessarily a good thing), a telling style of communication in which they actually take on some of the Trailblazer qualities.

Scores for the entire group show a profile described as highest in dominance, next highest in sociability, with substantially lower levels of relaxation and compliance. This profile of high dominance and sociability and low relaxation and compliance typify an entrepreneurial personality profile that is often seen in founders of new ventures. It is

FIGURE 5.9: **Female vs. Male Entrepreneur Graphs**

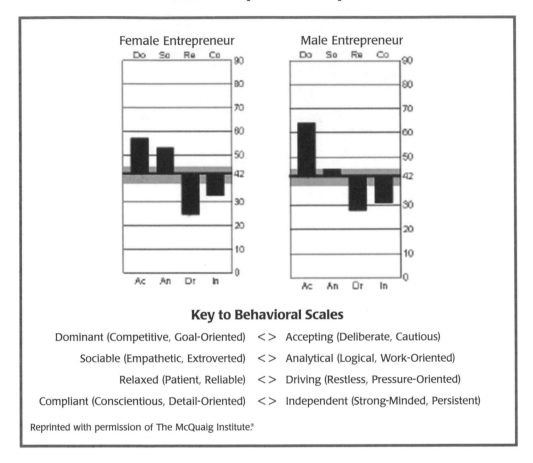

also of interest that women scored high on both dominance and sociability whereas men scored substantially higher on dominance than they did on sociability. Based on these scores, specifically the higher level of sociability, it can be said that female entrepreneurs will be better than their male counterparts at delegating authority and building consensus, relationships, and teams.

The total spread between the males' lowest factor, their drive, and their highest factor, dominance, is 36 points. (For women, the spread is 31.) As you can see in Figure 5.10, the further from the norm line (42 points) the stronger the personality is. The closer to the norm line, the more flexible or malleable is the personality.

This spread takes on greater meaning when you consider that 68 percent of the population has a personality with about a 20-point spread, between a low of 30 and

FIGURE 5.10: **Deviation in the McQuaig System**™

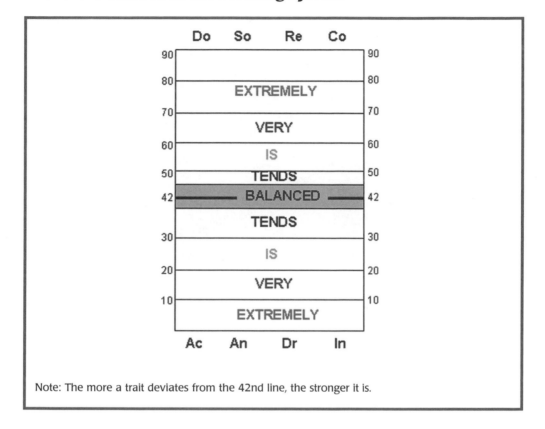

Note: The more a trait deviates from the 42nd line, the stronger it is.

a high of 50. The size of one's personality determines the size of the environment or organization that one can impact. Bigger is not always better. Due to the relationship between the drive and compliance, the study group would be able to focus on and control the details of the operation and at the same time be independent enough in order to deal with ambiguity. Because of the relationship that exists between the very high dominance and the much lower sociability, those individuals with the most extreme spread would display a very controlling side.

In its purest form, however, the Go-Getter personality represents 31.1 percent of the study group. In order for there to be such a high spread between the dominance and the sociability in the YEO mean scores, you have to look no further than the Figure 5.11 pie chart that shows Trailblazers represent 28.9 percent of the study group.

FIGURE 5.11: **YEO Chart of Personality Types (N=1,509)**

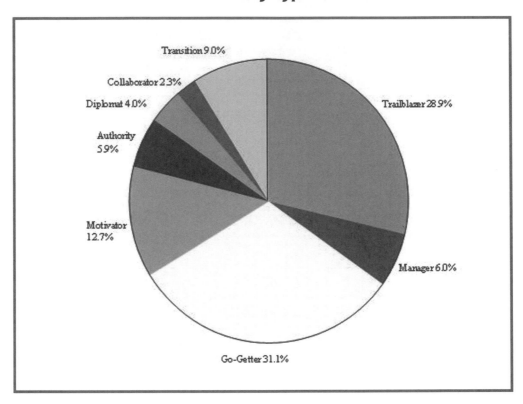

As you may very well know, motivation is short-lived. I know this flies in the face of many motivational speakers' messages, but we can rarely maintain changes based on emotional buy-in for more than 30 days.

I created the Performance Pyramid (page 11) so that the entrepreneurs I coach could have a concrete, cognitive model and process that they can rely on whether they happen to be feeling motivated or not.

We each predominantly fit one of the seven types listed initially in this chapter. Your personality type represents Tier I on the Performance Pyramid. If you are a Generalist, specifically a Go-Getter or Trailblazer, then it will feel more natural for you to enact the necessary job behaviors to become a successful entrepreneur. If you are not a Trailblazer or a Go-Getter personality then it is essential to look at Tier I in relationship to the requirements of the position, Tier II. The difference between these creates a behavioral gap and it is that gap that needs to be managed.

It is here that the model really began to develop as I realized that there were specific actions (Tier III) that support the Tier II requirements. An example of these actions for a shop owner might include visiting with the local chamber of commerce, joining a networking group such as Business Network International, creating a local neighborhood marketing plan that includes mail, welcome wagon, advertising or personal visits, and determining a way to measure these actions (Tier IV). If the shop owner is able to reach the acceptable Tier IV (Metrics) then I can almost guarantee that he or she will reach the desired Tier V (Results).

My associates and I have tested this model hundreds of times and based on our research, it works and works well. If an entrepreneur can accept the changes necessary from a cognitive perspective he can also reach his goals.

Because Trailblazers have a high level of dominance and a low level of sociability, they cause the spread to be greater in the overall comparisons. Women have more sociability and more drive than the men. This allows them to work at a faster pace, put more pressure on themselves and others, multitask at a greater level, and use their sociability to get what they want. They can manage others more effectively, handle relationships more smoothly and naturally, and build consensus and collaborate with others. The women's pattern has a spread of 31 points between highest and lowest personality factors (only 5 points less than their male counterparts) because the really significant sex difference is the spread between dominance and sociability. The women's differential is only 3 points compared to the men's 20 points. The men's differential allows the men's dominance to literally dominate their personalities.

The bottom line is all about job-fit. If you have a personality (Tier I) that matches the behavioral requirements of the position (Tier II), then the chances of doing well in that position go up exponentially. And, if you don't have the right personality . . . well, you will just have to work harder. But why not find an opportunity that is just right? For more on finding the right fit, see Chapter 17, The Goldilocks Theory.

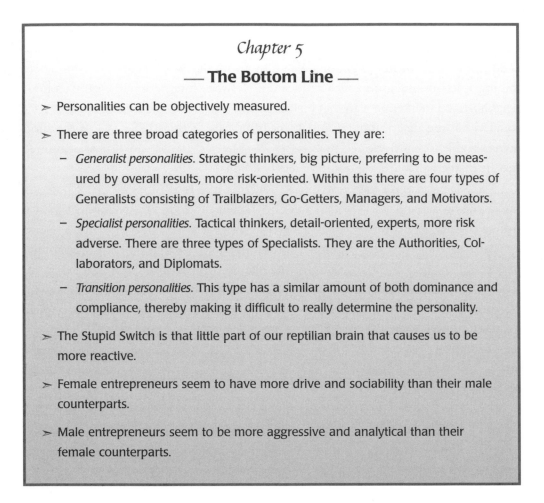

Chapter 5

— The Bottom Line —

➤ Personalities can be objectively measured.

➤ There are three broad categories of personalities. They are:

   – *Generalist personalities*. Strategic thinkers, big picture, preferring to be measured by overall results, more risk-oriented. Within this there are four types of Generalists consisting of Trailblazers, Go-Getters, Managers, and Motivators.

   – *Specialist personalities*. Tactical thinkers, detail-oriented, experts, more risk adverse. There are three types of Specialists. They are the Authorities, Collaborators, and Diplomats.

   – *Transition personalities*. This type has a similar amount of both dominance and compliance, thereby making it difficult to really determine the personality.

➤ The Stupid Switch is that little part of our reptilian brain that causes us to be more reactive.

➤ Female entrepreneurs seem to have more drive and sociability than their male counterparts.

➤ Male entrepreneurs seem to be more aggressive and analytical than their female counterparts.

The DNA of Entrepreneurial Success

EVERYONE IS GOOD AT SOMETHING. RARELY IS ANYONE GOOD AT EVERYTHING. AND like it or not, very few people achieve success in ventures that aren't good fits with their innate personalities. So if you want to start a company, get a job, or invest in an opportunity, doesn't it make sense to learn more about who you are and what makes you tick? If you're going to be hiring and managing people, wouldn't it be a good idea to know who they really are?

The Benefits of Understanding Personality

Understanding your personality and the personalities on your team gives you an incredible edge. If you're a believer in the golden rule, "Do unto others as you would have them do unto you," it's time to reconsider. Although the adage sounds good, it will please only the people who are just like you. Instead, consider doing unto others as they would have you do unto them. In other words, treat others as *they* want to be treated.

Warning: Don't assume you know how someone wants to be treated.

Secret: Knowing someone's personality type gives you accurate information on what type of treatment will trigger the response you want.

Even without knowing someone's personality profile, you can make a fairly educated guess at his personality type by paying close attention to what he says, what he does, and how he does it. For example, is he a risk-taker or a risk-avoider? Does he seem to enjoy working with people or systems? Does he seem to multitask, or does he prefer to finish a project before starting another?

Imagine that you walk into a conference room for a committee meeting with a handful of people you've never met. All of you have volunteered to be part of the committee, so you can assume that you either have some level of sociability or a need to achieve or control. Otherwise, the typical tendency would be to avoid (or at least *not* volunteer for) group or team situations.

> The first objective is to select a committee chairman. Before the introductions have even begun, Sally says, "Let's get down to business. We don't have much time, and I have a lot of experience in this area, so I'd like to get things started and make myself available to serve as the interim committee chair."
>
> George interjects, "Maybe it would make the most sense to review the objectives for our committee and then take a vote."
>
> Karen agrees with George: "We probably all have experience in this area, so to keep the process fair. I think, we should get to know each other a little and then consider our options. But I'm open to whatever the rest of you are thinking."
>
> Tom says, "Voting sounds good to me." With a soft chuckle he adds, "Just don't put my name in the hat. But if you need me, I'd be willing to help out." Everyone but Sally laughs.
>
> Karen turns to Stuart, who has been quiet up to this point, and asks, "What do you think?"

Stuart has the look of a deer in headlights. He swallows and says, "I'm here for your computer support. It doesn't matter to me who's in charge, so long as it's not me."

Of the profiles you read in the previous section, which one do you think fits each committee member? Take a moment to consider the possibilities before you read further.

Sally exhibits high dominance by suggesting that she be in charge. She shows she's more analytical (less sociable) by expressing more interest in the objectives than in meeting the rest of the people on the committee. She doesn't laugh when Tom introduces a little humor to the mix. Sally is probably a Trailblazer. (This doesn't mean Trailblazers don't have a sense of humor, but "fun" tends to take a back seat to results when they're on a mission.)

> **Humor**
>
> Those with higher levels of dominance and lower levels of sociability have a strong tendency toward sarcasm. Throw a little drive into the mix, and you get a quick wit. Think about Jim Carrey, Robin Williams, Ellen Degeneris, and David Letterman. They're all introverts that would often times prefer to be by themselves.

George is willing to disagree with Sally's suggestion and put forth his own idea and suggest a vote. The willingness to challenge Sally shows that he also has high dominance, but his desire for group consensus indicates that he has a higher level of sociability than Sally. George is most likely a Go-Getter but possibly a Manager.

Karen attempts to increase the comfort level in the meeting, showing a higher degree of cooperation and acceptance. She supports George's idea to vote but also says she'll go along with whatever the others want. She doesn't want to be part of a conflict, which is on par with her cooperative and accepting nature. She suggests that the members get to know one another a little, which indicates that she's sociable, but she's willing to express her own ideas. She also asks Stuart to share his thoughts, again showing her tendency to be cooperative or a consensus-builder. Karen is probably a Diplomat.

Tom makes it clear that he doesn't want to be the one in charge but suggests that he's willing to assist. This indicates that he has above-average dominance, though not nearly as above-average as Sally and George. He has an easy way about him and makes a joke, indicating high sociability. Tom seems to be a Motivator or possibly a Diplomat.

Stuart, who doesn't say a word until he's specifically asked to comment, shows a more accepting and analytical side. His statement that he doesn't want to be in charge indicates his accepting nature, and his assertion of his specific role as "computer support" indicates that he wants to stay in that role. Stuart is most likely a Specialist/Authority.

Short-Term Personality Changes

With all that said, keep in mind that people can exhibit behaviors that are significantly different from their natural personalities, at least for short periods of time. Introverts can behave like extroverts, especially when they're with a group of introverts that they trust and feel comfortable with. When someone they don't know walks into their environment, they may return to their more introverted roots. We all have the ability to stretch or hold back our natural styles for a relatively short period of time. The challenge is changing our personality for an extended period.

Just think back to your last job interview, and compare your behavior with the way you acted the last time you went out with one of your good friends. Notice any differences? Anyone who has ever interviewed for a job knows that his "interview personality" isn't necessarily his real personality. Interviewing and dating are basically "sales calls;" in those scenarios—if we're interested in the job or our date—we're selling ourselves. Our objective is for the person conducting the interview to offer us the job or for the person sitting across from us at a candlelit restaurant to be interested in future engagements.

For the most part, personalities, Tier I—developed largely during the early formative years of people's lives—change little over the course of their lives. Their behaviors, Tier II, however, are the manifestations of their personalities and are the aspects of their personalities that are changeable. People can change their behavior to get what they want in a number of environments. I like to use the typical dating personality or vacation personality to illustrate your ability to behave outside your natural personality because almost everyone can relate to it (see Figure 6.1). Regardless of your personality, the dating personality you exhibit, particularly on the first few dates, is probably quite different from what your parents and best friends see.

Imagine that you're on a date; perhaps it's the beginning of a relationship. Do you think that you'll be more aggressive or more accepting? The dating personality is usually accepting. "You're 35, and you live with your mother. That's great. What a wonderful way to show your love and support for her!" When you're on a date, do you think you'll be more calm and patient or be more impatient? The survey says more patient. Imagine it's time to pick up your date. You expect your date to be ready by

FIGURE 6.1: **Dating or Vacation Personality**

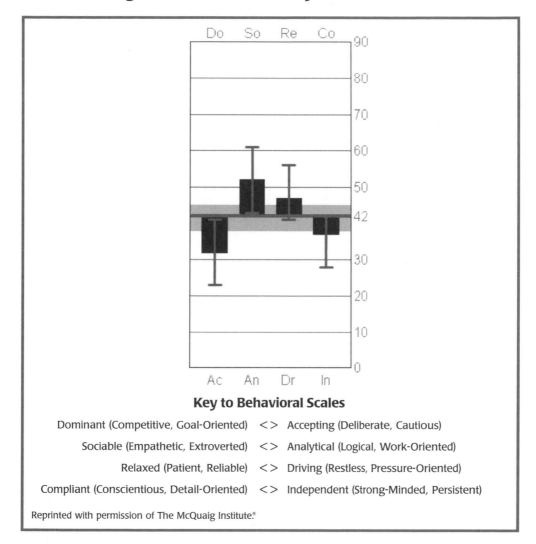

Key to Behavioral Scales

Dominant (Competitive, Goal-Oriented)	<>	Accepting (Deliberate, Cautious)
Sociable (Empathetic, Extroverted)	<>	Analytical (Logical, Work-Oriented)
Relaxed (Patient, Reliable)	<>	Driving (Restless, Pressure-Oriented)
Compliant (Conscientious, Detail-Oriented)	<>	Independent (Strong-Minded, Persistent)

Reprinted with permission of The McQuaig Institute.®

6:30. You have plans on seeing a movie at 7, but your date isn't ready. Do you blow a gasket or do you say, "That's OK. Why don't we just have dinner first and then play the rest of the evening by ear?" Right! You're more patient. For those of you who are now married, are you still as patient? I doubt it.

When dating, do you find that you're more sociable and outgoing or more shy, introspective in your thoughts? Most of us are more sociable. For those of us who think selling is just like lying, even we can increase our sociability in the dating process.

My wife and I took our three children, Josh, Rebecca, and Alex, to Hawaii. It was definitely a honeymoon-like environment (except for the kids). One day, Josh and I were lounging by the pool and he asked if he could get a smoothie. Do you have any idea how much smoothies cost in Hawaii? They are close to $8. (They justify the price by saying they have to import the fruit from the mainland.) I said, "Sure, just bill it to the room." I wanted to make sure I got both my miles and points. Several minutes later, Josh returns with his smoothie but with a grimace. I said, "What's wrong?" He said, "It taste more like mom's coffee, not like chocolate. Dad, why don't you take this one and I'll get another!" What would you do? It's vacation . . . we went back to the smoothie stand and traded in for a new smoothie. For two weeks I was being a *mensch*. That is Tier II behaviors for wonderful, accommodating, and agreeable. Can any of you relate to this story? To make a long story short, we were at the airport coming home and my wife, Renee, stops me, puts her palm on my chest and asks, "Who's getting on the plane with me? Is it the Bill I have grown to love all over again in this honeymoon-like environment or is it Bill the Butthead?" I responded, "Who would you like it to be?" Renee said, "If it is Bill the Butthead, perhaps he should think about staying here in Hawaii." We can change our personalities for short periods of time.

Do you feel more relaxed or driving when dating, and are you more compliant, wanting to do everything right, or more casual and independent? When dating, we have a tendency to be more relaxed and independent in that we're more flexible and uninhibited. This is a great personality to have in a dating environment.

The dating personality is very resilient, able to sustain itself for sometimes the entire dating process. The challenge with the dating personality is that you're able to be this person for a couple of years but then one morning, you wake up, look at your significant other and say, "I can't believe how much you've changed since we got married." With shock, they look at us and say, "I'm not the one who has changed. You're the one who has changed." The truth is, everyone changes.

While dating, interviewing, or in a selling or speaking role, you can project a personality that's completely different from your everyday nature. The bigger the difference between the way you're acting and your natural style, however, the harder and more stressful it will be to keep up the act. (Those of you who are attempting this know exactly what I mean!) Eventually, for most people, the mask falls off. If you meet someone who appears to be calm, cool, and collected, all you have to do is put him in a stressful situation to unveil the person behind the mask. The best novelists learn to do this with the characters in their stories to give readers the inside scoop on the characters' true nature, showing their strengths and revealing their weaknesses.

Find the Long-Term Personality

According to the Talmud, an important book in Judaism, before a woman shall marry a man, she should see him under three conditions. True personality traits tend to come out when someone is drunk, sick, or angry. I jokingly tell executives who are hiring, "If you really want to know what someone's like, take them out for bad sushi, offer them a couple of martinis, and then piss them off and see what happens" Of course, it would be easier and less painful to have them take a personality assessment.

Since founding and running a successful company is a long-term process, it's best for an entrepreneur to carefully choose a venture that's well suited for his natural personality. The bottom line is that each of the seven personalities is much more compatible with some types of businesses than with others. Rather than swimming upstream with the currents running against your potential success, why not focus on the types of situations and businesses in which you can thrive?

The value of understanding your own personality is that you can leverage your strengths, improve your weaknesses and limitations, and discover the type of organization that you're best served in creating. You have two choices; you can either choose a business that is well designed for you or be prepared and know that you will need to hire and surround yourself with the right people. Both work.

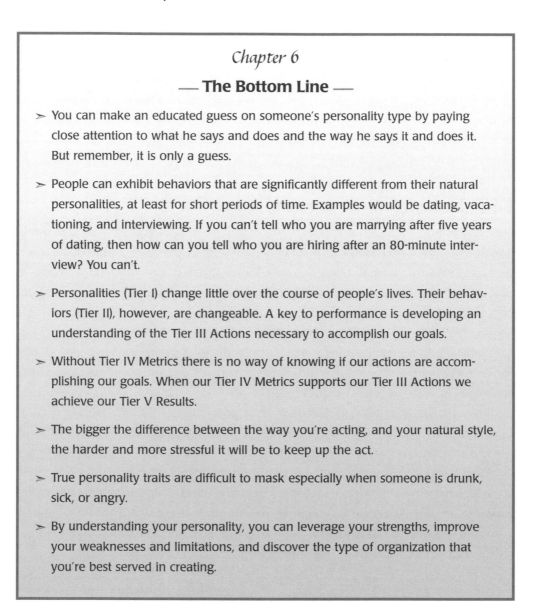

Chapter 6

— The Bottom Line —

➤ You can make an educated guess on someone's personality type by paying close attention to what he says and does and the way he says it and does it. But remember, it is only a guess.

➤ People can exhibit behaviors that are significantly different from their natural personalities, at least for short periods of time. Examples would be dating, vacationing, and interviewing. If you can't tell who you are marrying after five years of dating, then how can you tell who you are hiring after an 80-minute interview? You can't.

➤ Personalities (Tier I) change little over the course of people's lives. Their behaviors (Tier II), however, are changeable. A key to performance is developing an understanding of the Tier III Actions necessary to accomplish our goals.

➤ Without Tier IV Metrics there is no way of knowing if our actions are accomplishing our goals. When our Tier IV Metrics supports our Tier III Actions we achieve our Tier V Results.

➤ The bigger the difference between the way you're acting, and your natural style, the harder and more stressful it will be to keep up the act.

➤ True personality traits are difficult to mask especially when someone is drunk, sick, or angry.

➤ By understanding your personality, you can leverage your strengths, improve your weaknesses and limitations, and discover the type of organization that you're best served in creating.

7

Triumphs and Tragedies

At THE END OF THIS CHAPTER YOU WILL FIND TWO BLANK FORMS FOR YOUR HOME-work (Figures 7.3 and 7.4). These are Your Personal Action Plan forms for you to determine your strengths and your developmental areas. Those listed in this chapter only represent about 10 percent of those created by The McQuaig Institute®. These are for your private use only. Should you desire additional information about The McQuaig System™ or other assessments, you can find it at www.theentrepreneurnextdoor.com.

The greatest and perhaps only form of knowledge is self-knowledge. Highly successful people are not necessarily blessed with a higher intellect or more charisma than others (actually they may be but we don't like to say so), but they do know how to make the best use of their talents and how to avoid pitfalls that could limit their success. They are either naturally gifted in understanding themselves, have learned from their mistakes, and/or have had great mentors who coached and guided them. Many of those that have higher than average levels of self-awareness also have higher levels of emotional intelligence.

Dwight Sandlin, the senior partner and founder of Signature Homes in Pelham, Alabama, has a Trailblazer personality. Dwight hates to be sold but he loves to buy. As a leading homebuilder in the Birmingham area, Dwight was approached by the ABC television show *Extreme Makeover: Home Edition*. On "Bullhorn" Day, Monday, January 31, 2005, Dwight and hundreds of his employees and subcontractors pitched in and built a home for the Harris family. This was enough for the Harris family but it wasn't enough for Dwight. He went to work on his Rolodex and was successful in finding people willing to guarantee college experiences for Chris and Diamond Harris's seven children. When they say that charity begins at home, there's a new benchmark.

This chapter will help you identify your strengths and become aware of your weaknesses. If you're married, the weakness side is probably something someone has already shared with you. (This is a bit of humor. Not much.) It's these potential limitations that decrease your effectiveness. This knowledge will enable you to improve your performance, increase your job satisfaction, and achieve greater success.

The challenge in writing about great companies or their leaders is what if they are only great for a snapshot and not for the full-run motion picture? We see this all too often, especially when we look at the fastest growing companies. How many of the high tech companies of the 1990s are still around today? Very few. A number of years ago, *Inc.* magazine wrote a cover story about a young entrepreneur that they labeled the next Bill Gates. I believe that Bill Gates has either a Trailblazer or a Manager personality. This cover story was about a hypergrowth entrepreneur with a Motivator personality. He was one of the greatest sales people I've met. The challenge with that high level of sociability is that they have difficulty holding others accountable and they are not typically the most analytical. This was this entrepreneur's Achilles heel. Numbers were not his friend, and within 12 months of being written about, he was out of business.

As an aside, people usually figure this stuff out by the time they're 75 years old, but if you bought this book because you're of an entrepreneurial spirit, you don't have the patience to wait until you're in your 70s.

When people consider their strengths and their corresponding developmental considerations (what used to be referred to as potential limitations), they focus on their preferred or natural style of personality (Tier I). You may think that some of the examples I've listed are less relevant to you at this time. If I provided a list of ten suggestions to three people with the same personality and asked each of them to determine which of the ten suggestions fit them, they would probably choose different suggestions. These differences occur because people learn from life's experiences; therefore, what may be an issue today will more than likely not be an issue a year from now. Some learn sooner rather than later. So some of these suggestions may not apply to you, but before you disregard any of them, discuss them with someone who knows you well and whose opinions you respect.

This chapter provides you with information that will not only make you more effective in your current role but will also give you concrete ideas as you look forward and consider new opportunities, assignments, and roles. Ideally, you would make a list of actionable items, devise an action plan, and begin to work toward making the changes necessary for becoming a better leader or manager. Read the following pages, which detail in depth the strengths and weaknesses of the seven personality types. Then absorb the content, create your Personal Action Plan, and determine the most appropriate plan of action—*for you*. It's important to remember that as difficult a suggestion as this may be, your development starts and ends with you.

In Their Own Words
What Entrepreneurs Said about Their Defining Moments

Many of the participants in the young entrepreneur survey group came from lower, lower middle, and middle class income groups. Some spent time in jail, filed for bankruptcy, lost loved ones, were divorced, or had family members who survived the Holocaust. Yet they have survived life's big and little knocks and uncertainties. They've had every challenge that can be imagined. They looked at their problems and saw opportunities. These opportunities allowed them to grow, thrive, learn, and persevere.

The bottom line is that they didn't give up. I know that everybody has had challenges. The key is to learn from them. Here you have the opportunity to learn from someone else's challenges. These are only a small portion of the responses. More can be found on www.theentrepreneurnextdoor.com.

Q: *"What is your life's most significant event or defining moment that has affected your business life and why?"*

"Doing jail time at 20 helped me define my life's priorities. Also, hitting the glass ceiling in corporate life so I had to venture out on my own to progress."

"Having our major client (about three years ago) undergo a massive restructuring in an acquisition; this forced us to "grow up" as a company and pay more attention to process, sales, marketing, infrastructure, hiring, and personal development."

"When I quit drinking and using drugs. I made a lot of money selling drugs; the only problem was that I became my best customer. After I got sober, I focused all that energy into my current business."

"Growing up in Houston 1979 to 1985. Seeing the boom and bust and how it affected people close me. When I started high school, we knew no rich people. By the time I graduated, four close families were millionaires. By the time I was a sophomore in college, they were all flat broke. My father couldn't find work and had to work out of state. This taught me business discipline. Nobody that went broke had any. They thought the boom would never end. I have 'banker' mentality because of this."

"Taking a group of mentally retarded adults on a two-week camping trip. I learned that taking responsibility for the well-being of others was a monumental task—but the ability to do so while communing with nature was amazing and challenging."

"The fact that I have a profound hearing loss enables me to operate in a manner that requires accommodation while earning respect."

"Failing at my first business and going $75k in debt. It taught me what not to do and showed me I could do anything after I failed. Gave me a 'no-fear' attitude."

"The death of my stepfather—I realized that I would never be able to depend on anyone else for help."

"Father's embracing of capitalism (my father started six different businesses). I was taught early on that to have control, you need to be in control."

"The birth of my first child provided focus for achieving business success, to facilitate a stable environment for his development, and for me to share in that process."

"Getting fired from my own company by an investor who wanted to change everything about the business."

Trailblazers' Strengths and Weaknesses

Trailblazers have an edge that can be the bane of their existence as well as the source of their need for competition. They have a phenomenal ability to compete: They thrive on it, they love it, and they're good at it. They enjoy working with systems, concepts, ideas, and technologies. They're technically oriented, have a strong strategic orientation, and are so results-oriented that they can easily forget about the people side of their business. That is a nice way of saying they have a tendency to step on toes. When working around a Trailblazer, wear your steel-toed shoes. These Generalists like to assume a role involving freedom of action within known structures, with strong leadership or competitive selling responsibilities. They have a need for autonomy and authority, a predisposition toward communicating in a professional manner, an orientation toward achieving results and a sense of urgency about setting and realizing goals, an aptitude for keeping a variety of tasks on stream, and a preference for being able to initiate projects under defined parameters.

Trailblazers typically display a number of these qualities:

- Are extremely competitive, ambitious, and goal-oriented
- Tackle projects and situations aggressively

- Want responsibility for and authority over others
- Enjoy overcoming objections/resistance and achieving goals in the face of obstacles
- Are logical, work-oriented, and analytical

Rick Sapio of Mutuals.com has a Trailblazing personality. For years he lived in a hotel apartment suite that was in the same building as his office in Dallas. He lived there because he wanted to focus on his business and no commute meant that he had more time and energy to focus on his business. He had no television because he didn't want distractions. He did have hundreds of business tapes and was surrounded by hundreds of motivational and business books. He wanted to focus only on his job. In his closet, he had 40 white shirts all in a row. With his personality, delegating authority doesn't come naturally. He was, however, able to hire another Generalist, specifically a Manager, to manager his day-to-day operations, thereby allowing himself the opportunity to work on the overall strategy and the big-picture side of his business.

Carving Out a Niche

Trailblazers prefer being the driving force of an endeavor and, therefore, are typically the founders of many businesses. They occasionally don't buy a franchise or a distributorship but rather are the ones who start a company that competes with a franchise. They're usually highly innovative; they see what Burger King does and imagine their operation becoming Burger King Plus but within their own environment. They're strong, calculating risk-takers, are willing to invest in themselves, and are purposeful in that they don't like to take "no" for an answer.

If those with this personality don't surround themselves with those who can manage the people side, they can run good performers away. They can alienate others and are so comfortable keeping things to themselves that they have few close friends. But don't worry about them—they don't need many friends. Most Trailblazers have few friends, but the ones they do have are usually very close and maintained forever. They can go months or years without reconnecting with their friends, but when they rejoin these friends and begin exchanging their thoughts, it seems as if they were never apart.

If you want someone who's truly determined to get the job done, look to a Trailblazer. You just can't worry about the bodies they leave in their wake. It's important to remember that if they can learn from their developmental considerations, their learned behaviors (Tier II) take charge, and they can mitigate their edge.

Leverage Strengths for Greater Success

Action items for a Trailblazer are:

1. Take stock of your successes.
2. Conduct your own performance review.

Pushing for results is a strength of a Trailblazer.

- You are highly results oriented, ambitious, and assertive.
- You are unwavering in your desire to succeed.
- You are very comfortable expressing your point of view.

The strengths of most Trailblazers are typical of individuals who:

- are extremely goal-oriented and step in to take charge of situations
- are very competitive and need to win
- relish having authority and influence over others
- seek out challenges and tough problems to tackle
- like to take risks and hold themselves accountable for the consequences

To leverage your strengths, take stock of your successes. Think of the specific actions you took to achieve these results and recall situations where others helped along the way. Next time you face a challenge, draw on these experiences to guide you.

Then conduct your own performance review. Where are you compared to your goals? Determine what you are doing well and look for areas where a different approach might be beneficial.

Turn Development Considerations into Advantages

Action items for a Trailblazer are:

1. Take a back-seat role.
2. Be the last to speak.

Collaborating with others is a developmental area for a Trailblazer.

- You want control and will automatically take over in many situations.
- You can be overbearing, discouraging input from others.
- You may be seen as dominant or self-centered.

To manage your developmental areas more effectively, take a back-seat role. Approach your next project with the idea that you do not have to take complete responsibility for the outcome. Instead, seek out the contributions of others and be prepared to share the credit with them.

Be the last to speak. In meetings, try not to influence the discussion too early on. Filter your comments by asking, "Does this need to be said or do I just want to say it?"

Go-Getters' Strengths and Weaknesses

Go-Getters have an ability to assume a role of a Generalist nature, with strong leadership or competitive selling responsibilities. They enjoy and have a need for autonomy and authority, a clear preference for initiating and setting their own direction, an orientation toward achieving results and a sense of urgency about setting and realizing goals, an aptitude for keeping a wide variety of tasks on stream, and a predisposition toward persuasiveness, able to sell their ideas to others in a diplomatic manner.

Go-Getters typically display a number of these qualities:

- Are extremely competitive, ambitious, and goal-oriented
- Tackle projects and situations aggressively
- Want responsibility for and authority over people
- Enjoy overcoming objections/resistance and achieving goals in the face of obstacles
- Are independent, persistent, and decisive

Carving Out a Niche

Go-Getters work well in both ambitious and ambiguous environments. This means they can invest in, buy, or start a business that's new to them. They don't require a high level of expertise in their endeavors. In their opinion, expertise is helpful but not necessary. They're innovative, able to take the ideas of others to the next level. They're driven, work well under pressure, multitask, and seem to be in constant motion. They often have a chameleon-like quality that allows them to have a strong level of natural empathy. They are good collaborators and consensus-builders and are good at providing motivation for themselves and others. They appear to almost always be a positive influence on themselves and others.

Leverage Strengths for Greater Success

Action items for a Go-Getter are:

1. Encourage competition among your team.
2. Take charge of your personal development.

There's good news and bad news. The good news is that most people know what their strengths are. The challenge is that they don't always understand that with each strength comes a corresponding and diametrically opposed potential limitation.

Go-Getters' strengths are:

- You are extremely goal-oriented and step in to take charge of situations.
- You are very competitive, need to win and thrive on overcoming obstacles to attain your objectives.
- You relish having authority and influence over others.
- You seek out challenges and tough problems to tackle.
- You like to take risks and are willing to hold yourself accountable for the consequences.

Competing is a strength of a Go-Getter.

- You enjoy winning and the success that comes with it.
- You seek opportunities to go head-to-head with others and will put a competitive spin on just about anything.
- You do not hesitate to take on new challenges, especially if the rewards and the risks are high.

To leverage your strengths, encourage competition among your team. You can increase productivity and get everyone engaged with a little healthy rivalry. Look for opportunities to beat the forecast—or your competitors.

Then, take charge of your personal development. Meet with your boss/coach to discuss how your job relates to the goals of the organization, and find out what you have to master in your current role to take it to the next level.

Go-Getters have an amazing level of self-confidence. Because of this, they are challenged in understanding how others can't do what they themselves can so easily accomplish. A manufacturer of springs in the San Francisco Bay area has been growing his business at a double-digit clip for as long as anyone can remember. He refers to what he and his key people do as "the heavy lifting." This personality can do *a lot* of heavy lifting.

Turn Developmental Considerations into Advantages

Action items for a Go-Getter are:

1. Look for a team win.
2. Perform an unprovoked act of kindness.

Teambuilding is a developmental area for a Go-Getter.

- Your strong desire to "win the battle" may lead you to lose sight of the best solution.
- You may create long-term adversaries and discourage future alliances.
- You find it difficult to stay motivated when you do not feel personally challenged.

To manage your developmental areas more effectively look for a team win. When negotiating, rather than viewing a desired outcome in terms of "What's in it for me?" ask instead "What's in it for them?"

Perform an unprovoked act of kindness. For example, send a business opportunity to another division or volunteer to help an associate with whom you do not always see eye to eye. Create long-term allies who may help you down the road.

I knew a client's sales manager in a furniture store who was single, reasonably attractive, and a great closer. Many with this personality are great salespeople. On those Saturdays when he was without a date for the evening and an attractive, single female shopper was in the store, he would typically take the floor, make the sale, and then proceed to tell the store's new client that delivery typically took a week to ten days, but that if she were going to be home that night he would make arrangements to have the furniture delivered. He'd also bring the paperwork and a bottle of wine to celebrate her new purchase. Remember, I'm talking about potential limitations.

Managers' Strengths and Weaknesses

Managers have the ability to assume a Generalist role, with strong leadership or competitive selling responsibilities, along with a need for autonomy and authority, a preference for initiating and setting their own direction, a predisposition toward communicating in a professional manner, a disposition patient enough to cope with long-term projects, and an inclination toward a day-to-day, evenly paced routine.

Managers typically display a number of these qualities:

- Are extremely competitive, ambitious, and goal-oriented
- Tackle projects and situations aggressively
- Want responsibility for and authority over people
- Enjoy overcoming objections/resistance and achieving goals in the face of obstacles
- Are independent, persistent, and decisive
- Want to take their time to think things through
- Want to take charge and show initiative
- Have the strength to follow through and keep at it until they get results

Carving Out a Niche

Managers have a strong technical orientation and are analytical, highly results-oriented, stable, methodical, patient, and somewhat independent. They like doing things on their own, are great behind-the-scenes leaders, and are great at working with systems, concepts, ideas, and technologies. They like to think things through. Their decision-making process might be described as "ready, aim, aim, aim, fire." They're loyal and strongly independent. They like to do what they feel comfortable with and dislike being swayed with any form of emotional argument. They enjoy working by themselves and could be challenged to manage those in a more active environment.

Leverage Strengths for Greater Success

Action items for a Manager are:

1. Find a mentor.
2. Go to bat for someone else.

Managers strengths are that they:

- are extremely goal-oriented and step in to take charge of situations
- are very competitive, need to win, and thrive on overcoming obstacles to attain their objectives
- relish having authority and influence over others
- seek out challenges and tough problems to tackle
- like to take risks and hold themselves accountable for the consequences

Asserting yourself is considered to be a strength of a Manager.

- You have a great deal of confidence in your abilities.
- You have definite opinions and believe that your solutions and ideas are the best ones.

To leverage your strengths, find a mentor. Pick a person who has had a great impact on your company, someone who does a good job of influencing others while achieving consensus. Seek this person's advice the next time you have an idea you want to push through.

Then, go to bat for someone else. Use your assertive nature to help out team members who may be struggling with difficult situations.

Turn Developmental Considerations into Advantages

Action items for a Manager are:

1. Listen actively.
2. Solicit feedback.

Listening to others is a developmental area for Manager.

- You may not listen as well as you should.
- You often find yourself formulating your response before your colleagues have had a chance to finish and you can miss opportunities to get buy-in or build consensus.

To manage your developmental areas more effectively, listen actively. Look your colleagues in the eye and nod to indicate that you understand their points of view. Start your response by summarizing what they have said. Never assume you know what someone is going to say before he says it.

Also, solicit feedback. Accept the fact that your ideas may not always be the best ones. Bounce them off someone you trust and listen to his opinions before moving forward.

An ongoing challenge for those with Manager personalities is the difficulty they often experience working with the people side of the business. They're so good with the technical side that their analytical nature overshadows their ability to work well with others. Loyalty is one of their assets, and the corresponding challenge can be best described by the following story.

I was presenting to a group of business owners in Oregon. One attendee had an especially strong Manager personality. I asked him whether he's a creature of habit, and he said yes. I asked him whether his employees would consider him to be a highly loyal employer, and his answer again was yes. I asked him how long he'd been the CEO of the bank. He replied, "Fourteen years." And I finally asked how long he'd been thinking about firing someone but hadn't. He said, "About fourteen years now." In this case, loyalty is a limitation.

Motivators' Strengths and Weaknesses

Motivators have an ability to assume a role of a Generalist nature, doing best with leadership or selling responsibilities. They have an orientation toward achieving results and sense of urgency about setting and realizing goals; an aptitude for keeping a wide variety of tasks on stream; a predisposition toward persuasiveness, able to sell their ideas to others in a diplomatic manner; a need for autonomy and authority; and a preference for initiating and setting their own direction.

Motivators typically display a number of these qualities:

- Are restless, driving, and energetic
- Have a strong sense of urgency about getting things done quickly

- Work well under pressure and enjoy meeting tight deadlines
- Are very friendly, sociable, and outgoing
- Enjoy working with and selling ideas to people
- Are good communicators and optimistic, tending to see the positive side of things

Carving Out a Niche

Motivators do well in business with partners or in a business that involves others. In a service business, for example, their success can be based more on their location and concept than on the entrepreneur's directed approach to networking. Motivators keep clients for life because they enjoy long-term relationships and are good at nurturing those relationships. They work well in a strong team environment and can find it somewhat challenging to work in a confrontational environment. They have plenty of drive and multitask well but can have a tendency to procrastinate.

Leverage Strengths for Greater Success

Action items for Motivators are:

1. Share your enthusiasm.
2. Examine the processes your company has in place.

Most Motivators:

- Are very restless, energetic, and take action quickly when things go wrong
- Are change oriented and enjoy new projects
- Take a do-it-now approach
- Set tight deadlines, initiating and responding well to pressure

Driving change is considered to be a strength of a Motivator.

- You are active and eager for new experiences.
- You have a strong and immediate need for action.
- You enjoy fast-paced environments where there is great activity.

To leverage your strengths, share your enthusiasm. You may be just the shot in the arm that your peers need. Get your team to rally around a new idea—then be the one to step up and make things happen.

In addition, examine the processes your company has in place. There may be policies and procedures that have not changed with the times. Challenge them, but first take the time to understand them.

A friend and previous client, Mark Gordon of Washington, DC, had a data/wiring installation company. Mark struggled with holding others accountable, but he was wise enough to hire someone to handle the elements of his business that he didn't enjoy. He concentrated on the business relationships, put together a buying group, eventually sold his business, and is now living in Florida working as a COO with an underwater salvage (treasure-hunting) company. He is living his dream and was able to accomplish his goals through others.

Turn Developmental Considerations into Advantages

Action items for Motivators are:

1. Eliminate surprises.
2. Look before you leap.

Staying focused is a developmental area for Motivators.

- You would rather not plan things in advance.
- You change focus quickly, making it difficult for others to keep track.
- You can get bored easily and are always looking for the next fire to put out.

To manage your developmental areas more effectively, eliminate surprises. Respect that others may not share your sense of adventure. Make sure that everyone is on the same page prior to starting new activities.

Also, remember to look before you leap. Before jumping into something—and dragging everyone else in with you—take the time to think through the full ramifications of what you are about to do. List the pros and cons.

Authorities' Strengths and Weaknesses

Authorities and their Specialist counterparts make up more than 70 percent of the U.S. population. Remember our country's beginning—our roots were those of people who came to the New World to have freedom, autonomy, independence, and control over their destinies. They were our founders, and in essence they were our earliest-day version of today's entrepreneurs. Authorities have an ability to function effectively in a specialized, expert role with an aptitude for being a supportive team player, especially in a team-like environment; a preference for working within a clearly structured and closely supervised environment; a positive preference for precise, detailed tasks; an inclination toward a day-to-day, evenly paced routine; and a propensity for analyzing ideas/projects/tasks. If you want something done right, give it to an Authority. They're great with the details and are, therefore, challenged by letting go of those details, as no one will do it as well as they will. Better at delegating authority, their challenge is holding others accountable and dealing with confrontation. It's not that they can't deal with the difficult aspects of the business—they can—it just requires more effort.

Authorities typically display a number of these qualities:

- Are accepting, cautious, and deliberate in approach
- Make a point of avoiding friction with others
- Are good team members who will be careful about making decisions
- Are conscientious and cooperative
- Are good with detail and take their duties seriously
- Follow company rules and directions
- Are relaxed, patient, steady, and reliable

Carving Out a Niche

Authorities might refer to themselves as "accidental" entrepreneurs because they often end up running a business when that was never part of their original plan. Consequently, they're best served going into a business that embraces their level of expertise or allows them to develop a new level of expertise. Given their accommodating nature and dislike for prospecting, they need to be in a business where customers or clients are driven to them. In most cases, this personality type will either need a partner with a stronger natural sense of prospecting or networking or have other Specialist-oriented personalities working and supporting them. Authorities can succeed in running someone else's business concept such as a franchise or a distributorship, provided the organization is well supported with advertising and marketing.

Leverage Strengths for Greater Success

Action items for Authorities are:

1. Encourage teamwork.
2. Provide upward support first.

Your responses are typical of individuals who:

- are agreeable and obliging when working with others
- are careful to minimize risks before making decisions
- are unpretentious and work to get things done without fanfare
- foster a sense of harmony in the workplace and adopt compromise solutions

- support team efforts

Cooperating with others is a strength of an Authority.

- You like to keep the peace and will go out of your way to get along with others.
- You believe that teamwork is very important.
- You will take a collaborative approach on most issues.

To leverage your strengths, encourage teamwork. For example, this can be done by getting others to rally around a team member who has fallen behind or, at a higher level, by helping your team understand how your department supports the organization.

Provide upward support first. Be helpful in a way that will most benefit you. Be aware of the needs of your boss and other senior managers. Use your expertise to make them more productive.

T. Scott Gross is a professional speaker, author, restaurateur, and one hell of a great guy. A couple of years ago, Scott published the book *Why Service Stinks* (Kaplan Business, 2003). It is about the personalities that make the best customer service professionals. Scott has an Authority personality yet his position requires a Go-Getter personality. If you consider his three positions along with his personality type, being a writer is a perfect fit. Being the front person for his restaurant, especially one that really believes in delivering great customer service, requires a Motivator personality—a stretch for someone who's an Authority. His third role as a keynote speaker is the one that requires the high dominance, typical in a Go-Getter. When I first met Scott, he completed one of our personality assessments. When I presented him with his results, he categorically disagreed with his results. He challenged, "How can I not be a risk taker? I fly planes. How can I not be a risk taker? I'm a volunteer paramedic. I save lives."

I asked him, if he would ever consider taking off (flying) in order to beat an approaching storm front? Would he ever be able to do the things he does as a paramedic without training? A couple of weeks later he called and told me his reports were accurate. He's a great keynote speaker, but doesn't want anything to do with presenting a full-day program. Scott, on a daily basis—often several times in a day—needs to stretch his personality so that he can effectively do all of his jobs. And a good job he does!

I belong to a CEO group called The Executive Committee (TEC). There are more than 10,000 members, divided into relatively small groups. The 15 members of my group get together once a month for an all-day meeting where we discuss business issues, share our thoughts, hold one another accountable, and listen to professional presentations by outside experts. The only Specialist in my group is Wendell Keith,

CEO of the Keith Companies (which make blast furnaces). Wendell is an excellent CEO. Don't get me wrong—he has his issues—but he recognizes the wisdom of surrounding himself with those with the right personalities for their positions. In fact, Wendell uses the services of Accord Management Systems Inc., to assist him in his selection process.

The key is that Wendell does the heavy lifting. In spite of his natural personality style (Tier I), he understands the necessary behaviors (Tier II) to hold others accountable, handle the strategic side of his business, delegate details, and handle confrontational situations on a timely basis. These are the Tier III actions.

There are hundreds of examples of Specialists behaving like Generalists. It happens every day. It's not their natural style (Tier I), but it's due to their cognitive ability (Tier II) to understand the changes that are necessary for them to perform (Tier III).

The Specialist, when doing Generalist work, may very well be tired, even exhausted, but he can do the job. He can change his nature for short periods of time in order to have a greater impact on the position. You can read about these people and their successes at www.theentrepreneurnextdoor.com.

Turn Developmental Considerations into Advantages

Action items for Authorities are:

1. Create a "High Anxiety To-Do List."
2. Just say no.

Addressing adversity is a developmental area for Authorities.

- You can procrastinate when having to confront people or make difficult decisions.
- You are reluctant to voice your disagreement in group settings and will avoid rocking the boat.
- You can take on much more than is reasonable when supporting others.

To manage your developmental areas more effectively, create a "High Anxiety To-Do List." List the items that make you feel uneasy—for example, making a difficult decision, confronting an under-performing direct report or colleague, or selling your boss on a new idea—and make these a top priority.

Also learn to say no. Resist your desire to pitch in when you have a number of time-critical tasks already. Stay focused on the tasks that help you achieve your goals.

Collaborators' Strengths and Weaknesses

Collaborators are another form of Specialists. They're cautious and deliberate and go out of their way to get along with others. They know they're part of a team and will work for the good of the group rather than seeking out individual recognition. They enjoy working in an environment with clear direction and are careful about making decisions and good at doing so only after thorough examination of all the facts. They're great in new areas once they've developed the requisite level of expertise. They prefer a conflict-free working environment and will often try to mediate quietly, one-to-one, especially if co-workers are having problems with one another. They come across as thoughtful, sensitive, and caring people, and others will relate to them easily. They're accepting and cautious, and their challenge can be their desire to be liked at the expense of getting results.

Sociable and outgoing, they genuinely like people and enjoy working with them. They understand others, see their points of view, and get along well with others. At home with people and confident in situations involving others, they're optimistic and tend to see the positive side of things. They often make a good first impression and enjoy helping others. Outgoing and good communicators, they relate well to others. One of their challenges can be keeping it professional.

Reliable and patient, they establish routines to complete their tasks. They work well with systems and methods and keep calm, cool, and collected most of the time. Predictable in performance, they're steady and consistent contributors. They don't feel the need to challenge the status quo, tending to be a steadying influence on others and not needing to make frequent changes because they are comfortable working within the existing structure. Stable and dependable in approach, they like to pace themselves and develop their own work habits. Very loyal, they prefer a family-like environment, and because of that high degree of loyalty, they can find it difficult to confront employees and hold them accountable, let alone fire them.

Tending to be thorough, they tackle their responsibilities conscientiously. They enjoy preparing for contingencies. They follow directions and are good with detail. Of course, their difficulty with delegating details to others presents a challenge.

Collaborators typically display a number of these qualities:

- Are accepting, cautious, and deliberate in approach
- Make a point of avoiding friction with others
- Are good team members who will be careful about making decisions

- Are friendly, sociable, and outgoing
- Genuinely like people and enjoy working with them

Carving Out a Niche

It had better be about people, because Collaborators relish the people side of business. Consequently, they're well served in retail, customer service, or warm selling environments. They typically benefit by having a partner who is more aggressive about developing new business. Although Collaborators aren't usually comfortable with cold calling or pitching new ideas, they're far from pushovers and are adept at holding their ground when it comes to doing things right and following prescribed rules or guidelines. They aren't big risk-takers and want to be sure they avoid blame, which is why doing things "right" is so important to them. They run a tight ship.

Leverage Strengths for Greater Success

Action items for Collaborators are:

1. Help others reach agreement.
2. Create alliances.

Most Collaborators:

- are agreeable and obliging when working with others
- are careful to minimize risks before making decisions
- are unpretentious and work to get things done without fanfare
- foster a sense of harmony in the workplace and adopt compromise solutions
- support team efforts

Building consensus is considered to be a strength of a Collaborator.

- You take a safety-first approach to decision making and get buy-in before moving forward.
- You collect input from others and work to accommodate their needs.

To leverage your strengths, help others reach agreement. Your ability to seek compromise combined with your nonthreatening demeanor can be a great asset when egos start to clash.

Also learn to create alliances. Let others know their opinions have been factored into the solution or have at least been considered. By developing allies, you will find it easier to have your positions accepted and increase your confidence in your ability to make tough decisions.

Turn Developmental Considerations into Advantages

Action items for Collaborators are:

1. Challenge your desire to get advice.
2. Present a solution.

Influencing others is a developmental area for Collaborators.

- Your efforts to gain acceptance from all sides can result in a watered-down solution.
- You may yield too much authority in areas where you are the expert.

To manage your developmental areas more effectively, challenge your desire to get advice. Next time you are about to seek input of others, before moving forward ask yourself if their contribution is necessary or whether you can make the decision yourself.

Present a solution. Rather than taking an open-ended approach to gathering input, start by proposing a solution. For example, start with "Here's what I recommend. What do you think?"

Diplomats' Strengths and Weaknesses

Diplomats are driven individuals who get things done quickly, work well under pressure, and enjoy working with tight deadlines. They can adjust to change, are quick to respond to new situations, and work well in a changing atmosphere. They have a high sense of urgency, enjoying variety and working at top capacity. They enjoy it when things are really happening and moving and they can keep a variety of jobs going at once. Active and energetic, they vigorously attack the parts of the job they enjoy and push themselves and others to get results quickly.

Conscientious, they take their work seriously. They're good planners, and they like to be prepared for contingencies. Following directions carefully, they're thorough and good with detail. They respond well to guidance and direction. They learn the systems and procedures, becoming authorities in their field. Thorough and always putting their emphasis on the quality of their work, they adapt well to situations where they can do the work themselves and check details personally.

Sociable and outgoing, they genuinely like people and enjoy working with them. They understand others and see their points of view. They're optimistic and tend to see the positive side of things. At home with people and confident in situations involving others, they often make a good impression and enjoy helping others when possible. Outgoing and open, they're good communicators and relate well to others.

Tending to be good team players, they seek consensus in their dealings with others. They take a fairly careful approach to decision-making, preferring to examine available options before moving forward in an effort to avoid needless risks. They're inclined to respect authority, and they adjust well to supervision as long as it's fair and understanding.

The Diplomat is excellent working in retail or other people-oriented environments. For each strength, though, there's a challenge. The Diplomat's challenges are as follows:

- May have difficulty holding others accountable
- May have difficulty dealing with confrontation
- May want to be liked at the expense of getting results
- May procrastinate
- May have difficulty letting go of details

Carving Out a Niche

As Diplomats are both outgoing and empathetic, they often prefer to hold roles that support the leaders of an organization rather than being in charge themselves. Since they promote harmonious relationships and tend to be well liked, however, people are often happy and willing to follow their lead. The flip side of the coin is that Diplomats tend to avoid conflict and have a hard time asserting themselves and holding others accountable. Therefore, to be successful business leaders, they typically need to hire stronger, more results-oriented people to make sure that deadlines are met, commitments are kept, and staff members are following through on projects.

Leverage Strengths for Greater Success

Action items for Diplomats are:

1. Share your enthusiasm.
2. Examine the processes your company has in place.

Your responses are typical of individuals who:

- Have a sense of urgency and are quick to react
- Like variety and enjoy taking on new projects
- Like pressure and deadlines
- Seek out fast-paced environments

I recently worked with a female franchisee with a Diplomat personality working in the early-childhood development industry. Her challenge was marketing the concept. The difference between the successful franchisees and those who weren't was largely their ability to market. We devised a plan of action in which she and one of her employees visited with schools, church groups, day-care facilities, and other organizations where the parents of her potential students might congregate, and through the collective strength of both their personalities they were able to successfully market their concept. Today, Gina is a very successful entrepreneur.

Responding urgently is a strength of a Diplomat.

- You can quickly shift your focus to more critical priorities.
- You are action oriented and want to do things now.

To leverage your strengths, share your enthusiasm. You may be just the shot in the arm that your peers need. Get your team to rally around a new idea, then be the one to step in and make things happen.

Examine the processes your company has in place. There may be policies and procedures that have not changed with the times. You can look for ways to improve them, but first take the time to understand why they are there in the first place.

This is definitely one of the best customer-service or retail profiles you'll find anywhere. They are still a Specialist, but they're great at building consensus and collaborating with others.

Turn Developmental Considerations into Advantages

Action items for Diplomats are:

1. Look before you leap.
2. Eliminate surprises.

Staying focused is a developmental area for Diplomats.

- You may jump in without taking the time to plan first.
- You can get bored easily and seek out new activities, making it difficult for others to follow.

To manage your developmental areas more effectively, look before you leap. Before jumping into something, take the time to think through the full ramifications of what you are about to do. List the pros and cons.

Eliminate surprises. Respect that others may not share your desire for something new. Make sure that everyone is on the same page prior to starting new activities.

Strength and Weakness Self-Assessment

Based on what I've read in this chapter, I feel that my strengths and developmental areas are most like:

Trailblazer   _____

Go-Getter   _____

Manager   _____

Motivator   _____

Authority   _____

Collaborator   _____

Diplomat   _____

I also have qualities similar to: _____

Personal Action Plan

On the next few pages, you will begin to complete your Personal Action Plan (Figure 7.1).

- First, transfer the key strength or developmental area that you selected in the Self-Assessment, based on your personality type. If you were unable to find a match, then proceed by determining those items that you know to be your strengths or developmental areas.
- Then, use the suggested Action Items to help you set concrete, on-the-job Action Items.

For example, suppose your developmental area is "focusing on numbers" and your Action Item is to make numbers your friend. Get to know percentages, dollar figures, and bottom-line financial details, any information that is important to success in your role and to your organization. Your own Action Item might translate into being prepared to make a better contribution at the next quarterly review, study the YTD financials, and clarify any figures you don't understand with the controller. Your desired outcome might be to use specific elements from the YTD financials in your presentation at the quarterly review.

Figures 7.1 and 7.2 illustrate two of my Personal Action Plans. Use them to gain an understanding and help you fill out two of your own in Figures 7.3 and 7.4.

FIGURE 7.1: **Personal Action Plan—Strengths**

STRENGTH: USING LOGIC—Link your skills to strategy

DEVELOPING ON-THE-JOB ACTION ITEMS (Review the Action Items that will help you leverage this Strength.) • Personalize the Action Items related to the key strength you have selected or create your own Action Items below. • State your desired outcome.	TARGET DATE
1. Determine my best job fit, which is to be the front person, the person presenting, speaking, and developing the direction and strategic alliances.	Done
2. Create the organization necessary to free myself of the day-to-day operations. To accomplish this I will need very strong key indicators, a comp plan to drive growth, engaged employees, and someone to take day-to-day operating responsibilities.	In process
3. Staff the organization with the skills necessary to allow me the opportunity to accomplish #1 listed above. This will include a great marketing person, a trainer, three sales people, and a solid administration team.	In process
4. Step out of the day-to-day operations, and select a Managing Director to manage the tactical side of the business. Don't sabotage them or yourself.	Done

POTENTIAL OBSTACLES (Identify any potential barriers to success)	WAYS TO OVERCOME OBSTACLES (What might you do to overcome these barriers?)
Inability to retain core personnel or their inability to perform at the level necessary to accomplish our goals	Nurture our employees and become an employer of choice. Lead by example, Hold one-to-ones monthly so that I am not surprised by outcomes. Let people always know where they stand.

FIGURE 7.1: **Personal Action Plan–Strengths, continued**

ASSESSING YOUR PROGRESS (To be completed once you have had the opportunity to implement your Action Plan). How did it go? What was the outcome? In what ways could you further leverage this Strength to achieve greater effectiveness?

Currently have solid sales reps that have been with us now for 2-plus years. Our managing director has been in position for six months and is accomplishing great things. Have hired one new sales rep dedicated to engagement and hiring one or two others before year end to also dedicate to engagement. Both EE reps have a strong "C" level presence. As of December 1, we will have a fully staffed admin team. Still need to have someone to support me.

FIGURE 7.2: **Personal Action Plan–Developmental Areas**

DEVELOPMENTAL AREA: COMMMUNICATING YOUR MESSAGE—Anticipate Emotional Concerns and Put Yourself in Your Listener's Shoes

DEVELOPING ON-THE-JOB ACTION ITEMS (Review the Action Items that will help you manage this Developmental Area more effectively). • Personalize the Action Items related to the key Developmental Area you have selected or create your own Action Items below. • State your desired outcome.	TARGET DATE
1. Utilize Guinot's work in listening to what is being said, cognitively determine the motivation of the comment, and respond with a favorable response eliciting greater feedback from the speaker. Don't become defensive, look for the best in others, and concentrate on what people are able to accomplish. Become a world-class teacher of others (teach them to fish).	Ongoing
2. Use the objection process of Feel, Felt, Found, i.e., I understand how you must be feeling. When I consider what you are saying, I have felt the same way when I experienced the same situation. What I found was…	Ongoing

FIGURE 7.2: **Personal Action Plan—Developmental Areas,** continued

3. Develop procedures and systems to improve the training of others so that we can better measure their advancement, accomplishments, and understanding of the process… Embrace numbers and key indicators so that others know where they stand at all times and be engaged in mentoring or coaching them.	Ongoing

POTENTIAL OBSTACLES (Identify any potential barriers to success)	WAYS TO OVERCOME OBSTACLES (What might you do to overcome these barriers?)
My own stupid switch preventing me from accomplishing my goal. My drive and lack of patience getting in my way, thereby causing me to be short with others.	Interject more humor into the situation, don't take myself so seriously, and be patient with the speed that others learn at and process.

ASSESSING YOUR PROGRESS (To be completed once you have had the opportunity to implement your Action Plan). How did it go? What was the outcome? In what ways could you further manage this Developmental Area to achieve greater effectiveness?

Still struggling with #3 as we have not yet begun tracking our metrics with the sales reps. I am paying much closer attention to the overall numbers including our P & L's. Sub Chapter "S" begins on January 1, New CPA begins on 12/1/05.

Goal for December is to have graphs that track metrics posted.

FIGURE 7.3: **Your Personal Action Plan—Strengths**

STRENGTH: _____	
DEVELOPING ON-THE-JOB ACTION ITEMS (Review the Action Items that will help you leverage this Strength.) • Personalize the Action Items related to the key strength you have selected or create your own Action Items below. • State your desired outcome.	**TARGET DATE**

POTENTIAL OBSTACLES (Identify any potential barriers to success.)	WAYS TO OVERCOME OBSTACLES (What might you do to overcome these barriers?)

FIGURE 7.3: **Your Personal Action Plan–Strengths**, continued

ASSESSING YOUR PROGRESS (To be completed once you have had the opportunity to implement your Action Plan). How did it go? What was the outcome? In what ways could you further leverage this Strength to achieve greater effectiveness?

FIGURE 7.4: **Your Personal Action Plan–Developmental Areas**

DEVELOPMENTAL AREA: COMMMUNICATING YOUR MESSAGE–Anticipate Emotional Concerns and Put Yourself in Your Listener's Shoes

DEVELOPING ON-THE-JOB ACTION ITEMS (Review the Action Items that will help you manage this Developmental Area more effectively.) • Personalize the Action Items related to the key Developmental Area you have selected or create your own Action Items below. • State your desired outcome.	TARGET DATE

FIGURE 7.4: **Your Personal Action Plan–Developmental Areas,** continued

POTENTIAL OBSTACLES (Identify any potential barriers to success.)	WAYS TO OVERCOME OBSTACLES (What might you do to overcome these barriers?)

ASSESSING YOUR PROGRESS (To be completed once you have had the opportunity to implement your Action Plan). How did it go? What was the outcome? In what ways could you further manage this Developmental Area to achieve greater effectiveness?

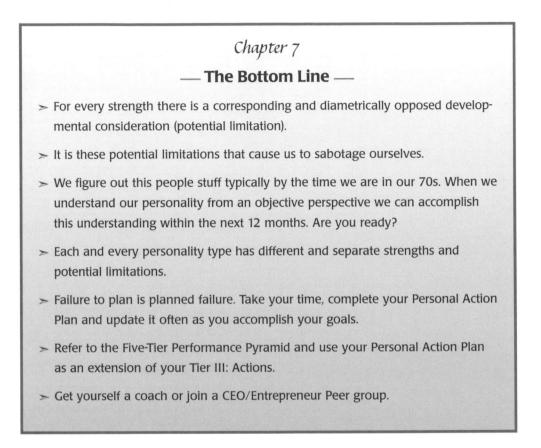

Chapter 7

— The Bottom Line —

➤ For every strength there is a corresponding and diametrically opposed developmental consideration (potential limitation).

➤ It is these potential limitations that cause us to sabotage ourselves.

➤ We figure out this people stuff typically by the time we are in our 70s. When we understand our personality from an objective perspective we can accomplish this understanding within the next 12 months. Are you ready?

➤ Each and every personality type has different and separate strengths and potential limitations.

➤ Failure to plan is planned failure. Take your time, complete your Personal Action Plan and update it often as you accomplish your goals.

➤ Refer to the Five-Tier Performance Pyramid and use your Personal Action Plan as an extension of your Tier III: Actions.

➤ Get yourself a coach or join a CEO/Entrepreneur Peer group.

Entrepreneurs and Wantapreneurs

What Drives Them

I T ISN'T NECESSARILY OBVIOUS REWARDS LIKE MONEY THAT TURN ENTREPRENEURS AND wantapreneurs on and keep them going. Indeed, for most workers the motivations aren't always obvious.

Personality affects people's attitudes toward work, according to Frederick Herzberg's theories on motivation. From his research, he concluded that such factors as company policy, supervision, interpersonal relations, working conditions, and salary are important but not necessarily motivators. He believed that the absence of these factors can create job dissatisfaction, but their presence does not necessarily guarantee motivation or create satisfaction.

131

Herzberg determined from his research that true motivators are elements that enrich a person's job. He found five factors in particular that are strong determinants of job satisfaction: achievement, recognition, the work itself, responsibility, and advancement. These motivators (satisfiers) are associated with long-term positive effects in job performance, whereas the basic factors (dissatisfiers) consistently produce only short-term changes in job attitudes and performance. Satisfiers describe a person's relationship with what he does, and many are related to the tasks being performed. Dissatisfiers have to do with a person's relationship to the context or environment in which he performs the job.

What makes entrepreneurs and wantapreneurs tick? What motivates them, often against seemingly insurmountable odds? The answers to these questions are ego, status, sense of urgency, and independence. While successful business leaders make it look easy, there's more to their success than meets the eye.

You will no doubt relate to the motivational factors that are most in line with the type of entrepreneurial personality that you, or the entrepreneurs you know, possess. By looking at the behind-the-scenes operations, thought processes, and strategies of successful entrepreneurs, you can discern what will work for you and how to leverage that knowledge and awareness. You will also find out where you might be tempted to compromise your integrity or get into trouble. Fortunately, I was able to learn some of these lessons in my youth, when the stakes were much lower.

Looking at each of the four behavioral factors, there are particular motivational needs for each:

- If I have a high level of Dominance, I am often motivated by independence, control, authority, autonomy, and a certain degree of power.
- If I have a high level of Sociability, I am typically motivated by recognition, being a part of a team, social stimulation, and being able to work with others.
- If I have a high level of Relaxation, I am motivated by things like stability, working in an environment without a great deal of change, and loyalty.
- If I have a high level of Compliance, I will usually be motivated by security, understanding what is expected of me, having a book to go by, and being in an environment that is relatively free of risk. I want to be rewarded for my level of expertise.

Understanding these motivators is important not merely for increasing your own self-awareness, but also for increasing your awareness of what motivates others. Successful leaders have to know how to motivate others, especially others with complementary talents.

Lessons Learned

I was seven years old, and it was a warm spring in Peoria with blankets of colorful flowers blooming all over the neighborhood. It was also the opening day of a new Spudnut Donut shop at the corner of University and Main. I became an avid customer, and with my loyal visits the owner immediately took a liking to my chutzpah. He made me an offer I couldn't refuse: two doughnuts and $4 a day to deliver free doughnut samples to the neighborhood. This was his way of attracting the neighbors to his new store. Pretty good idea; I'm still a big believer in sampling.

I started on a Saturday morning and delivered doughnuts for several blocks, giving away more than 50 a day. All the neighbors loved the idea—so much so that they started giving me tips for the service. Sometimes they paid me as much as 50 cents.

The second week, I was caught in a dilemma. The neighbors, becoming accustomed to the service, wanted to pay for the doughnuts rather than going to the doughnut store. So here I am with my 50 sample doughnuts, $4 a day from Mr. Spudnut, and a thriving doughnut business, supplying customers ready to pay top dollar. Well, I'm sure you can see the dilemma from a seven-year-old's perspective. What would you do?

In Their Own Words
What Entrepreneurs Said about Defining Moments in Their Personal Lives

As in *The Millionaire Next Door* and *The Millionaire Mind*, in which many of the respondents gave credit to their spouses, this survey base also indicated it is their spouses and children that motivate them and have defined their lives. Not just their business, but their *life*. Without that, according to these participants, it would be a shallow happiness.

Q: *What is your life's most significant event or defining moment that has affected your personal life and why?*

"My parents are Holocaust survivors. They taught me the importance of respecting others and treating people with kindness. I also learned that most setbacks in life, including business difficulties, are relatively minor when you lose family members to hatred and bigotry."

"Three months ago, my wife of ten years passed away from complications associated with the birth of our daughter, seven days prior. Obviously, this has been the most difficult time in my life, and my life is now changed forever in ways that I am just beginning to understand."

"Divorcing my first husband and moving out of the area to a 100 percent commission job—I had no choice but to make it. My three children needed me to succeed."

"My youngest daughter, Chelsea, was diagnosed with a malignant brain tumor at age two and a half (1993) with a 20 percent chance of survival for one year. I sought extra treatments and methods to save her life and quality of life. Today she is nine and doing well."

"Getting married and having two wonderful children! If down to the event level, the moment I met my wife in 1986."

"Death of both of my parents. You learn that nothing lasts forever and that you in the end must take responsibility for your own life."

"My marriage to my wife. Because she is my soul mate, she provides the ultimate balance to my personality and allows a foundation and calm in my personal life that would make life miserable otherwise."

"The birth of my children. Because I would still be working 70 hours a week, with no other life than my work life. They taught me that there is more to life than work."

"Attended Gallaudet University, learned sign language, and was among peers. I operate in the deaf and the hearing world."

"Turning my life over to Jesus Christ as a teenager was the defining moment . . . although it has been a continual struggle over the years to maintain a spiritual perspective in everything I do . . . ."

"I never, ever quit. In my first marriage, my wife continued to have an affair. My tenacity exacerbated an unhealthy marriage. Since my divorce, I realized that only I could commit to what I can bring to the table. Plus, I am a recovering perfectionist."

"Serving a mission for the Mormon Church—it helped me understand the importance of serving other people and to get my priorities in order."

"When I finally gracefully exited/resigned from the company I started. This gave me time to finally focus on my personal life and a renewed perspective on my strengths and weaknesses and how to gain more overall balance in my life between work and play."

"My wife. I met her in second grade. We started dating in high school. She was my only date. She wouldn't let me marry her until she finished school."

"Leaving corporate life and going into my own business with the support of my wife. I was successful in the corporate environment, and my friends said I was nuts to leave. This decision allowed me to achieve the personal satisfaction and financial freedom we so highly value."

Trailblazers' Motivation

The Trailblazer is the granddaddy of all Generalists. Trailblazers are doggedly determined to get their own way and equally focused on results. They're much more analytical than their more sociable Generalist counterparts. Therefore, their Achilles heel is the people side of business; they're much more apt to enjoy focusing on the number side.

With a strong focus on winning, they promote internal competition and set genuinely ambitious, challenging goals with short time frames. With an emphasis on quantifiable results, they communicate their ideas in a straightforward, bottom-line way. They're careful to keep a professional distance from their people except when a more congenial approach is essential to attaining their business goals. Although they can be patient coaches if the situation warrants it, they can also light a fire under their team when appropriate. Although they accept some innovation from their team, they still expect them to follow defined parameters.

In Accord Management System's consulting practice, we have the need to hire a diverse group of personalities. Most are Generalists, and one of the most difficult to manage is the Trailblazer personality. Their favorite question is "Why?" as they challenge everything. They have the capacity to be somewhat, if not very, difficult to manage. The good news is that they are great at business development. The better news is that if you know they are going to be challenging, then it becomes easier to direct them. Tell them what you want, give them the tools, and get out of the way. If they are willing to let you know what is going on, then you have done very well.

They want constant challenge, control, and room to maneuver. They want their accomplishments to be recognized—both publicly and tangibly. They process information largely by using logic, keeping to the facts, and making sure they understand the people ramifications. They hold their emotions in check and keep things moving as they set their own deadlines. They want some variety in their jobs in order to keep from becoming bored. They can follow rules, especially if they have input into what the rules are.

Many of the entrepreneurs you hear about are Trailblazers. That's because they're able to make the difficult decisions that often adversely affect their employees. These are the CEOs or entrepreneurs who are able to lay off their entire workforce to break a union effort. They don't enjoy confrontation, but they don't avoid it either. You probably don't want to negotiate with Trailblazers, because they rarely lose. Their primary style of negotiation is a "win at all costs" approach that is often mitigated by a nice compromise or more conciliatory style. They can appear to come across as warm and friendly, but don't let your guard down—they'll take you to the proverbial mat.

It seems that many of our clients have a Trailblazer personality. They're often the founders of their destiny, seldom embracing the ideas of others. You won't find many Trailblazers serving as franchisees, but you will find them in the ranks of the franchisors.

Within the corporate environment, Trailblazers usually occupy positions that are more analytical, such as those of distribution and production managers. They're the CEO, the CFO, the COO, the CIO, the CTO, and the E-I-E-I-O. (A little humor.)

What Works and What Doesn't

When working with or managing Trailblazers, *do*:

- Challenge them to excel and set stimulating goals, or they will become bored very easily.

- Build accountability into their role. They don't mind playing by the rules; they just want to have input.
- Communicate with them from a logical perspective, and keep to the facts because they do not want to be swayed by emotional argument. They, as most introverts, have tremendous capacity for making extroverts absolutely crazy
- Be professional in your dealings with them; as they don't warm up to others quickly or easily. Once they trust you, they will do almost anything for you.
- Involve them as a sounding board to test the validity of an argument or a case you're developing. But be careful what you ask for. They can be so analytical that they come across as being terse or rude.

If you don't do these things, they will make your life miserable.

I asked a client I was working with, "When was the last time that you screwed up a people decision?" He replied, "There was a time when I wasn't a very effective manager. It may have been as recent as this morning. I know that I have cost myself literally hundreds of thousands of dollars largely because of my need to control. I need to control the outcome, the process, and yes, even the people." This need to control has caused very talented and capable employees of Trailblazers to seek their opportunity elsewhere. I am sure this client created much of his own competition.

When working with or managing Trailblazers, *do not*:

- Control their activities too closely. They enjoy freedom and will fight for it.
- Demand that they report every little detail to you. They prefer to be measured on overall results. They are willing to perform to metrics as long as they are playing on a level playing field.
- Compliment them unless there's a good reason. They aren't comfortable with superficialities as they think you are up to something. They don't mind compliments, but they prefer them in private.
- Get upset if they are a little less than diplomatic. They sometimes let their intensity obscure the possible impact on others. Their style of communication is somewhat matter of fact, strictly business, to the point where they can be considered rude. It is important to know that they aren't; they can just come across that way.

Trailblazers are very creative and strong advocates of their own ideas, so don't become defensive if they constantly want to change things. They naturally look for different solutions.

Go-Getters' Motivation

With a strong focus on winning, Go-Getters promote internal competition and set genuinely ambitious, challenging goals with short time frames. Focusing on outcomes rather than processes, they maintain a more or less hands-off approach and are generally comfortable with delegating the "how" to their staffs. They share their excitement with their teams and motivate those around them to fast action. They gather input from those around them and are good mentors for their teams. They share their knowledge, encouraging others to do the same, and provide positive feedback when needed.

Go-Getters are looking for constant control and the room to maneuver. They want their accomplishments to be recognized—both publicly and privately. They'll set ambitious goals and targets for themselves. They have strong convictions and want to do things their own way. They want to know that they're in control. They may occasionally need to be refocused. They may also disagree with an idea unless they are part of the thought or unless it is presented by someone they truly respect. They work well under pressure and keep things moving. They prefer a variety of assignments and don't want too much routine. They want to interact with others and desire a higher-than-average level of social stimulation. Go-Getters are an awesome force as long as they get their way. Remember that their motivational needs are independence, control, authority, autonomy, and a certain degree of power.

A CEO client by the name of Tom once told me a story about the time he was a sales manager in a fast-growing company. He was next in line for the general manager's position. He'd been on board for only about a year when the previous general manager prematurely retired. Tom wasn't ready for the position—or so the owner thought—and the promotion went to one of Tom's peers, who proceeded to micromanage Tom. (If you were being micromanaged, how long would you stay?) Tom was gone within 60 days and went to work for the competition. That is where the story takes a turn for the amazing. The company that Tom went to work for was in the same industry as his previous employer. Tom's new company grew largely through acquisitions. One of the first companies it acquired was Tom's old company, and the first person that Tom fired was . . . Well, you get the story don't you?

What Works and What Doesn't

When managing Go-Getters, *do:*

- Challenge them to excel, and set stimulating goals, because they love to play the game and always play to win.

- Make sure they're aware of the potential if there's room for advancement. Not everyone wants to get ahead, but the Go-Getters typically do. Because of this trait, it can be challenging to keep them motivated and focused.
- Entrust them with authority. They will look at your company as their own, and as long as they maintain this perception, they will stay.
- Urge them to delegate some of the more intricate details. This becomes a real challenge for Go-Getters because they can handle the intricate details; they just don't enjoy them. Again, if you maintain their buy-in, they will handle the details.
- Acknowledge their contributions when you act on one of their suggestions. It makes them feel that they are being appreciated and that goes a long way in motivating them.
- Build strategies with them so they can stay in focus.

A CEO client of mine met with her director of sales at least once every six months for the specific purpose of determining and maintaining the employee's focus. The last thing she did at every meeting was ask if he still bought into her vision. She felt that she was able to keep him years beyond her expectations. In order to forestall his departure, she opened a subsidiary with him at the helm. She had designed a set of golden handcuffs.

When working or managing Go-Getters, *do not*

- Encroach on their authority. They're protective of their autonomy. Actually they are protective of just about everything. They can be territorial when necessary.
- Take credit for their ideas/work. Recognition is important to them. There is no quicker way to get a Go-Getter to quit than to take credit for his accomplishments. On the other hand, you now know what to do if you want one to quit.
- Let them get away with anything they shouldn't; they are OK with accountability. Their independence just gets the better of them at times.
- Hesitate to stand up to them when necessary. They can need reminding that there are good reasons that their way isn't always the best. Just be careful how you go about it. They are not fond of public criticism. Then again, I don't know too many people who are.
- Be insincere. They can accept the good and the bad in people.

Managers' Motivation

With a strong focus on winning, Managers have personalities very similar to their Go-Getter cousins in that they promote internal competition and set genuinely ambitious, challenging goals. Focusing on the outcome rather than the process, they maintain a more or less hands-off approach, generally comfortable with delegating the "how" to their staffs. With an emphasis on quantifiable results, they communicate their ideas in a straightforward, bottom-line manner. They're careful to keep a professional distance from their people except when a more congenial approach is essential to attain their business plan. In their own way, they show a good deal of patience when working with and coaching others even while maintaining an arm's-length relationship.

> When coaching, I use the four-penny technique, and this concept works well for all analytical leaders because it provides them with a metric to gauge their Tier II and Tier III actions. It helps them work better with others. Start every day with four pennies in your right pocket. Your job prior to the end of the day is to have four positive conversations with four different employees, and with the completion of each conversation you get to move one penny from one pocket to the other. By the end of the day, all four pennies should be in your left pocket. A positive conversation should take less that 60 seconds. One last thought: A comment or compliment can't end with the word "but."

Managers want to be challenged as well as to have control and room to express their ideas. They typically have strong metrics that support and guide their goals. They look at their numbers on a daily basis and are strong cause-and-effect thinkers. They have firm convictions and will insist on doing things their own way. They need to feel that they're in control, and they can get downright cranky when they're not. They can be respectful of authority, especially if they sense they've made an error. All they want is for others to explain their positions logically. They keep to the facts and attempt to make sure they understand the people ramifications. They keep their emotions in check. They prefer having the ability to think things through; if there's an emergency, they want to be notified as soon as possible. They want to hear the bad news before it happens and the good news after it happens. They hate surprises.

Managers are doggedly determined to win, but they approach their world from a rather analytical and methodical perspective. They don't say much, but what they do say is usually important. One of my clients is Frank, a minority owner of a $20 million-a-year implementer of computer systems. In 2005, Frank's company installed a new accounting package. I have learned that such packages should be run in tandem for a minimum of three months, i.e., both accounting packages should be run simultaneously so as to make sure that there are no glitches. Frank's controller did not recommend this, and about six months later, the company discovered that its bank account had $500,000 less than it should have. One accounting package looked at invoicing and collections differently than the other. But that wasn't the really bad news. The really bad news was that the company was outside its loan covenants, its line of credit was called, and its relationship with Cisco Systems was at risk. It took six months of hard decisions, ones that would cause most mortals to lose sleep, but Frank didn't flinch. Today his company is back in the black.

The challenge for Frank is that he and his majority partner have almost the same personality. Frank wants his independence, and his partner wants to maintain his control. Frank is an introvert, and so is his partner. Frank doesn't want to be rushed to make decisions and is a loyal person, and so is his partner. That loyalty is their saving grace—they're both high in the loyalty index and not quick to change the status quo. Both Frank and his partner were wise enough to bring in a third-party business coach who forces each of them to sit down once a month and bring their issues to the surface, working with them to mitigate their respective edges—and they do have them.

There are several great coaching organizations you may want to consider. I'm a member of an organization called Vistage (formerly TEC, The Executive Committee). I attend a monthly meeting, but the most important aspect of my membership is that I have a one-on-one with my TEC chair every month where we discuss my issues. His job is to hold me accountable. You will find a list of CEO or Entrepreneur Peer-to-Peer groups listed on our web site www.theentrepreneurnext door.com.

What Works and What Doesn't

You will notice that the Manager is very similar to the Trailblazer. The only difference is the Manager's level of relaxation. When managing or working with Managers do attempt to provide the following:

- Because of their analytical style, it is important to coach them to adopt a team perspective. This is not easy for Managers because they prefer to handle the heavy lifting themselves.
- They have been accused of being somewhat opinionated and stubborn; therefore, it is important to resolve your differences privately and together.

> If you are highly driven and are comfortable working under pressure, then you may have difficulty developing and maintaining an appreciation for those who are more relaxed. The challenge that you as a leader have is having an appreciation for why others can't do what you can so easily accomplish.

- Communicate with them from a logical perspective, and keep to the facts. Emotional argument is lost on them as are many of the nuances that more social individuals might possess.
- They prefer working on their own, so provide as many opportunities for them to fly solo as possible, but let them know that if they plan on growing in your organization that they will need to do so by working with and through others.
- Managers are somewhat private individuals and professionalism is important to them. Do not take liberties or get too touchy unless you want to buy a harassment issue. Respect their privacy.
- Remember that they are creatures of habit and enjoy the stability of their lives. They do not enjoy a chaotic environment, so do what you can to maintain a stable work place.

When working with or managing a Manager, do yourself a favor and *do not*:

- Expect them to become instant friends. They prefer to take their time to get to know someone. Once you become a member of their inner circle, feel confidant that they will go to the mat for you (or in nonsports terms, they take care of those that take care of them).
- Compliment them unless there's a good reason. They aren't comfortable with superficialities.
- Get upset if they're a little less than diplomatic. They sometimes let their intensity obscure the impact of their analytical skills because they prefer dealing with the technical side of the business more than the people side.
- Don't put pressure on them unnecessarily. Managers have a high level of relaxation, and with this can come a desire to have as much notice as possible when things are about to change. They function best in a calm, predictable environment. You don't have to go overboard on this, just provide as much advance notice as possible.
- Leave everything till the last minute. Be sure to respect their need to schedule tasks methodically.

Motivators' Motivation

The Motivator is a Generalist with high dominance, higher sociability, and both drive and independence. Motivators are encouraged by internal competition and enjoy challenging yet attainable goals. They aren't as aggressive as Go-Getters or Managers. Very energetic, they'll light a fire under their teams, motivating them to immediate action. Sympathetic and empathetic, they understand their staff members' individual concerns and get buy-in or agreement accordingly. They share their knowledge and are genuinely interested in mentoring, providing positive feedback, and maintaining an atmosphere that encourages personal growth and empowerment.

Motivators keep things moving and use their sense of urgency to get things done quickly. They work well with deadlines and not only place themselves under pressure but also are comfortable putting others under that same pressure as well. Make sure they finish what they start, because they can have a tendency to go off on tangents. This is a challenge that all people with low levels of relaxation face. They multitask well, they work well under pressure, and they're very flexible. But the flip side is that they may have a tendency to procrastinate, find constant focus challenging, and be easily distracted. They need to interact with others—and like being asked for their insights about the people side of the business. Don't give them too many projects in which they have to work alone because they tend to excel in environments where they have a high level of social stimulation. Challenge them, let them set some of their own goals, and give them the freedom to accomplish those goals.

Jay Sweet is the CEO of Boyd Lighting in San Francisco, a family business. Having a Motivator personality puts him in a great position to sell and market his company and himself. Remember the first scene in *Mr. and Mrs. Smith* where there was a shooting? Remember the beautiful lighting fixture that was destroyed in a hail of bullets? That was one of Jay's products. He knows people, appreciates them, and is a tremendous motivator, hence the title Motivator.

Boyd Lighting is a very entrepreneurial company. It would be almost impossible to succeed in a creative endeavor unless you have the drive to push for results. Because of Jay's high level of sociability, he knows almost everyone in the industry. If a designer has a new idea, Jay will be one of the first people he goes to.

What Works and What Doesn't

The Motivator is similar to the Go-Getter except his dominance and sociability are reversed; that is, he usually enjoys the people side more than the technical side of business.

When managing or working with Motivators, remember the following:

- The Motivators are great at keeping a number of projects on track, so give them the opportunity to work on a wide variety of projects simultaneously.
- One of the advantages that driven people have is that they work well under pressure. Because of that, they can have a tendency to go off on tangents. They

will usually be open to the relationship in which together you can build a strategy for them to stay in focus.

- Motivators are usually great communicators. Make the most of their ability to communicate, and seek their insights into people. They can be great in sales or management roles as long as they are working with others.
- The Motivator personality has been called a behavioral barometer. You can feel comfortable seeking or soliciting their input into others, and they are often accurate gauges of office morale.
- Depending on the relationship between their dominance and independence, you can feel comfortable providing opportunities for them to make decisions. The reason I mention these two factors is that if their dominance is higher or their independence is very low, they will want to make decisions. As their dominance gets closer to the norm line, they will have less concern about making the decisions themselves.

When managing or working with Motivators, *do not*

- Assign them too many routine, repetitive tasks. They get bored quickly and have to work at maintaining their focus. It becomes a challenge for the innovative CEO because Motivators always want to do more.
- Dampen their enthusiasm by never letting them go off on a tangent. Sometimes those tangents can produce unexpected options.
- Object if they let things go till the last minute as long as they come in on time. They work best under pressure. Why is it that many of us wait until the last minute to complete our projects? It is because we can.

My grandmother was a Motivator, and she was the one who lent me the money to go to college. Naturally, my first approach for financing was our neighborhood banker. The bankers were cordial enough because Grandma was an important customer, but I had no collateral and was turned down—can't blame them. So I approached Grandma. She said she'd lend me the money, and I gallantly suggested that she charge me interest. She agreed and said, "How about 10 percent?" Astonished, I told her I could borrow the money from the bank at only 5 percent. (It was a long time ago.) She said, "Then perhaps you should borrow the money from the bank." After graduating from college, it took me years to pay off the loan. When my grandmother passed away, I was notified that the entire amount of the loan, plus the 10 percent and compound interest, was sitting in a special account with my name on it. Grandma was a pretty sly lady.

The Role Self-Awareness Plays

People can understand and predict how Motivators, Managers, Go-Getters, and Trailblazers find their success, but what about the other 70 percent of the population? They are able to achieve success (you noticed I didn't say, "enjoy a similar success") by knowing the behaviors necessary to being successful (Tier II). Once they understand the right behaviors, they must define and take the right actions (Tier III) and accurately measure those actions (Tier IV) to achieve the right results (Tier V).

Now it's time to look at these personalities that are more wantapreneurial. These are the Specialists or experts. They prefer having structure, are motivated by security and stability, and are more risk-adverse. But success need not elude them. They can be *very* successful.

Authorities' Motivation

Authorities lead by example, focus on output, seek consensus, and are willing to subordinate their own agendas for the good of the whole, striving to eliminate conflict situations. Focused on getting the job done as it should be, they seek well-defined, formal parameters for themselves and their staff, ensuring that proper procedures are understood and followed. In their own quiet way, they show great patience when coaching others. They're loyal and work hard to ensure that their teams can progress at a comfortable pace. They communicate their ideas in a rational, straightforward way. They prefer to maintain some professional distance, concerned that becoming too friendly might hamper their ability to treat their teams objectively.

They prefer being subject-matter experts. They like others to show their appreciation for their contributions and provide strong support when and if they ask for it. They don't make tough decisions easily or readily. They prefer to have enough facts to allow them to prepare thoroughly. Wanting to know what's expected, they dislike dealing with ill-defined projects. They prefer to have their questions answered fully.

> We make the concept of change sound easy, and for the most part, the process of embracing change is almost an easy process to follow. What is difficult is doing it. Knowing the behaviors we need to change is simple; we hear these messages daily—lose weight, exercise more, work harder, relax. The lifelong challenge is turning these behavioral expectations into actions. Based on my experience, a defining factor is passion. Those that have and maintain passion for what they do have all the motivation one could ever want.

They prefer that others take their time when explaining things and want to set their own pace. They want things around them to remain as calm as possible, especially if they can maintain their routines. They want time to prepare and really keep their emotions in check.

Authorities are rarely the founders of their enterprises, but they're often the franchisees, the distributors, or the second- or third-generation entrepreneurs. They just do it differently.

Several years ago, I was giving a presentation to a TEC group of entrepreneurs located in New York City. The topic was personality and leadership. As preparation for the presentation, I surveyed the personality of each of the attendees and their key executives. A member with an Authority personality came up to me after the presentation and asked whether I would consider hiring someone with his personality as a CEO? I said, "No." He wasn't surprised. He wasn't too wild about his position, considered himself to be an accidental CEO, and was, in fact, a second-generation entrepreneur. Interestingly enough, he was successful. His business generated about $3 million in annual revenue. He enjoyed the financial side of the business and the manufacturing or outsourcing side, but he didn't enjoy the sales or people side. Nor did he enjoy confrontation or holding others accountable. Therefore, he hired only those who were easy for him to manage. He hired other Specialists. Therein lies the problem.

I presented to this same group a couple years ago, and the same CEO approached me before the meeting and asked whether I remembered him. I did, largely, because I'd met with his TEC chair the night before and discussed his success. Paul was the benefactor of ongoing coaching, and because of this, he'd hired a great vice president of sales—one with the right personality. The CEO granted him the necessary authority to make decisions and the autonomy to enjoy his position, and today they have annual revenues in excess of $25 million.

Paul was able to develop the behaviors necessary to be an excellent CEO because he knew who he needed to be to accomplish his goals. Even better, he was able to hire those who could make him successful. Letting go of the details was and is his challenge. The way coaching helped Paul get around this was the agreement he had with his VP of sales. He agreed to provide him with his

> If you read *The Millionaire Next Door*, you may recall the professions that many of their survey respondents had. Many were Specialists. That is another difference between my survey group and theirs.

authority and autonomy in exchange for the VP providing him with constant updates on performance, pricing, and other issues that were important to Paul. The more the VP was able to do this, the less important it became to Paul that he do so. Both parties won. Cool!

What Works and What Doesn't

When managing or working with Authorities, it is important to recall the following:

- As Specialists, the Authorities want to understand exactly what is expected, so be sure to reach agreement with them on their specific goals.
- They like to make carefully considered decisions, and it is important to provide them the environment that allows them to take the time necessary to think about their decisions before they make them.
- Authorities are relatively serious individuals. Management should actively solicit their perspective in meetings and rely on their specialized focus, because they will see a side of issues that others may miss.
- They are very dependable workers. Because of this, you can count on them to follow through carefully. If I were an astronaut going up in the space shuttle, I would want an Authority putting in the "O" Rings in the Space Shuttle.
- Sometimes Authorities can make managers crazy, especially Generalist managers. It is important to spend the time necessary to answer their questions about how a specific project or task should be done. Their favorite question is "how."

When working with or managing Authorities, be sure you *do not*:

I have discussed how people come in different flavors, and that extends to the choice of questions or words they use. The more compliant Specialists have a tendency to be more concerned with the "how" side of the business. If they know how, then they can do it right. If they do it right, they avoid blame. Simply stated, Authorities will do anything they can to avoid blame. The challenge is they often work for or with a Generalist personality who is primarily a "why" person. To bring this story full circle, the Authority asks the Generalist how he wants a project done, and the Generalist says, "Don't worry about how to do it. You've done the job before, just get it done and have it on my desk in the morning." The Authority does his best. The job is on the Generalist desk in the morning, and the first question the Generalist asks is, "Why did you do it this way?" No matter what the Specialist does, without the "how," his life can be challenging.

- Put Authorities in positions where they have responsibility for difficult people. They don't want to make tough people decisions. They can do it if they absolutely have to, but they will not enjoy it.
- Give them vague instructions. They prefer specifics.
- Expect them to make big decisions quickly or easily. They base their decisions on solid research and clearly defined rules. Yet when doing something the right way is important, you want an Authority working on the project.
- Give them too many things at once. Because of their high level of relaxation, they prefer to finish a project before they begin another.

Collaborators' Motivation

The Collaborator is another Specialist personality. The difference between Collaborators and Authorities is that Collaborators have a higher-than-average level of sociability. They're able to build consensus, motivate their employees, and work with and through others. They can "sell" easily, provided they're selling to a warm market in which the customer is attracted to their business based on location, brand, or possibly tenure in the business or area of expertise. An example of this type of position would be a convenience-store operator. The difference between a national brand such as Circle K or 7-Eleven and its local competition is that the national brand may generate twice the annual revenue based largely on brand awareness, the standards it maintains, and the similarities of store layouts (stability, knowing what to expect). This is of tremendous benefit to Specialists' personalities because their success may be more brand or location dependent than on their personality.

In the recent best seller *Follow this Path* (Warner Business Books, 2002), the authors (Curt Coffman and Gabriel Gonzalez-Molina) say, "Customers are five times more likely to return to a specific location because of the people who work there." When the Collaborator is the one running the store, return business is almost a lock. It's the Collaborator's extra bit of sociability that makes the difference.

Collaborators lead by example and focus on the team, seek consensus, are willing to subordinate their own agenda for the good of the whole, and strive to eliminate conflict situations. They concentrate on inspiring team cooperation. They share their knowledge and are interested in both mentoring and encouraging an atmosphere of personal growth. They show a good deal of patience when working with and coaching their team. They strive to make sure that they and their team can prepare for contingencies at a reasonable pace. They set parameters for their staff, careful to ensure proper procedures.

Collaborators want to become subject-matter experts. They want to be appreciated for their contributions, and they may want strong support. They don't make tough decisions readily. They do enjoy interacting with others and feel valued when their opinions are shared. They don't want to be too isolated, nor do they enjoy unnecessary pressure. It's important for others to recognize that some things may not be that urgent and that Collaborators don't enjoy doing too many things at once. They want to have all the information they need before making decisions. They prefer to be able to ask their questions in advance and may occasionally seem to expect too much detail.

At Accord Management Systems, we have two Collaborators on our staff: Wendy Dowl and Susan Ingram. They are absolutely wonderful because they will do whatever they can to do it right. The more thorough we as managers can be, the better Collaborators they are. You will find that Collaborators have high levels of energy, are loyal, enjoy working with clients, and most importantly, they always want to do a good job. Wendy and Susan are not on the market, but if you embrace personality testing, you can find Collaborators just like them to support your business.

What Works and What Doesn't

You will notice that the difference between Collaborators and Authorities is their level of sociability. From an entrepreneurial perspective, this can be a dramatic advantage because the Collaborator is able to use his sociability to sell, convince, and manage.

When managing or working with Collaborators, *do:*

- Be specific and reach agreement with them, and make sure the Collaborator understands the expectations and specific goals.
- Keep their trust. The Collaborator personality has a tendency to want to do things right and to keep things professional. They build their relationships over time and trust is an important part of those foundations.
- Minimize their deadlines and changes because of their high relaxation, and be sure to explain why a change is necessary.
- Make sure they understand their roles in relation to the project as a whole. Because of their expertise, they may have some good alternatives and ideas.

When working with or managing Collaborators, *do not:*

- Give them vague instructions unless you want to make them crazy. They prefer specifics. The challenge for most Collaborators is they often end up working for or with a Generalist. This can make all parties frustrated unless each understands what makes the other tick and what ticks the other off.

- Give them responsibility for difficult people. They don't want to make tough people decisions. Most Specialists are more authoritative in their management styles. Collaborators have a particular challenge in that they also have high levels of sociability, and this factor can create additional stress if they want to be liked at the expense of getting results.
- Let them feel as if they're out on a limb. Be sure they have the support they need. They like to know they have backup.

Diplomats' Motivation

Diplomats prefer to lead by example and enjoy focusing on team spirit, seeking consensus, and working to eliminate conflict as much as possible. They use their own need for speed to demonstrate the appropriate response time to their staff. They set well-defined, formal parameters for their staff, ensuring that the proper procedures and boundaries are clear. They concentrate on inspiring team cooperation. They share their knowledge, and are interested in mentoring and in encouraging an atmosphere of personal growth.

They keep things moving and prefer to set their own deadlines. They want a variety of assignments and don't appreciate having too much routine. They'll check details and follow through to make sure that the details are handled correctly and thoroughly. Don't expect them to make big decisions by themselves—they prefer to build consensus when making their decisions. Diplomats won't appreciate being too isolated. They want to specialize and make sure they have the opportunity to do things right. They want whatever information is pertinent to their success. Don't let them feel as if they're on their own.

From an entrepreneurial perspective, the Diplomat is the king of Specialists; he has all the right things going on. Diplomats have the sociability to handle the customers and employees alike. They have the drive to put pressure on both themselves and others. They have the compliance to ensure that the details of the business are handled in a satisfactory fashion. Their challenge is that they're tactically oriented. They won't typically be the founders of businesses, but they can be great at *running* retail operations. Do you have any idea how many retail franchise opportunities there are? Lots! There is, however, a difference between running a franchise where the customer is attracted to the location based on a national brand and owning an individual retail store.

Successfully operating an independently owned retail location could be much more challenging because the Diplomat would be responsible for the marketing and networking, areas more associated with the Generalist personality. It is not that they can't handle the Generalist expectations, it can just be more stress and challenge than they want.

A number of years ago a friend by the name of Gary asked me to teach him my business. I told him that it really took a strong Generalist personality to be successful in my line of work. I had known Gary for a number of years, and he kept asking me. Finally, I relented and told him that he could join me on a training trip to Charlotte, North Carolina. Everything was fine until the first morning. We were in downtown Charlotte. It was beginning to rain, and we were ready to cross the street when I realized that Gary was not walking with me. I turned around, walked back to Gary, whose feet appeared to be cemented to the curb, and said, "Let's go. What are you doing?" He said, "There is a police officer in his car, and I don't want to get a jaywalking ticket." This actually happened. I then said, "Gary, it's raining, let's go." Gary walked to the corner, waited for the light to change, and then crossed. Those were the behaviors of a Specialist, specifically a Diplomat.

What Works and What Doesn't

When working with or managing Diplomats, *do:*

- Provide a fast-changing environment. They can handle a number of different projects provided that they have the right level of expertise. If they know what they are doing, then they can handle and even enjoy a fast pace.
- Give them a well-defined, clear structure. As Specialists, the better their understanding of the expectations, the better they are able to perform.
- Make them an integral part of almost any team. The Diplomat is a great leader of other Specialists.
- Remember they are "how" people and will want to make carefully considered decisions.

When working with or managing Diplomats, *do not:*

- Assign them too many routine, repetitive tasks. They get bored quickly.
- Become defensive if they constantly want to change things. They naturally look for different solutions.
- Expect results before they've finished the project. Their thorough approach requires that they complete assignments fully.

- Ask for decisions in areas outside their expertise. Instead, let them become your expert advisers.
- Give them vague instructions. They prefer specifics.
- Put them in situations where they have responsibility for difficult people. They don't want to make tough people decisions.

Motivation Self-Assessment

Based on what I've read in this chapter, I feel that my motivational needs are most like:

Trailblazer	_____
Go-Getter	_____
Manager	_____
Motivator	_____
Authority	_____
Collaborator	_____
Diplomat	_____

I also have motivations similar to: _____

Working Style Self-Assessment

Based on what I've read in this chapter, I feel that my style (including the "dos and don'ts) is most like:

Trailblazer	_____
Go-Getter	_____
Manager	_____
Motivator	_____
Authority	_____
Collaborator	_____
Diplomat	_____

I also have motivations similar to: _____

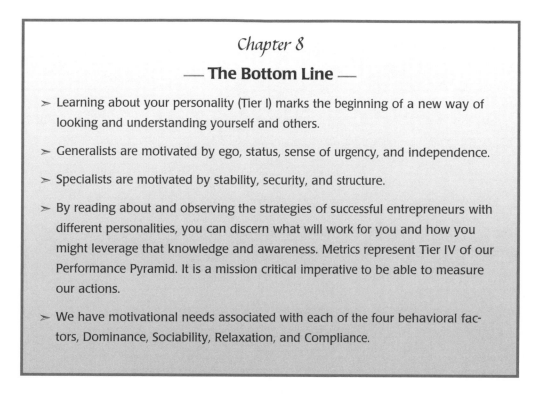

Chapter 8

— The Bottom Line —

➤ Learning about your personality (Tier I) marks the beginning of a new way of looking and understanding yourself and others.

➤ Generalists are motivated by ego, status, sense of urgency, and independence.

➤ Specialists are motivated by stability, security, and structure.

➤ By reading about and observing the strategies of successful entrepreneurs with different personalities, you can discern what will work for you and how you might leverage that knowledge and awareness. Metrics represent Tier IV of our Performance Pyramid. It is a mission critical imperative to be able to measure our actions.

➤ We have motivational needs associated with each of the four behavioral factors, Dominance, Sociability, Relaxation, and Compliance.

How Entrepreneurs and Wantapreneurs Operate

CHAPTER

9

Education and Experience

STATISTICS TELL US THAT THOSE WITH A COLLEGE DEGREE HAVE GREATER EARNING capacities than those without. But does an entrepreneur or wantapreneur really need it? Mightn't experience do? Book smarts vs. street smarts. In Donald Trump's third iteration of *The Apprentice,* his book-smart graduates competed for honors with those without a college degree. The book-smarts group won. But did they really? And would that same level of success take place in a real world environment? After many weeks of grueling tasks, the final episode came down to one book-smart applicant and one street-smart applicant.

157

Education

In the research on the YEO group, the college graduation rate was three times higher than the national average. See Figures 9.1 and 9.2.

FIGURE 9.1: **Graduation Rates**

The Entrepreneur Next Door Survey Group (High School Graduates)

Entrepreneurs	Graduated	Not Graduated
High school	100%	0%
College	81%	19%

General population*	Graduated	Not Graduated
High school	83.4%	16.6%
College	25.2%	74.8%

*Per U.S. Census, March 1999

This is not to say that if you go to college, you will be more successful. Well, actually, the statistics do say that, but what my company found for this survey group was that entrepreneurs with the right personalities had acquired the same level of success regardless of their educations. This is a major thought, and a major finding.

This group may have attended and graduated from college, but that's not the same as saying they were all "A" students. In fact, only about 13 percent of our college graduates were "A" students, as Figure 9.2 shows.

Comparing Dr. Danko's research in *The Millionaire Mind* with the YEO research indicates some differences in the two groups' GPAs.

	High School Average	*College Average*
The Entrepreneur Next Door	3.26	3.12
Millionaire Mind	N/A	2.92

According to *The Millionaire Mind,* the average grade-point average for millionaires while in college was 2.92, with an average SAT score of 1,190 out of a possible 1,600. *The Entrepreneur Next Door* research group shows a college grade-point

FIGURE 9.2: **Grades***

	High School	College
A	22.90%	13.60%
B+	33.30%	27.70%
B	21.90%	36.20%
C+	17.10%	16.00%
C	4.80%	4.30%
D+	0.00%	2.10%
D	0.00%	0.00%

*Figures have been factored to reflect institutions that have a five-point system.

Source: YEO survey.

average of 3.12 and SAT scores of 1,235. There are a number of conclusions that can be drawn from this information. Perhaps *The Entrepreneur Next Door* group as a whole was smarter, worked harder, etc., or perhaps it was nothing more than that the groups were 25 years apart in age and our educational system, including SAT test preparation classes, have changed. What you can surmise is that the members of the YEO study group have worked hard their entire lives and the investment they made in their educations was viewed as critically as the investments they have made and continue to make in their lives.

It appears the entrepreneurs married people with a similar education level. The couples' graduation and post-graduation statistics are within 5 percent of each other. This suggests that they're more comfortable with peer relationships.

	High School Graduate	College Graduate	Postgraduate
Entrepreneur	100%	81%	24%
Spouse	97.7%	76.1%	20%

Who did better in school? It should be noted that this answer was provided only by the entrepreneur. The term *better* was not clearly defined. It shouldn't surprise anyone that these entrepreneurs think they did better in school than their spouses with Self 58.3 percent and Spouse/Partner 41.7 percent.

Two hundred members of The Young Entrepreneurs Organization and their significant others attended an educational event held on a cruise ship in the Caribbean. During the cruise, I gave three presentations. The third was a spousal program where I surveyed the personalities of both the entrepreneur and the spouse. Ninety percent of the entrepreneurs were very strong Generalists and 90 percent of their spouses were Specialists. It didn't matter if the entrepreneur was a man or a woman. Ninety percent of their spouses had the opposite personality. From the perspective of education, it doesn't seem to matter if you are a Specialist or a Generalist. Anyone can get great grades and do well in school.

When I was in college (it now seems like a past life), I took a placement assessment called the Strong Campbell Inventory of Skills. (Today it is called the Strong Interest Inventory of Skills.) This test has hundreds of questions and compares your answers to the answers of people who are successful within certain jobs. It then suggests the type of job you may want to consider. My test results said that I could be successful as either a preacher or a funeral director. I was surprised because: (1) I am not even the right religion to be a preacher and (2) I would not be comfortable working around dead people.

Today, I look at these responses differently. What are the qualities that both of these positions require? Empathy and an ability to be convincing. Here I am 30 years later preaching to readers, clients, and employees and doing my best to close the deal. And although most of my clients and associates can be described as "live wires," every now and again, I do have to deal with the walking dead. So while the jobs the test suggested were not on par for me, the abilities needed to successfully fulfill those positions are very similar to the abilities that I use daily. I took the same test ten years ago and that time the responses compared favorably with that of consultant or director of marketing, two of my passions.

Experience

In terms of experience, members of the study group learned their entrepreneurial craft the hard way: they did it themselves. And if you look at the age when most of them began their entrepreneurial experiences, you can see that more than 25 percent of them gained their experience before graduating from college. See Figure 9.3. When was your first entrepreneurial experience?

My study depicts very few late bloomers. (That doesn't mean those older than 40 aren't successful—they are. But they aren't the emphasis of our research.) Our survey

FIGURE 9.3: **Age When Started First Business**

Year	Percent
Before 11 years of age	3%
11 to 20	22%
21 to 30	52%
31 to 40	19%
41+	4%

respondents started their first businesses before the age of 25. In fact, the average age was age 24. Twenty-five percent of our survey group was in business before they turned 21. They've been in business for only a little less than seven years and have experienced a phenomenal level of success. The professions of these people aren't nearly as important as their personalities and how they use their personalities to succeed.

According to a study of nascent entrepreneurs by The Kauffman Foundation in Kansas City:

1. About 6.2 of every 100 adults 18 years and older are engaged in starting a new business. That means that right now, there are about 10.2 million adults attempting to start a new business.
2. All ages with the exception of those older than 65 are involved with the entrepreneurial process.
3. Among the most active are young men ages 25 to 34.
4. Blacks are about 50 percent more likely to engage in start-up activities that whites.
5. Hispanic men are slightly more likely to engage in a start-up than white men.
6. Hispanic women and white women are about as likely to attempt a start-up, but both are less likely than black women.

As early as ten, I remember selling cookies to raise money for summer camp. I shoveled snow, mowed lawns, and had a paper route. I had no idea at the time, but on reflection, I was different from others. How were you different? When did you notice those differences, and how did they manifest themselves?

7. Approximately 26 of every 100 black men, 20 of every 100 Hispanic men, and only 10 of every 100 white men with a graduate education are interested in going into business for themselves.

Obviously, entrepreneurship is pervasive regardless of color, education, or background.

Background

Is entrepreneurship nature or is it nurture? The answer is still unclear, but for a moment ponder the following:

The court case with the twins that I mentioned in Chapter 1 is winding its way through the Maryland legal system. At question is the guilt or innocence of two identical male twins. One has been married for a number of years, has two children and a good job, and is considered by those who know him to be an upstanding citizen. His brother, on the other hand, has a rather spotty reputation, with a number of brushes with the legal system.

The question is which of the brothers has committed a heinous act. Although the authorities have DNA evidence and have looked at more than 120,000 DNA markers, the evidence isn't conclusive because all the DNA markers are identical. This case points to the fact that even with the exact same make-up, two people can choose very different paths.

Do you know any identical twins? At what age did you begin to see differences in their personalities? Do they behave the same? Do they appear to have the same personality? What are some of the more striking differences?

When I present to executive or CEO groups, among the questions I ask are: "When did you notice that you were different from others? At what age? How did it manifest itself?" I recently asked those questions during a CEO presentation in New Jersey. A CEO with a Trailblazer personality said he first noticed he was different when he played sports in high school. Given his low level of sociability, I asked him if they were individual or team sports. He said, "Team sports." I asked if he could give me an example. He said, "The wrestling team." If any of you know anything about high school sports, wrestling isn't really a team sport. You are on the mat all by yourself.

When we go back to our formative years, most of us can identify a point in time when we realized we were different. Some of us were neater, some messier, some enjoyed the company of others, some didn't. We were all different, and those differences became engrained at a relatively early age. Consider the implications of Figure 9.4.

FIGURE 9.4: **Occupation of Entrepreneur's Parents***

	Father's Profession	Mother's Profession
Professional	24.8%	15.2%
Entrepreneur	45.7%	14.3%
Homemaker	1.0%	50.5%
White-collar worker	15.2%	16.2%
Blue-collar worker	13.3%	3.8%

*Most recent occupation during the ten years before retirement.

According to our survey of young entrepreneurs, both parents have equally influenced these entrepreneurs. Their fathers were doctors, lawyers, CPAs, or entrepreneurs 70.5 percent of the time. The mothers also influenced these entrepreneurs by promoting strong marriages and providing tremendous stability in their upbringing. They had someone to check to see if they were doing their homework and to supervise their free time, so they may have been less likely to get into trouble. The fact that 50.5 percent of mothers were homemakers most likely led to strong expectations that the entrepreneurs' spouses would not work outside the home. Children are also a great motivation for spouses to be at home. But there were only a few stay-at-home spouses in this study group, so these female entrepreneurs have difficult decisions to make as they try to balance work and family.

Job-Fit

A benchmark study published by the *Harvard Business Review* looked at the relationship between performance and age, gender, race/color, education, experience, and personality. The research question was, "Who would make the best salesperson?" More than 1,500 salespeople working in 14 different industries were surveyed. Seven were high-turnover industries such as automobile and insurance sales, and seven were low-turnover industries such as pharmaceutical and heavy equipment sales. The study differentiated the results into four groups; 1st quartile, 2nd quartile, 3rd quartile, and 4th quartile. (See Figure 9.5.) The 1st quartile represented the top 25 percent in performance. When looking at the performance of those who reached the first quartile, the study authors found that there was only a 1 percent differential between men and women, between those over 40 and those under 40, between Caucasians and people of color, between those with experience and those without, and between those with college degrees and those without. There was, however, an 18 percent differential between those with the right personalities for the job and those without. The authors referred to this matching as "job-fit."

If you recall the five-tier pyramid, having the right personality represents the concept of job-fit, matching the personality of the individual with the behavioral requirements of the position.

Notice in Figure 9.5 the percentage associated with those that either quit or were fired. The majority of those who left did so during the first six months when the cost of turnover is less. But still, the cost of losing a good salesperson can be in the tens of thousands of dollars. Even losing a bad one can be expensive. If you would like to have a formula for determining the cost of turnover, please go to www.theentrepreneurnextdoor.com. Turnover for sales and executive positions can cost a company more than 100 percent of the position's annual salary.

FIGURE 9.5: **The Best Salespeople**

Months after Hiring	Performance Quartile				Quit/ Fired
	1st	2nd	3rd	4th	
6-month/job-fit	11%	26%	23%	14%	24%*
6-month/not job-fit	2%	10%	18%	24%	48%*
14-month/job-fit	19%	42%	7%	4%	28%
14-month/not job-fit	1%	6%	14%	22%	57%

*Due to rounding there is a slight difference.

Source: *Harvard Business Review*, July/August 1985

In Their Own Words
What Entrepreneurs Said They've Learned from Their Experience

Q: *What have you learned from your experience?*

"Never let anyone analyze and negotiate the deal for you."

"Well, my current venture is in danger of not living up to my expectations, due to partnership friction and overwork—but we're working on it by hiring more/smarter, and trying to put processes in place and more clearly defined roles."

"I once invested the majority of my savings with a fellow in a start-up idea in an area I was unfamiliar with, based on the enthusiasm of a close friend. He immediately squandered my investment. I learned never to jump in blindly without full personal understanding and checking it out first."

"Don't have partners. Figure out what you want to do. Prove it. Do it well yourself. Hire people and train them how to do it your way."

"Hire experienced people, get professional advice, pay attention to the details, and stay focused."

"Don't trust people."

"People will screw you. Things take time. Always be willing to change your plan on a dime. People are your most important asset (but stay close to them)."

"Without focus, even the best ideas may not be successful. Almost anything is achievable with vision and desire."

Who's King?

Do not depend on a local economy. Do not work within only one industry. If you are in the construction industry, you either need to control the purse strings or be on the beginning of the pay cycle. (Those at the end always wait longer for their money.) Remember cash flow is the King. Be diversified. Only work with paying customers.

"Trying to work with partners was futile. Working alone worked much better for me. I could do things my way, make my own mistakes, take responsibility for them, and learn from them."

"Don't ever invest in a small business that you do not control."

"Learn from your mistakes."

"I learned to divide the success of the business into discrete steps and try to remain open to new information. I also have learned the need to rely on other people"

"Many don't walk their talk. It taught us to pick our partners/customers very carefully."

What Entrepreneurs Said about Surprise Business Challenges

Q: *What are the challenges to your business success that have surprised you?*

"How much the government takes in taxes and how expensive a good medical program is. Those two issues make it extremely difficult to pay my employees on the top end of the scale for my industry and that is one point that always stays on my annual business plan."

"The challenge of building a complete, strong, and complementary team—how hard it is to find people who have the passion, the power, the wherewithal, and the desire to go for the same goal."

"People get so hung up on the details; so few hold the big picture."

"I lived my whole life thinking I was different from others and came to learn that other entrepreneurs are just like me. This was a huge surprise to me."

"People screw you."

"Juggling feelings of self-doubt with the pressure to succeed."

"Being a woman in business, especially a young woman, opens you up to a ton of criticism. I am not talking about the glass ceiling; rather, what happens when you start to become successful, get lots of press, etc. Naysayers come out of the woodwork; it's weird!"

"The only real surprise was how little most employees really care, and how most of them just don't get it."

"I am surprised at how difficult it is to get front-line workers to buy into the concept of excellence (basically the 'I'm only here for the paycheck attitude')."

Chapter 9
— The Bottom Line —

➤ The success of the entrepreneurs in my study did not take place because of a college education, but because they had the right personalities for their chosen business ventures. Those without a college degree enjoyed as much success as their peers with college degrees.

➤ Only about 13 percent of the college graduates in our survey were "A" students.

➤ On the average, our survey respondents started their first businesses before the age of 25 and 25 percent before the age of 21.

➤ People are all different, and those differences became engrained at a relatively early age.

➤ Success is not determined by age, gender, race, education, or experience; it is determined more by personality.

> Not having the right personality doesn't preclude success: it just makes it more difficult.

> When Tier I (Personality) and Tier II (Behaviors) match (job-fit), then the chances for success increase by a 19 to 1 margin.

> Without Tier III (Actions) to support our direction we are bound for failure.

> With Tier IV (Metrics) we have a better sense of our pace and direction. It is via this accomplishment and only through these measured actions that we are able to achieve Tier V (Results).

> Turnover for sales and executive positions cost a company more than 100 percent of the position's annual salary.

10

How Entrepreneurs and Wantapreneurs Learn

W̲E ALL LEARN SOMEWHAT DIFFERENTLY. THIS RESEARCH, BASED LARGELY ON REPORTS generated by The McQuaig Institute,® covers an individual's personality and learning style, which stems largely from temperament (personality). It does not take into consideration level of IQ (Intelligence Quotient), EQ (Emotional Intelligence Quotient), knowledge, attitudes, skills, or experience.

Learning style is important because if you are a Generalist, you're a fast study and learn new material quickly and easily, which is the good news. The bad news is that you're going to have very little appreciation for why things may not be so easy for your employees to learn. If you're a Specialist, then the challenge is that it will take you longer to grasp certain concepts, but the reward is that once you learn them, you'll have them forever.

Trailblazers' Learning Style

Trailblazers are naturally competitive, goal-oriented individuals who respond best to training that lets them compete based on their capabilities and what they can accomplish. They're big-picture thinkers who like to have an understanding of the direction of the training as well as a sense of control over where the training or learning is going. They want to know how their participation will contribute to achieving their goals. They are tuned into WIIFM, which is "what's in it for me?" If they are going to invest their time and energy, they want to know what their return on their investment will be. Programs that give them an opportunity to try things for themselves will generate the best results. If you think this personality sounds challenging and disruptive, you're right, but all personalities have their challenges.

Because they have an analytical, objective, and rational perspective, they learn best from programs that present issues in a logical, methodical manner. They expect the topics to be explained factually and realistically, without an undue amount of selling or motivating. In fact, when you attempt to sway Trailblazers with an emotional argument, you run the risk of losing their interest. They, like many introverts, believe that selling is tantamount to lying. They excel when given an opportunity to analyze the pros and cons and to come up with creative solutions to problems. They want to make up their own minds.

Training programs that move things along at a sensible but not overly hectic pace are perfect for them. They like to see a good variety of topics covered and to have enough time to handle them each in turn. They look for and appreciate reasonable time frames. This latter can be a tricky element, as those with higher levels of relaxation want the pace to be slower whereas those with more drive want a faster pace.

Trailblazers adapt well to training that provides sufficient detail while leaving some room for innovation. They understand process without having to spend a lot

> While this chapter is designed to help you learn how you learn, there is also an ancillary benefit for those who must sometimes teach. Wouldn't it be nice to know the personalities of the attendees in the class or meeting you are about to instruct so that as a trainer or teacher you can change your style to make it more effective? Do unto others what they want you to do unto them.

of time on it. They're fairly comfortable voicing their opinions about issues, although they may keep their opinions to themselves if faced with strong opposition.

Go-Getters' Learning Style

Go-Getters are naturally competitive and goal-oriented. They respond best to training that lets them rise above the crowd and show others what they can accomplish. They're very competitive, like to be the main attraction, and refuse to take "no" for an answer. They're also strategic in their thinking and gravitate to a global perspective but may come up short when it comes to the details. They want to know how their participation will contribute to achieving their goals. Programs that give them an opportunity to try things for themselves will generate the best results.

Experimenting, thinking for themselves, and doing things their own way come naturally to these strong-minded, determined individuals. They have their own opinions and will express them freely. They prefer training that focuses more on the overall concept than on the details, but they can stay on track if the rationale for why the details are important makes sense. Overall, though, they learn best in programs that offer them the opportunity to fill in the blanks for themselves. The meek trainer may find the Go-Getter to be a bit over the top, and therein lies a tremendous challenge: We want Go-Getters in our businesses because of what they can accomplish, but at what cost? You'd do well to take a Go-Getter aside before the training and solicit his input—you're now speaking to his motivational need.

Go-Getters thrive in a fast-paced, action-packed, happening atmosphere. They do their best work when the training is exciting and when they can see the momentum building. They expect programs that match their own sense of urgency—moving quickly, energetically, tackling a wide variety of topics all at once. They welcome the opportunity to be physically active during the session—moving around, joining new breakout groups, etc. Part of the challenge of their personality is that they learn very fast, but without use and application, they can forget just as fast—a case of in one ear and out the other.

> A fellow speaker with a Go-Getter personality recently commented on how he had just completed a PowerPoint class and had created a 20-page presentation after attending the six-hour class. Much to his own chagrin, he proceeded to change and update that same presentation some 30 days later and lamented that he couldn't even find his PowerPoint icon on his computer.

Genuinely outgoing, Go-Getters profit from interesting, entertaining, and enjoyable training situations in which they have plenty of opportunity to interact with others. They want to discuss what they're learning as they're learning it, participate in role-playing simulations, and use their people skills to help facilitate breakout sessions. Training that takes an upbeat approach and stresses the positive appeals to their optimistic nature.

Managers' Learning Style

Managers have a high level of dominance and are analytical, relaxed, and independent. They have a Generalist personality similar to the Trailblazer's and the Go-Getter's but are more relaxed, wanting to think things through before responding. They're naturally competitive and goal-oriented and respond best to training that lets them rise above the crowd and show others what they know and what they can do. They're big-picture, strategic thinkers who look at learning from the 30,000-foot level. They want to know how their participation will contribute to achieving their goals and can come across as somewhat rude if they don't get their way. This pseudo-rudeness is due to their low level of sociability. Programs that give them an opportunity to try things for themselves will generate the best results.

Experimenting, thinking for themselves, and doing things their own way are natural for these strong-minded, determined individuals. They have their own opinions and express them freely—sometimes too freely. They prefer training that focuses more on the overall concept than on the details or the process, but they can deal with the details if they clearly see how they're linked to the overall outcome.

Because they have an objective and rational perspective, they learn best from programs that present issues in a logical, step-by-step, methodical way. They expect the topics to be explained factually, to the point, and realistically, without too much selling or motivating. Training can be entertaining, but without substance it is a waste of their time. Be careful, as Managers can be quite sarcastic. They excel when given an opportunity to analyze the benefits and drawbacks and come up with creative solutions to problems.

They relate well to training situations that give them an opportunity to try things more than once so that they can become comfortable with the routine and have enough time to assimilate what's being taught before moving on. They're creatures of habit, and unlike those who have a fast learning style, Managers prefer to learn at their own pace. The greater the level of relaxation in their personality, the longer it may take them to learn. From a training perspective, this can be frustrating because when you ask a Manager a question, he often hesitates before answering. You may believe he doesn't get it. Quite the contrary, he does get it—it's just that he's thoughtful and wants to think things through before responding. If topics are covered too quickly, Managers may have difficulty keeping up; therefore, pressure and deadlines are better kept to a minimum. They prefer things to move at a steady, consistent pace.

One of the challenges for Managers is that they have a low level of sociability and most trainers have a high level of sociability. This can and often does become a behavioral bottleneck that can prevent either trainer or participant from gaining the insights they are looking for.

Motivators' Learning Style

Motivators are also Generalists, but their level of sociability is greater than their dominance, so most training environments will be all about them. They're also driven and independent, meaning they want a relatively fast-paced environment and can figure most things out for themselves.

They thrive in an exciting environment. They do their best work when the training stimulates their own ideas and when they can feel the momentum building. They expect training programs to match their own sense of urgency—moving quickly, energetically, keeping the pressure up, tackling a wide variety of topics all at once. They welcome the opportunity to be physically active during the session—moving around, joining new breakout groups, etc. In fact, getting Motivators to sit still for an extended period of time can be difficult, so plan frequent breaks. Otherwise, they can become disruptive.

Genuinely outgoing, they'll profit from training situations in which they have plenty of opportunity to interact with others. They want to discuss what they're learning as they're learning it, participate in role-playing simulations, and use their people skills to help facilitate breakout sessions. Training that takes an upbeat approach and stresses the positive is a perfect fit for their optimistic nature. You can more than likely count on the Motivator for participation.

Naturally competitive and goal-oriented, they respond best to training that lets them rise above the crowd and show off a little. They're big-picture thinkers who like to have an understanding of and a sense of control over where the training is going. They want to know how their participation will contribute to achieving their goals. Programs that give them an opportunity to try things for themselves generate the best results.

If you are involved in a training environment and need people to participate, call on a Go-Getter, Motivator, Collaborator, or Diplomat. If you call on a Trailblazer, you are likely to be challenged. The Mangers and Authorities will want to think it over before responding—often leaving the trainer frustrated and wondering if anyone is getting it.

Years ago I was working with Mohammed Fathelbaub, the then YEO Executive Director. We were conducting a forum training in Pittsburgh for a group of YEO members. They were all introverts, every one of them. By the end of the training, Mohammed was exhausted. He felt he did a horrible job because he received so little positive feedback during the training. His evaluations, however, were all excellent. The attendees were learning. They just weren't sharing that with anyone.

Motivators adapt well to training that provides sufficient detail while leaving some room for innovation. They understand process without having to spend a lot of time on it. They're fairly comfortable voicing their opinions about issues and are good at swaying others with a strong argument. They're not necessarily ones to get in your face about an issue; they're more likely to use their high level of sociability to get what they want. They have a very strong chameleon-like quality.

Authorities' Learning Style

Authorities are Specialists, meaning they prefer doing things the right way. They're accepting, analytical, relaxed, and compliant. They take a careful and unassuming approach into any training situation. They benefit most from programs that allow them to add to their expertise. They ask questions, probe, and seek direction in order to satisfy themselves that they understand and have the necessary answers. They recognize the value in being an individual contributor and don't feel a need to compete for a team-leader role. As trainers, you may love having Authorities in a training environment, but you have to earn their trust and make them feel safe before they'll fully participate.

Meticulous and conscientious, they are most comfortable in well-structured, organized training programs that focus on process and cover the details. They want to know exactly what's going on, the who, what, when, where, why, and how of it—specific information rather than general parameters. They concentrate on their own assignments and review their work carefully to ensure accuracy.

They relate well to training situations that give them an opportunity to try things more than once so that they can become comfortable with the routine and have enough time to assimilate what's being taught before moving on. If topics are covered too quickly, they may have difficulty keeping up; therefore, pressure and deadlines are best kept to a minimum. They prefer to see things moving at a steady, consistent pace and don't need or want lots of excitement.

Can you imagine what happens when Motivators and Authorities are in the same learning environment? At the same time? The Motivator is much more forceful in sharing his emotional arguments, and the Authority can become overloaded.

> Years ago my local bank was changing its computer systems, so the tellers were all required to become proficient in this new system. The teller I had been going to for years was not terribly adaptable to change. But the assistant bank manager spent more time with her than with any of the younger tellers, and guess what? She got it and is still there today. Authorities may not be the quickest learners, but once they have it, they keep it forever.

Collaborators' Learning Style

Collaborators are another type of Specialist. Collaborators are much like Authorities but have a higher level of sociability. They take a careful, unassuming, and yet enthusiastic approach to training. They benefit most from programs that allow them to add to their expertise. They don't appreciate an overview that covers a topic too broadly, without providing for specifics. They'll ask questions and seek direction to satisfy themselves that they understand and have the answers they require.

Genuinely outgoing, they'll profit from training situations in which they have plenty of opportunity for interaction with others. They want to share what they're learning as they're learning it and hear what others in the group are learning and experiencing. They like role-playing and other forms of active learning. Training that takes an upbeat, positive approach appeals to their fun-seeking nature. They prefer the more social aspects of learning, such as a training class that has to do with their interactions, as opposed to more technical training about computers.

They relate well to training situations that give them an opportunity to try things a few times so that they can become comfortable with the new information or skills before moving on. If topics are covered too quickly, they may have difficulty keeping up, so pressure and deadlines are best kept to a minimum. They prefer a steady, consistent pace and don't need or want lots of excitement. They can deal with change but prefer not to have to just for the sake of it. Give them a valid reason for the change, with ample time to think it through, and they will become more adaptive.

They do best with training that provides sufficient detail while leaving room for innovation. They understand process without having to spend a lot of time on it. They're fairly comfortable voicing their opinions about issues, although they may keep their own counsel if faced with strong opposition.

Because they have an objective and rational perspective, they learn best from programs that present issues in a logical, methodical manner. They excel when given an opportunity to analyze the pros and cons and come up with new solutions to problems. They may not appear to be natural leaders because their desire to think things through before making a decision can come across as wavering or being indecisive. However, once they come to a conclusion, they are good at putting it into action.

Diplomats' Learning Style

Diplomats are Specialists, but they are much more driven than Collaborators or Authorities. They have an accepting manner and high levels of sociability and compliance. Their sociability is a natural gift because it allows them the opportunity to really enjoy the more social aspects of business.

Diplomats thrive in a fast-paced environment. They do their best work when the training is exciting and they can see the momentum building to a crescendo. They expect training programs to match their own sense of urgency—moving quickly, energetically, keeping the pressure up, tackling a wide variety of topics all at once. They welcome the opportunity to be physically active during the session, moving around, joining new breakout groups, etc.

Meticulous and conscientious, they are most comfortable in well-structured, organized training programs that focus on process and cover all the details. They prefer specific information rather than a general overview. They concentrate on their own assignments, review their work careful to ensure accuracy, and don't necessarily seek out responsibility for someone else's work. They legitimately care about the team and will do what they can to help others.

They profit from entertaining training situations with lots of interaction. They like to talk about what they're learning and hear the insights of the other participants. They're naturally optimistic, and it takes a really bad experience for them to become involved in negativity.

Given the opportunity, they may prefer training that provides them with an opportunity to stand out. They can focus on the overall picture but not at the expense of the specifics. They look for training programs to give them just the right balance of information—an amount they can assimilate comfortably, without being overwhelmed by minutiae.

Learning Style Self-Assessment

Based on what I've read in this chapter, I feel that my learning style is most like:

Trailblazer   _____

Go-Getter   _____

Manager   _____

Motivator   _____

Authority   _____

Collaborator   _____

Diplomat   _____

I also have qualities similar to: _____

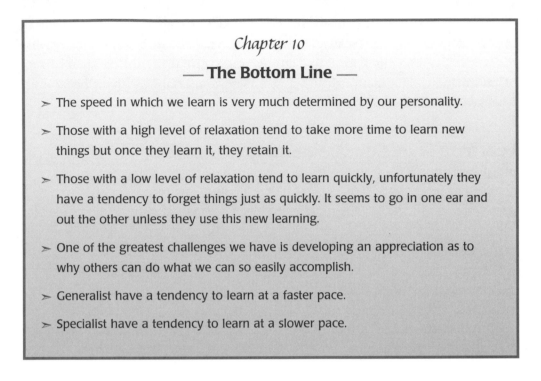

Chapter 10

—— The Bottom Line ——

➤ The speed in which we learn is very much determined by our personality.

➤ Those with a high level of relaxation tend to take more time to learn new things but once they learn it, they retain it.

➤ Those with a low level of relaxation tend to learn quickly, unfortunately they have a tendency to forget things just as quickly. It seems to go in one ear and out the other unless they use this new learning.

➤ One of the greatest challenges we have is developing an appreciation as to why others can do what we can so easily accomplish.

➤ Generalist have a tendency to learn at a faster pace.

➤ Specialist have a tendency to learn at a slower pace.

11

How Entrepreneurs and Wantapreneurs Lead or Manage

ENTREPRENEURS ARE RARELY SATISFIED WITH EITHER THEIR PERFORMANCE OR THE PERformance of others. See Figure 11.1 if you doubt that. On a survey question about business challenges, most respondents think they're better leaders than they are managers. In other words, they're saying it's easier to handle the strategic or leadership side of the business than the management or tactical side. The challenge is that almost every business, especially start-ups, requires more day-to-day management than leadership. Initially, the entrepreneur spends more time working *in* the business than *on* the business. An exception to this might be a well-funded launch where the entrepreneur is

FIGURE 11.1: **Surprise Business Challenges**

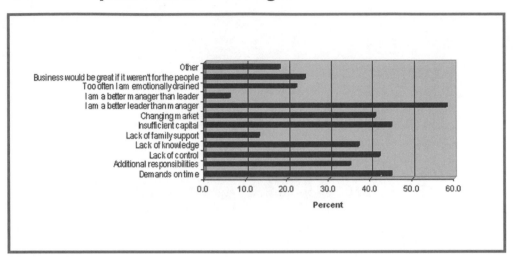

the visionary and has surrounded himself with those who will handle the implementation and the day-to-day operations.

Respondents also mentioned the constraints of capitalization, lack of control, and demands on one's time. Interestingly enough, lack of control is really a behavioral issue in that most Generalist personalities rarely feel they have enough control, which makes sense for a controlling personality. Specialists, on the other hand, have an equally difficult time letting go of the details. The Generalist has a need to control the "authority," and the Specialist has a need to control the details.

The People Factors

"Selecting the right people" is the number-one challenge of the entrepreneur (see Figure 11.2), followed by "developing leadership capabilities" and "tapping the thinking power and creativity of your people." Managing people is, at best, difficult, and leading them can be overwhelming for the faint of heart. That's why it becomes so important to understand your employees, your partners, and even your significant other.

The greatest concern that the entrepreneur has is selecting the right people. The Generalists have difficulty hiring strong personalities because they often have trouble working with types that are a lot like themselves. They also have a higher level of

FIGURE 11.2: **Top Three People Challenges**

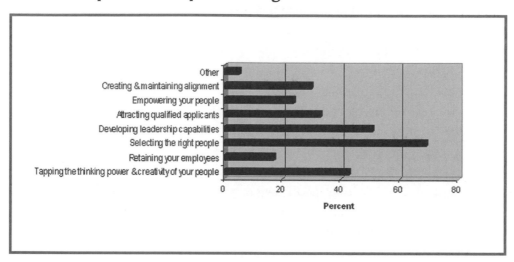

sociability, which means they tend to be internal optimists and believe the best about everyone.

Specialists have a hard time hiring the right people because they have a tendency to only want to hire other Specialists, people they know will do it right. Therefore, they have tremendous difficulty hiring for sales or management positions.

All of the entrepreneurs realize that they rarely have a sustainable advantage technologically and they rarely have more money than their competition. The only competitive advantage they can sustain is achieved by having the best people in the right positions and this knowledge can make their quest to hire and retain the right people even more frustrating.

Developing leadership capabilities is difficult for the Generalist because they function as if everyone is like them. One of their greatest difficulties is developing an appreciation for the differences between themselves and their staffs. They are ultimately quite short with their employees, which may get them the results they want short-term, but long-term will lead to frustrated employees and possibly high turnover. Generalists have difficulty with the introverts because they never know where they stand and they have difficulty with extroverts because they feel like the extroverts are always lying or trying to sway them with an emotional argument.

Specialists have difficulty developing leadership capabilities because they always want to make sure that what they're doing is right. Their fall-back position will tend to be more education, rather than learning more leadership skills.

Tapping the thinking power and creativity of employees can be challenging for Generalists because they tend to go with their own ideas and sometimes don't even think about enlisting the thoughts of their team. For Specialists it can be challenging because asking for employees' ideas can be like opening a can of worms.

Unlike most human resource organizations that are bound by their legal departments and therefore unwilling to take a risk, the entrepreneurs will do anything they can to maximize their business edge and advantage. That's why so many of them embrace the concept of hiring and managing others based on personality surveys and skill testing. They are doing what many larger companies wish they could do, and they were doing them way before they became popular.

The leaders surveyed were more than willing to use tools, technology, and systems to evaluate personnel.

Skills testing	31.6%
Personality testing	51.6%
Intelligence testing	5.3%
Background checking	47.4%
360-degree assessments	9.5%
Reference checks	78.9%
Creativity models	5.3%
Emotional Intelligence testing	6.3%
Exit interview	66.3%
Other	10.5%

The number-one response outside of the normal Human Resources (HR) focus of reference checks and exit interviews was personality testing. Of those surveyed, 51.6 percent used personality testing. This is *three times greater* than in most businesses within the United States. Obviously, the younger entrepreneur is more willing to use technological accelerators in order to maintain or achieve a competitive edge.

Rarely do we meet a business owner who's satisfied with either himself or his managers. In their responses to questions of leadership effectiveness detailed in Figure 11.3, 43 percent of the entrepreneurs gave a 3 on a scale of 5 when asked to rate the effectiveness of leaders in their organizations. And very few of the entrepreneurs gave their managers a 5. As I mentioned before, business owners have a hard time

FIGURE 11.3: **Effectiveness of Leaders in Your Organization**

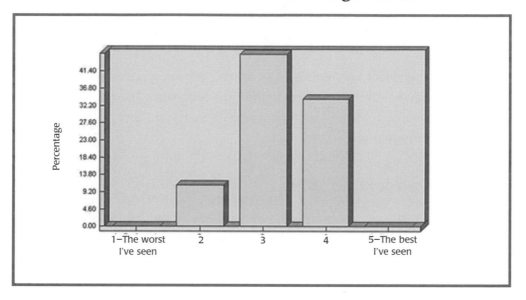

understanding why others can't do what they so easily accomplish. If I don't think I'm a 5, how can I possibly give a 5 to others?

In a 1985 article in the *Harvard Business Review*, Pete Drucker said, "At most, one-third of our hires turn out right, one-third are mediocre at best, and one-third are outright failures. In no other area of our business would we put up with such miserable performance."

This study group indicated that only 28 percent of their employees were truly exceptional performers. Among the rest, mediocre employees are more of a concern than the poor ones. The poor ones leave or should be asked to, but the mediocre ones stay, become bitter, and can sabotage companies. I've asked the following question of CEOs in my presentations thousands of times: What percentage of your employees are truly awesome performers?

> There are very few college classes that future leaders can take that prepare them for managing the people side of business. In fact, unless one is in an MBA program with an HR bias, it is fair to say that they would have very little (if any) class work that helps them learn to understand and manage the people side of business.

Effective Employees	CEOs
0 to 20%	29%
21 to 40%	36%

Effective Employees	CEOs
41 to 60%	24%
61 to 80%	8%
81 to 100%	3%

The answer given most often is between 20 and 25 percent. When we ask the same question of human resource managers in the same companies, the answer is closer to 60 percent. Both are right based on their perspective—it's just that the entrepreneurs are looking for more from people.

Growing Leadership Skills

"Like parenthood, leadership will never be an exact science. But neither should it be a complete mystery to those who practice it. In recent years, research has helped parents understand the genetic, psychological, and behavioral components that affect their job performance (parenting). With new research, leaders too have obtained a clearer picture of what it takes to lead effectively. And perhaps as important, they see how they can make it happen.

The business environment is continually changing, and a leader must respond in kind. Hour to hour, day to day, week to week, executives must play their leadership styles like a pro — using the right one at just the right time and in just the right measure. The payoff is in the results."

—Excerpt from "Leadership That Gets Results,"
by Daniel Coleman, in the *Harvard Business Review*

"A leader is best when people barely know that he exists, not so good when people obey and acclaim him, worst when they despise him. Fail to honor people, they fail to honor you; but if a good leader who talks little when his work is done, his aim fulfilled, they will all say 'we did it ourselves.' "

—Lao-Tzu

Entrepreneurial inspiration could almost be an oxymoron. It's an interesting concept, however, when looking at entrepreneurs as purists. They inspire by their own doggedly determined level of tenacity. Most employees know that if they attach themselves to these rising stars, they too may have a phenomenal ride. Employees are

A client came to us and lamented that his company was suffering from low morale. His employees thought he was overbearing, a micromanager, and controlling. The rumor was that the employees considered the CEO to be a "butthead." The CEO was beside himself because he provided great benefits and flexibility, and legitimately cared about his employees and their well being. My company asked his employees to complete a McQuaig Job Survey,® which is a tool that we use to determine Tier II behavioral attributes for the CEO's position. The survey results, almost without exception, were identical to the CEO's real personality (Tier I). At this moment, the employees had an immediate shift in their thinking. They understood that the things they didn't like about the CEO were "necessary evils" in order for the CEO to deliver the goods. Their CEO was no longer an ordinary butthead but was now "their butthead." And it was because of his difficult nature that they were part of a very successful company and had their complete benefit package, 401K, stability, and tremendous security.

inspired by the vision of the entrepreneur—the big-picture attitude, the ability to look and see beyond. With the exception of the entrepreneur's executive team, employees most often have the opposite personality. It's almost like a moth being attracted to a flame. The challenge is for the employees to deal with the entrepreneur's ability to create constant chaos. Entrepreneurs rarely understand their employees, and their employees rarely understand their bosses.

One of the greatest things about the entrepreneur is the tendency to be innovative and often creative and imaginative as well. Being creative is producing original thought, whereas innovation is turning original thought into something different, greater, or better.

Creative people are inspired, and they often inspire others. If they are more introverted, then motivating others may be difficult. This is where entrepreneurs can fall short, especially those who aren't gifted with high levels of empathy. To them, dealing with people may not be either natural or enjoyable. A Trailblazer's or Manager's idea of motivation might be lacking when viewed through the perspective of one of the more sociable personality types. For example, when an employee asks, "How am I doing?" a Trailblazer or Manager might reply, "You got a pay check, didn't you?" I

> Thomas Edison was the creator of basic light bulb technology. Those who followed him were the innovators. I am not the first person to write about personality. I am one of a few that sees it as a model of predictability and strategic understanding, and as a tool for succession.

hope you realize I'm taking a bit of literary license, but the personality types with low sociability can be on the terse side.

One of the greatest challenges for an entrepreneur is having an appreciation as to why others can't do what he can so easily accomplish. This is a major thought so let me repeat it. One of the greatest challenges for most leaders is the challenge they have in developing an appreciation as to why others can't do what they so easily accomplish. "My greatest challenge is myself," a successful entrepreneur told me. "Unfortunately, not many of the people that I do business with perform at my level. It is very difficult to sit back and watch them make mistakes."

This is the root cause of many an entrepreneur's impatience and challenging demeanor: *Why did you do it that way? Why didn't you make that sale? Why can't you work that extra ten hours this week and get it done? Why can't you work overtime? Why did you take "no" for an answer?* If other people could do the things entrepreneurs accomplish so easily, they wouldn't be the employees—they'd be the competition. On the other hand, how long could entrepreneurs do some of the jobs done by others in their companies? How long could entrepreneurs handle the details or work at a slow, repetitive task? Not very long, indeed.

My first real paying job was when I was 16 years old. My father got me a job sorting bottles at a Coca-Cola® bottling plant. In the old days people actually returned their empty bottles to the grocery store to get the deposits refunded. I thought this was a pretty great job. I got to drive the family Chevrolet Impala, I got to wear a yellow hard hat, and I got all of the ice cold Coca-Cola that I could drink all day long. I was working with three other bottle sorters who also thought this was the greatest job in the world. One had been sorting bottles for 15 years, one for 12 years, and one for 8 years. On my third day at work, we ran out of bottles to sort. The forklift driver got tied up elsewhere in the plant. When we ran out of bottles, it was like a free break. Once they delivered more bottles, I found that I was sorting bottles faster than ever. My motivation was that we would again run out of bottles, and I would get another unplanned break. As I was in my sorting frenzy, these three men looked at me, and said almost in unison, "Hey college boy, slow down, slow down, we ain't going to run out of bottles." I thought running out of bottles was a good thing. They saw running out of bottles as a bad thing because it affected their job security. Lesson learned . . . to be a great leader one must either have or develop an appreciation as to the motivations of others. I wanted my independence, and the others wanted their stability and security.

> Generalists can do almost any job in the company. They can do it faster, better, and more accurately but only for a short period of time. If they had to do the job all day long, they would then find it too tedious.

Can you think of a time or two that you got it wrong? In light of the fact that many of you have a spouse with the exact opposite personality, how often do you get it wrong in that environment?

Many entrepreneurs have a "telling" style of communication that comes from their technical orientation, which comes from a high level of dominance and a low level of sociability. Unfortunately, a telling style of communication isn't limited to those with high levels of dominance. Trailblazers, Managers, and Authorities all usually have a strong directive styles of communication.

The challenge for the entrepreneur who has a dominant style of management is to avoid creating an organization of highly compliant "yes" people. This is a natural tendency. What he needs is an organization of leaders, people like him, an organization of self-confident employees who are willing to fight for their authority and autonomy. The Generalist has a tendency to hire Specialists, and Specialists also have a tendency to hire Specialists. Hiring is mostly a counter-intuitive process. I discuss this further in Chapter 17, The Goldilocks Theory: Creating an Organization That Is Just Right. There is also a great body of knowledge available at www.theentrepreneur nextdoor.com.

The more sociable entrepreneurs are challenged because they delegate authority too freely. They sometimes have more of a need to be liked than to deliver results. Not only do they tend to overdelegate, but they often don't follow up as closely as they should. This overdelegation can lead to loss of control and accountability. Do you see yourself in either of these examples?

The difficulty for entrepreneurs with a high level of dominance, especially those who aren't gifted with an equally high level of sociability, is that they're overly controlling. They control not only themselves but also everyone and everything around them. They have difficulty delegating real authority. This becomes the entrepreneur's trap.

The entrepreneur's trap is the inability to delegate authority or give up control. This may limit entrepreneurs to a family or lifestyle business, as opposed to a larger,

Delegation and Authority

There are two main aspects of delegation: delegation of authority and delegation of details. Authority is the legal right to say "yes" or "no." With that also comes responsibility, and with responsibility the task of getting the job done. The second area of delegation is the delegation of details, e.g., giving someone a task to complete.

scalable business. While there is nothing wrong with a family or lifestyle business, it can limit the ultimate goals of the owner.

The real authority that highly dominant entrepreneurs delegate will usually only be given to those they know and trust, and even then they follow up excruciatingly closely and demand both metrics and results. If they don't get the results they're looking for, they can be downright nasty. And once they've lost trust in others, it can take a long time to regain their trust. On the other hand, they can delegate responsibility when necessary or required.

Last year, America's businesses spent close to $50 billion on purchases of information systems and technology. At the same time, only a tenth of that amount was invested in the training and development of employees. With objective systems, people know exactly what to expect. Therefore, it is essential that they adopt more objective measures for measuring both employees and their positions. These measures are extremely valuable because they allow people to better predict desired outcomes. It comes down to the old axiom: if you can't measure it, you can't manage it.

In Their Own Words
The Single Most Important Experience/Knowledge that Prepared Entrepreneurs to be CEOs or Leaders

CEOs are prepared more for their jobs behaviorally than in terms of their skills sets. They see the world differently, not because they want to, but because they have to. No one wakes up in the morning and decides that they want to become a CEO, CIO, EIEIO, or an entrepreneur. It just happens. And it happens because they can't stand the person they're working for, or they get fired, or they believe they're good enough and smart enough to take that risk. And typically, there are one or two people who entered our lives and made very dramatic changes or provided us with the experience, knowledge, or mentorship that prepared us for our leadership positions.

Q: *What was the single most important experience and/or knowledge that prepared you for your role as CEO or leader?*

"I actually believe that I could use some coaching to improve my skills as the company leader."

"My willingness to learn."

"It's a combination of personal traits that started with natural God-given ability and have been honed through years of experience and hard work."

"Personal counseling by a professional."

"Failing at some areas and learning from my mistakes. I credit my mentor with allowing me to fail and then learning how to avoid the same problem next time."

"Whatever you can do or dream you can do, begin it now. Boldness has power and energy in it."

"Learning that the CEO is the leader. Never show fear or doubt in yourself or your ideas."

"My willingness to take responsibility."

"Parenting."

"Learning how to treat the customer as a sole proprietor of my lawn mowing service at age 12."

"Being able to make a decision—right or wrong."

"Every day you should do something that scares you."

How Specific Personality Styles Lead

Have you noticed that not only do we look different from one another, but we also behave much differently? That's because we're hard-wired differently. When it comes to leadership, the chasm becomes even greater because you're not only dealing with the differences between personalities, you're also dealing with different skills, education levels, experience, and learned styles.

This section paints a picture of how each of the seven personality styles, four Generalist and three Specialist styles, lead and manage.

The Generalist personality is usually managing from 30,000 feet, which is great if they have organizations that are large enough that other strategic employees are in charge of execution. Where the entrepreneur struggles is handling both the strategy and the execution. Their difficulty is delegating and letting go of authority because they know that very few people will have a vision similar to theirs.

The Specialist personality on the other hand, has almost the exact opposite issue. Their challenge isn't delegating authority; it's delegating the details because they know that no one will do the job as well as they will.

Remember, in this segment you can gain an understanding of your employees' strengths and weaknesses as well as your own.

Trailblazers' Leadership Style

Because they have high levels of dominance and low levels of sociability, they're analytical, driven, and fairly independent. As leaders, they have the following behaviors:

- Depending on their level of dominance, they can be highly self-assured and decisive. Not only do they expect to be the ones who make the key decisions, but also they're most comfortable in that position—comfortable making the difficult and even unpopular decisions.
- They see themselves as resourceful problem solvers and believe that decisions should be based on facts, logical thinking, and impartial analysis.
- They think the best changes are ones that are balanced by a respect for existing systems and processes. In other words, they don't feel a need to reinvent the wheel.
- They're usually creative, imaginative, and innovative. They often come up with original ideas, and they also have the ability to take other people's ideas to the next level. This can be frustrating for others, as the Trailblazers always seem to

be a step ahead. They don't always talk about their ideas but their actions show what they're thinking.

Because they have high levels of self-confidence, they're prone to taking calculated risks; they believe they can make things happen. They have a need for change and are comfortable with it. They use their drive to maintain momentum and are careful to avoid letting emotions get in their way.

Potential Limitations

Their strong egos and aggressive natures can be intimidating, inhibiting input from others. They can easily give the impression that their minds are made up, therefore negating the need even to ask for opinions. They can be seen as setting unrealistic goals, which can instill a crisis mentality in their staffs and increase the risk of burn-out.

They focus more on facts than on people. They aren't prone to being swayed by emotional argument and, therefore, find managing sales or customer-service people a real challenge. Because of their matter-of-fact style of communication, they can come across as rude, even abrasive, especially when under pressure. They don't necessarily recognize the need to provide positive feedback, giving their staff members the impression that their work is unappreciated. They've been known to intimidate their employees by their sparse style of communication.

Go-Getters' Leadership Style

They have a high level of dominance, their sociability is high but still less than their dominance, and they are highly driven and independent. Go-Getters are risk-takers who not only make things happen, but make them happen fast. They embrace fast-paced environments and opportunities for change. They use their innate sense of urgency to maintain momentum and are comfortable putting pressure on both themselves and others. They're innovative in their approach and have a "Clintonesque" quality, a strong sense of empathy, and typically a high level of emotional intelligence that gives them the ability to read people. They can be optimists who sell their positive viewpoint to others, and they're good at addressing the needs and concerns of others.

This profile is typical of people who are highly results-oriented and assertive and come to work for one reason: to push for a win. Having a strong leadership style, they demonstrate the characteristics required to deal with challenging situations. Being people-oriented, they use their sociability to mitigate their potential edge.

They adopt an unstructured approach to getting things done, are comfortable with delegating the details, and are willing to look for alternative ideas. They're energetic and hard-driving, respond quickly, and cultivate a fast-paced, change-oriented workplace. Naturally outgoing and persuasive, they are able to build consensus and collaborate with others.

Self-assured and decisive, they expect to make the key decisions, seeing themselves as resourceful and influential problem solvers who focus on the big picture. They enjoy seeking out inventive solutions and firmly believe in their convictions, so they tend to make most decisions fearlessly. They put pressure on themselves and others to respond quickly, sensing a finite window of opportunity for action.

They're comfortable relying on their intuitive abilities and believe that the best decisions take the people factor into account.

Potential Limitations

Their strong confidence, ego, and aggressive, challenging nature can intimidate others and dissuade them from offering input. Unlike Trailblazers, Go-Getters rarely come across as rude, but they can be seen as way too intense. They try to control their environment and can set unrealistic goals. They can appear to have a vested interest in their own solutions and to be unreceptive to suggestions. Given their natural dislike for administrative concerns, problems can occur during the implementation phase of their initiatives because of a lack of a clear and specific plan of action. Go-Getters can delegate too many of the details, leaving projects open to ultimate failure. Their lack of patience and need for immediate resolution can lead to hasty decisions and result in their putting too much pressure on their team. Go-Getters are leaders who are good at dealing with pressure and multitasking, but they can also have a strong tendency to procrastinate. Their need for rapid change can lead them to overlook the long-term ramifications of their initiatives. They are 30,000-foot thinkers who can find implementation to be their challenge.

Their empathy and concern for others can make it difficult for them to hold others accountable, and they sometimes place a higher value on being liked than on getting results.

Managers' Leadership Style

Managers have a high level of dominance and a low level of sociability. They also have a high level of relaxation and are more independent than compliant. They're risk-takers who believe they can make things happen. They have a "ready, aim, aim, aim, fire" style of leadership—as opposed to the Go-Getter style which has been described as "fire, ready, aim." Their high level of relaxation makes them patient, relaxed, methodical, and calm, whereas Go-Getters and Trailblazers are much more driven, working at a faster pace. Managers' patience is also such that they're comfortable with the status quo and don't change things for the sake of changing. If it ain't broke, don't fix it. They'll want to review the alternatives before making a change, and given their analytical nature, they're equally careful not to be swayed by emotional argument.

They're more systems-oriented than people-oriented but can force themselves to deal with and lead others. They're much more comfortable managing by the numbers and metrics than by having long, drawn-out conversations. What this means is that direct reports need to accomplish specific goals on a daily, weekly, or monthly basis, and employees are being held accountable to these numbers. When you hit your numbers, you get to keep your job; when you don't hit your numbers, then you are the first one to know. They can adopt an unstructured approach to getting things done and can be comfortable with delegating the details. They provide practical, matter-of-fact, focused solutions and can be demanding of others. They don't enjoy

---

There is a new certification program available for those who need to be fired. It's called a CDE, for Career Development Elsewhere. (OK, I could be more sensitive.) No, actually, I suggest two questions of my clients to get them to determine when it's time to fire someone:

1. If the employee you have issues with were to come into your office tomorrow to turn in his resignation and you knew of someone as good, if not better, to replace him with, would you accept his resignation or try to persuade him to stay? If you're willing to accept his resignation, then perhaps it's time to let him go.

2. Think about the person that you have issues with and imagine that you are now writing him a weekly check from your own account. Would you be willing to write the employee a check from your own checking account, instead of using the business account? If not, then why are you willing to pay him with someone else's money?

---

emergencies or firefighting because they prefer a more long-term approach to decision making. Knee-jerk decisions are definitely not their style.

Potential Limitations

Their aggressive nature, which can be intimidating, is their primary limitation. Their approach limits communication, and their demanding nature can come across as rudeness. They aren't rude. They're just matter-of–fact, strictly business. Their preferred method of communication is usually e-mail or voice mail, which entrenches the reclusive perception that others have of them.

Their high level of relaxation presents another challenge because it often manifests itself as stubbornness. They're typically very loyal individuals, often viewing their employees as an extension of the family. But this loyalty can also lead to the difficulty they experience in firing employees. As a result, Managers keep people on long after they've served their purpose.

Motivators' Leadership Style

Motivators have high levels of both dominance and sociability, but their sociability is greater than their dominance. They're also driven and somewhat independent. Their high level of drive gives them a tremendous ability to work well under pressure, but more importantly, they're able to put a lot of pressure on others. They move quickly, think quickly, and act or react quickly. They're real people people, and their high level of sociability gives them, in turn, a high level of empathy. They read people well and have a clearly defined leadership style that invites participation. Strong consensus-builders, they actually care about and often solicit the opinions of others.

Because of their belief in others, they're willing to let go and be more delegative of authority. They are equally good at delegating the details. They can have a fairly loosely structured leadership approach to getting things done and have the ability to collaborate. Being an agent of change, they embrace it. They're great at selling their ideas and can create a strong emotional argument in order to get their way.

Potential Limitations

Their main limitations ultimately stem from their strengths. Because of their delegative style, they can find it difficult to hold others accountable and follow up closely with them. And because of their desire to be liked, they may find it difficult dealing with challenging employees. They may want to be liked at the expense of getting results. They can also have a hard time keeping their relationships with employees professional and will therefore want to avoid making unpopular decisions. They're fortunate that they have a high level of dominance that provides them with their self-confidence, but with their high level of sociability, they can be easily swayed or influenced. Numbers may not be their friend, and dealing with the operational side could be equally challenging.

> If you want to make a Motivator crazy, approach him, tell him there is something important that you wanted to discuss and when you see him smile and show interest, do an about face and walk away. This leaves the Motivator scurrying after you saying, "I have time, I have time." Cruel but fun.

Motivators are often heavily involved with the sales or customer-service side of the business. They enjoy being with and working with others so much that they may avoid being by themselves. They need a fairly constant level of social stimulation, and this puts them in the position of being easily taken advantage of.

Authorities' Leadership Style

Authorities have a Specialist personality in that they prefer doing things one way, the right way. They're risk-adverse and seek to have a high level of expertise. From a personality perspective, they have a high level of compliance, which is where their adversity to risk comes from. They have a high level of relaxation, which is their source of stability and loyalty. They're analytical, accommodating, agreeable, and cooperative.

As leaders, they lead by example and focus on output, seeking consensus and delegating authority. They do, however, have difficulty delegating the details. They're the true experts and lead based on the rules. Organized and systematic, they take a disciplined approach to leadership. They usually manage based on numbers, metrics, and expectations. They're better able to hold others accountable if they can accurately measure their performance. They're careful to not overreact and have a steady, methodical approach. They focus more on the practical, work-oriented side of the business than on the people side.

They seek authorization, approval, and a sign-off from others before they take a risk. They're good troubleshooters and problem solvers, having a strong analytical nature. Typically good with details and numbers, they're often well-served when working in the back end of the business. Rarely the founders of a business, they're more comfortable buying an ongoing business.

They aren't known as agents of change because they think things through thoroughly and seek others' expertise before making decisions. The decisions they make are weighed carefully, composed of detail, made analytically, and designed to avoid as much risk as possible.

Potential Limitations

They have a need to avoid confrontation and may have difficulty asserting themselves and taking a proactive approach to change and accountability. They may also have a tendency to put off important decisions because they will rarely think they have enough information to make the right decision.

Their focus on details can hobble their decision making, and their lack of big-picture perspective can lead them to analyze situations so long that they lose what little edge or initiative they had. They may have great difficulty demonstrating the determination or initiative necessary in many entrepreneurial endeavors. Like Managers, Authorities have high levels of relaxation, and the resulting loyalty is both an asset and an obstacle, making it difficult to deal with poor performers. Because of their analytical natures, it could also be difficult for Authorities to really motivate their employees.

Collaborators' Leadership Style

The main difference between the Authority profile and the Collaborator profile is that the latter has a higher level of sociability. This allows Collaborators to build stronger teams and work by, with, and through others. They have accommodating, agreeable natures and high levels of relaxation and compliance.

As leaders, Collaborators assume the role of supportive team leaders, focusing on the team and discouraging internal competition among their staff members. They see their role as one of providing guidance rather being authoritative or confrontational. They can be confrontational on occasion, but this usually occurs when someone isn't following the rules, policies, or procedures. They take it and take it and take it, and when they finally explode, no one knows where it comes from. Because Collaborators are so sociable, they typically are challenged by dealing with difficult people or situations. This challenge also takes itself to dealing with confrontation. To help them, my company uses a system we call "Point Easy." See Figure 11.4. Point Easy is not necessarily limited to a specific personality, as everyone can benefit from being more proactive, but it's particularly effective with Collaborators and personality types with

FIGURE 11.4: **Point Easy**

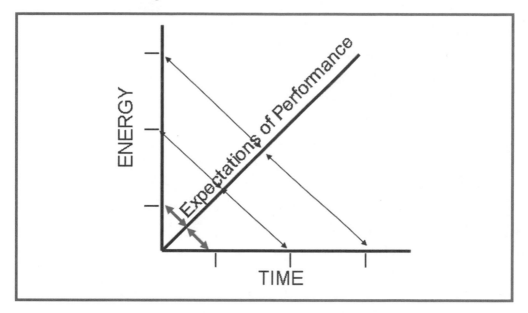

higher sociability than dominance because it provides a means to confront issues, without being confrontational.

People almost always know what the expectations for the job are. The challenge takes place when the employee (or yourself, for that matter) falls away from those expectations. The only way to get back to that point is to change or confront the situation. There is a direct relationship between the amount of time it takes to coach or confront an employee or situation and the energy that confrontation requires. Therefore, take the high road and confront the situation early in the process. It requires less energy and stress. In the long run, you'll feel better.

As leaders, Collaborators prefer to be in an environment where they have a sense of structure. Before they make decisions, they prefer having the authorization that comes from working within a well-structured environment. They rely on their intuition and their optimistic natures. As opposed to less sociable personalities, Collaborators are strong at building consensus that they also ask for and value the opinions of others.

Naturally sociable and outgoing, they try to maintain team harmony and take care of their employees. They like to think things through carefully and aren't quick to react. They want to promote a stable environment for both themselves and their organizations and work with established procedures whenever possible.

The need for Point Easy goes something like this: It is Thursday morning, and one of your employees is late. You hesitate to bring this to his attention because you don't want to create an issue, ruin his morale, or have it cost you another day's worth of wages, so you decide to mention it right before the end of the shift. Guess what? You got tied up and forgot to mention it. You justify this by saying, "I'll mention it to him first thing in the morning." Guess what? On Friday he was absent. By the time Monday rolls around, you've worried about it even though you missed your opportunity. Do you think the employee in question gave his tardiness and absense more than a moment's thought? I doubt it, but you spent hours fretting over what to do and when to do it. Use the Point Easy concept and get on with life.

They're reluctant to initiate change until they can ensure that they have the necessary support, and they do what they can to minimize disruptions and confrontation. They're comfortable selling their ideas to others in a warm safe environment. When it comes to change, they take a fairly low-key approach and always maintain a high level of sensitivity to other people and their opinions.

Potential Limitations

Collaborators will often do just about anything to avoid confrontation. Because of their high level of sociability, their optimistic natures, and their desire not to alienate or offend others, they can have difficulty holding others accountable. Our experience is that through the use of the Point Easy concept, they can hold others accountable by using a system and therefore removing themselves from the equation.

With their need to avoid conflict, they may have difficulty asserting themselves and providing a proactive direction. They may also have a tendency to procrastinate when faced with decisions outside their areas of expertise. In these situations, they'll do what they can to develop that expertise, but until they do, their decision-making skills will degrade until they have the requisite knowledge.

Diplomats' Leadership Style

Of all the Specialists, Diplomats probably have the best service-related leadership profile because they are very caring by nature and need to do things by the book. They have high levels of compliance and sociability and low levels of dominance and relaxation, meaning that they're driven as well.

As leaders, they typically are more comfortable guiding their team and employees, as opposed to telling them what to do. This selling style of communication works well in retail and customer-service environments. In particular, Diplomats encourage cohesion rather than conflict or competition, especially among their staff. They respond to situations quickly and work well under pressure. They have a high sense of urgency and need to get things done quickly. They take an organized and systematic approach to administration and leading others. Because they're naturally sociable and outgoing, they make a concerted effort to maintain team commitment and are especially willing to address the needs and concerns of their employees and customers.

They prefer to lead by example and really focus on the team. They'll use their own need for speed to demonstrate their concern for getting things done quickly. Because of their drive, they'll act quickly but with a careful approach to doing the right thing. They systematically look at precedents before choosing a course of action and seem to focus on the tactics rather than on the big-picture, strategic side of the business. Generally risk averse, they have a safety-first approach.

> The potential limitations of all personality types can be mitigated, provided they understand and embrace the right behavioral changes. Remember Tier I: Personality provides people with both their strengths and potential limitations. Tier II: Behaviors provides them with the direction necessary to do their jobs and change. The change is reflected in their Tier III: Actions, which when accomplished, provides us with the appropriate Tier V: Results.

Potential Limitations

Diplomats need to do things one way, the right way, so they have difficulty dealing with ambiguity. Their desire to be liked can make it difficult for them to keep it professional, to hold others accountable, and to make difficult people decisions. They're so good at managing by consensus that they can have difficulty asserting their position. This can also manifest itself in acceptance of lower levels of performance, because of Diplomats' challenge in dealing with confrontation.

Their by-the-book natures and need to monitor their teams' activities can leave employees feeling micromanaged. Diplomats may also have difficulty dealing with widely varied and often unpredictable entrepreneurial activities. They are, therefore, best in moderately structured work environments such as a franchise or distributorship that has a retail or a strong social orientation.

Leadership Style Self-Assessment

Based on what I've read in this chapter, I feel that my leadership style is most like:

Trailblazer _____

Go-Getter _____

Manager _____

Motivator _____

Authority _____

Collaborator _____

Diplomat _____

I also have qualities similar to: _____

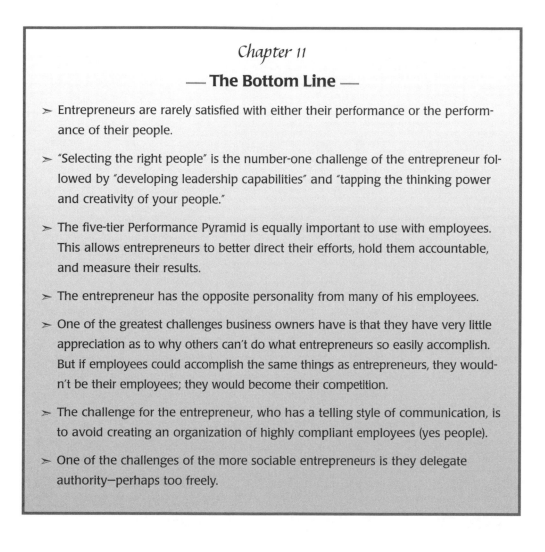

Chapter 11

— The Bottom Line —

➤ Entrepreneurs are rarely satisfied with either their performance or the performance of their people.

➤ "Selecting the right people" is the number-one challenge of the entrepreneur followed by "developing leadership capabilities" and "tapping the thinking power and creativity of your people."

➤ The five-tier Performance Pyramid is equally important to use with employees. This allows entrepreneurs to better direct their efforts, hold them accountable, and measure their results.

➤ The entrepreneur has the opposite personality from many of his employees.

➤ One of the greatest challenges business owners have is that they have very little appreciation as to why others can't do what entrepreneurs so easily accomplish. But if employees could accomplish the same things as entrepreneurs, they wouldn't be their employees; they would become their competition.

➤ The challenge for the entrepreneur, who has a telling style of communication, is to avoid creating an organization of highly compliant employees (yes people).

➤ One of the challenges of the more sociable entrepreneurs is they delegate authority—perhaps too freely.

Knowledge Is the World's Equalizer

THERE'S A DIRECT RELATIONSHIP BETWEEN THE AMOUNT OF TIME AN ENTREPRENEUR invests in his education and his success. I once heard two successful entrepreneurs say, "The harder I work, the luckier I get." And one of them added, "I have more good luck than my competition has bad luck." You can rest well assured that there is definitely a relationship between how smart you work and the results you achieve.

> *There are no exceptions to the rule that everybody likes to be an exception to the rule.*
>
> —MALCOLM FORBES

Building consensus isn't a natural act for the majority of entrepreneurs because they're more controlling and have a need to be very hands-on in their management style. Because of this, building consensus is a learned skill for most of them, and this learning comes only through hard work. The currency the entrepreneur spends in his development is the number of hours he invests in himself.

The entrepreneurs I surveyed invest an average of 110 hours a year in their training, learning, and development. Assuming an eight-hour workday, that amounts to a whopping 13 days, or over two weeks, a year. Knowledge is the world's equalizer and provides the greatest advantage when it comes to retaining that all-important competitive edge. Learning is one of the greatest investments in success that anyone can make. See Figure 12.1.

It seems as if employees stop learning at about the same time they graduate from college. I've interviewed hundreds of applicants in the past several years, and one of the questions I ask them is, "What are several of the last business books or publications you've read?" Unfortunately, most applicants stopped reading when they were last in school. I also ask applicants to write a 1,000-word SWOT (Strengths, Weaknesses, Opportunities, and Threats) analysis about our business. Several applicants

FIGURE 12.1: **Time Spent on Personal Development/Education (Annual)**

Hours	Percent
0 to 100	55%
101 to 200	21%
201 to 300	10%
301 to 400	2%
401 to 500	4%
501 to 600	2%
601 to 700	2%
701 to 800	1%
800 +	3%

Source: YEO Survey

have indicated that they weren't willing to write a 1,000-word report to get a job. If they aren't willing to invest 1,000 words to get a job, what are the chances that they'll be willing to write 1,000 to *keep* a job? Not very good.

Building Consensus

How the entrepreneur builds consensus: The Trailblazer and Manager may say, "What, me care about someone else's opinion?" The Generalists think, "I am right." The Specialists think, "It is right."

Consensus building is the one process that must occur in order for us to get buy-in from our employees, partners, and those whom we need on our team. For about 50 percent of male entrepreneurs and 70 percent of female entrepreneurs, building consensus is part of their nature because they have a higher-than-average level of sociability. But not all entrepreneurs are concerned about building consensus. They're more likely to think, "This is what I want to do, and either you're with me or against me." Unfortunately, it's often the latter. Many entrepreneurs are so self-confident that they can't imagine asking others for their opinions or buy-in.

People who are more accepting than dominant are most apt to build consensus. You can hear it in the way they talk to others. For example, they might ask, "Well, how do you feel about this?" Or, "What do you think about . . .?" Listen to their words. Are they concerned with how to get others on board in order to achieve agreement and eventually a goal? Have you taken care of your staff's needs? Does an inability to build consensus limit your ability to grow a company? It could, and often does, but on the other hand, there are times when building consensus gets in the way of getting the results you want—when you want them. It is a balancing of priority and timing.

The highly dominant entrepreneur thinks, "I am right. I know about this, and this is what I want to do." People who are more compliant are concerned with whether

> I have been a member of TEC since 2002. I can honestly say that I have finally become a good leader. From a Jim Collins, *Good to Great* perspective, I still have a way to go. But I have the right Tier I: Personality, I know the right Tier II: Behaviors, and about 80 percent of the time am able to muster the right Tier III: Actions. Between my monthly TEC meetings, my monthly one-on-ones with my TEC chair, the educational events sponsored by the National Speakers Association and the Institute of Management Consultants, and my sensitivity coach, I easily invest 140-plus hours each year in my own development. School only gets us so far; the rest we have to do ourselves.

The Challenger Disaster

Remember the Space Shuttle Challenger disaster? The "I am right" administrators were under a lot of pressure from the Reagan administration to get the Challenger into space. There were months of delays. This was to be a great PR opportunity for NASA. Before a launch, each area of responsibility has to acknowledge its readiness and grant its approval. Needing its sign-off, the administrators at NASA spoke with one of the engineering groups in Utah. Its recommendation was to delay the launch because it was going to be too cold that night. Engineers explained that when they'd previously retrieved the spent external fuel tanks after other launches, they found a degradation of the "O" rings. This was believed to be related to the low ambient temperature during pre-launch. When the rings become cold during the night, they harden. When they're quickly exposed to thousands of degrees of temperature, they have a tendency to crack.

So, there were the Authority engineers being told by the Trailblazers that they wanted to get this bird in the air. The Trailblazer (the "I am right" people) were forcing the issue. The engineers (the "It is right" people) were saying, "We don't recommend it." Finally, it came down to a Trailblazer's asking, "Can you tell me if we launch that we are going to have a problem?"

Obviously, the answer was "No, we can't *tell* you we're going to have a problem, but we don't recommend it." When push came to shove, the engineers gave in. Although they felt they were doing the wrong thing, they couldn't stand up to the "I am right" people. The rest is history.

something is *right*, with the right way to do things. The battle lines are thus drawn: "I am right. This is the way I want to do it" vs. "It is right."

Many partners, of both the business and spousal variety, encounter a similar challenge, the "I am right" versus "It is right" conflict. In business, they battle until the partnership dissolves, and the "It is right" Specialist is often left with the business. Meanwhile, the "I am right" entrepreneur goes off to start another business. The "I am right" guys are the ones who make it all happen and are usually the founders of new businesses. It is, however, their Specialist partners that make the back end of the business work. You will notice throughout the comment sections here and on the web site, the survey respondents had very few positive comments about partners. The partnerships that work the best are those where both partners understand each other—really understand each other.

"Evaluate your potential partners as closely as you would your potential spouse," said one entrepreneur surveyed. I think that you have to evaluate your potential partners even more than you do your spouse. You spend more time with your partners, and in good times, it's real easy getting along. In bad times, they create the worst of times.

Another battleground exists between the extroverts and introverts. Generally those in finance, accounting, and the legal department are more introverted; their extrovert opposites are found in sales. The extroverts are more optimistic, upbeat, and selling-oriented in their style of communication. Since introverts prefer a realistic and analytical approach, the selling style of communication can lead to a lack of trust. Introverts can't stand the thought of being swayed by emotional argument.

> If a company finds friction between different areas of the company, we typically find it between two specific areas or departments. Of the following five areas, which two do you think we see more friction between: operations, sales, finance, research and development, or HR? The friction takes place between sales and almost any of the other areas of the company. Have you figured out why?

In Their Own Words
What Entrepreneurs Said about Sound Advice

Q: *Is there one piece of advice you received early on that positively impacted your business life? If so, what was the advice, the situation, and your relationship with the person providing it?*

"The first year I was in business by myself, I was reinvesting my wages back into the business and not paying myself in order to feed the business. My CPA, a well-respected professional who rarely took on clients as small as me, admonished me to ALWAYS pay myself first. The business would take care of itself. That was valuable advice."

Mentor Wisdom

"My mentor advised me to never compromise the quality of advice I hired (accounting, legal, etc.) based upon the belief that I couldn't afford it. His advice has proven true time and again. Pay for the best advice up front, and it will minimize a lot of heartache later on!"

"My mentor (my first board member) gave me two key thoughts on being an entrepreneur: 1) Don't do it for the money, and 2) Don't believe your own B.S."

"You can do anything that you put your mind to."

"Reading Peter Drucker's books (on tape) while commuting to work in my early career."

"'You can't change a Shetland pony into a thoroughbred.' This is my dad telling me not to waste my time training the wrong people to sell life insurance/financial products. In addition, my best friend's grandfather sat us down and explained how he did not take vacations, drive new cars, buys new houses, etc. He saved his money for many years, and now he gets to enjoy the fruits of his labors. He helped me understand how important it is to save-save-save, and I do.

"Balance all your responsibilities. Time and Money."

"I only wish I had someone to give me such advice."

"Always be willing to walk away from a deal that is not to your terms, or to terms you can be happy with—learned from my partner."

"A professor at art school told me that there was no such thing as the concept of 'try.' You either do or don't do. That clarified a lot for me at just the right time."

"Watch the pennies, and the dollars will take care of themselves. Told to me by my father."

"The customer's dollar is a vote—it will tell you if what you are doing is right or wrong, and you just simply have to do more right than wrong."

"Save more than you spend, the power of compounding. Read a ton of self-help stuff in early 20s."

Personal Development Self-Assessment

How many hours of personal development and education do you invest in yourself each year? Is it enough?

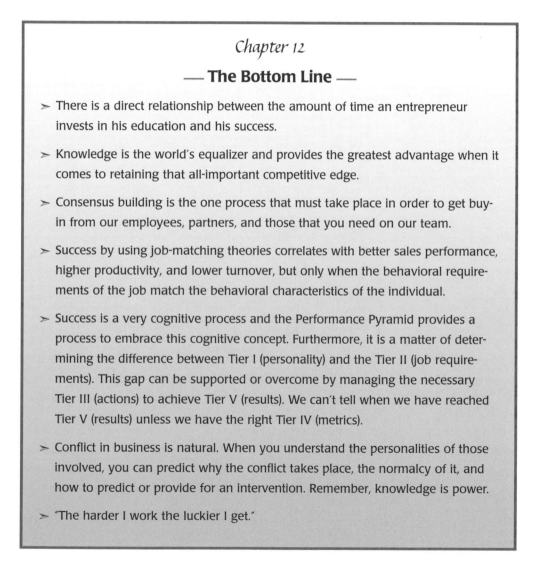

Chapter 12

— The Bottom Line —

➤ There is a direct relationship between the amount of time an entrepreneur invests in his education and his success.

➤ Knowledge is the world's equalizer and provides the greatest advantage when it comes to retaining that all-important competitive edge.

➤ Consensus building is the one process that must take place in order to get buy-in from our employees, partners, and those that you need on our team.

➤ Success by using job-matching theories correlates with better sales performance, higher productivity, and lower turnover, but only when the behavioral requirements of the job match the behavioral characteristics of the individual.

➤ Success is a very cognitive process and the Performance Pyramid provides a process to embrace this cognitive concept. Furthermore, it is a matter of determining the difference between Tier I (personality) and the Tier II (job requirements). This gap can be supported or overcome by managing the necessary Tier III (actions) to achieve Tier V (results). We can't tell when we have reached Tier V (results) unless we have the right Tier IV (metrics).

➤ Conflict in business is natural. When you understand the personalities of those involved, you can predict why the conflict takes place, the normalcy of it, and how to predict or provide for an intervention. Remember, knowledge is power.

➤ "The harder I work the luckier I get."

How Entrepreneurs and Wantapreneurs Sell

THERE'S A VERY SIMPLE DIFFERENCE BETWEEN SALES AND MARKETING. SALESPEOPLE GET paid for their results, and marketing people get paid for their efforts. That really just about sums it up. I could be more erudite and say sales is more tactical and marketing is more strategic, but the truth is that nothing happens until someone makes a sale.

Right before our daughter Rebecca's last birthday, she received a catalog in the mail displaying all the latest electronics: iPods,® Palm Pilots,® Blackberries,® cell phones. It had just what every teenage daughter wants. What took place next was marvelous. Rebecca looked at the catalog, looked at her mother, and said, "Mom, I remember you said I should get an iPod or a cell phone for my birthday. Which would you say would be best?" I'm thinking, "Go, girl. An assumptive close and a choice close all in one sentence." My wife looked at me and asked, "What are you teaching the children?" I said, "Survival skills."

Those of us who consider sales to be an art form and a profession know what the following terms mean: choice close, assumptive close, warm market, cold market, and reduce it to the ridiculous. The average close doesn't take place until you ask for the order more than five times, and the average salesperson stops after the second "no."

Sales Terms/Insider Jargon

- *Choice close.* Do you want the red car or the white car?
- *Assumptive close.* Mom, didn't you tell me I should get a new car?
- *Warm market.* The market created when people respond to a mailing or phone call or come into your store or location. (They are just one step away from being a friend.)
- *Cold market.* Those you don't know. For example, a telemarketer dialing for dollars every day.
- *Reduce it to the ridiculous.* When you buy our program for one year, the cost per day is only a dime.
- *Selling cycle.* The length of time it typically takes to go from an introduction to the close of business.
- *Professional visitor.* A salesperson who is unable to ask for the business for fear of ruining the relationship.
- *Professional closer.* A sales person who is able to ask for the order until he receives it.
- *Trial close.* The sales person asks, "If I could get this product for you at that price, would you then be interested in proceeding?"
- *Transactional sale.* When you sell based on a single transaction or a single event.
- *Relationship sale.* When you sell based on the relationships you've developed

In Chapter 9, you read about a *Harvard Business Review* study on salespeople, and the results continue to prove accurate today. You can invest in all the training in the world, but if you're training the wrong people, you won't get the right results. This is really a critical point.

Therefore, part of people challenge is the fact that, while everyone needs to sell, each personality type goes about it differently, some more and some less effectively. As you read the following descriptions of how each personality type sells, give some thought to what your style is and what you can do to improve it to grow yourself and your business.

Sales is a three-prong process:

1. Prospecting and closing business
2. Delivery
3. Administrivia (Excuse me, Administration)

People should be spending about 70 percent of their time prospecting and closing business, 20 percent on delivery of their products or services, and the remaining 10 percent on the administration. Fortunately or unfortunately, it is your personality that determines where you spend your time and with what ease. If you have a Go-Getter or Trailblazer personality, for example, you will prefer spending your time prospecting and growing the business. Managers and Diplomats would rather be handling the delivery. Motivators, Collaborators, and Diplomats would enjoy the delivery and the Authorities and Managers would enjoy the administrivia.

Consider Jerry Maguire in the movie *Jerry Maguire*. Was Jerry a closer, or was he more of a professional visitor? Have you thought about it? If not, think about it. If you thought he was a closer, perhaps your rationale is the fact the he exhibited a very high level of energy and was aggressively all over the place. But when you look at the other side of his frenetic approach, did it really land him a client? It didn't. Throughout the entire movie, one prospect after another was closed by someone else. He had no clients and was down to one prospect. If he didn't close by signing Rod Tidwell, he'd be out of business. He had one shot. He was standing outside Tidwell's home in Tucson, Arizona. He bent over, covered his face with his hands, took a deep breath, and as he raised his head, he slightly raised his arms from his side, indicating a moment of triumph. He was ready, he was jazzed, he changed his behaviors, and the rest is history. What was Jerry doing? To be more technical as well as precise, Jerry knew the Tier II: Behaviors that were necessary and he was able to manifest the right Tier III: Actions in order to get the right Tier IV: Metrics. "Show me the money," and lastly . . . the Tier V: Results, a new client

As you read about the various personalities, see whether you can tell which type most fits Jerry. And see if you can determine whether he is a closer or a professional visitor. (The answers are at the end of this chapter.)

Trailblazers' Selling Style

Trailblazers have a high level of dominance and are analytical, driven, and relatively independent. Despite their dominance, they sometimes lack the sociability that can be so valuable in selling or building relationships.

Many Trailblazers lack a strong people approach. However, they *do* share the other three characteristics found in many aggressive closers, specifically dominance, drive, and independence. They love the challenge of opening new businesses and closing new accounts but aren't so enamored with account maintenance (convincing a client to invest additional amounts in their products or services, or up-selling).

Taking a direct approach, they concentrate on the measurable benefits of the sale itself and therefore favor a more transactional sale where the relationship is secondary. Given a choice, they'd much rather deal in the factual, objective side of selling.

Because of their high level of drive, they aren't gifted with a high level of patience. This puts them in a position where they want to close often and quickly. This is just as well because they can easily get bored with a long-term selling cycle. They're more detail-oriented and controlling than most salespeople, prepare carefully for their calls, and take an organized approach to selling. Thanks to their high level of dominance, they need to control the sales process, and they get downright cranky if they can't.

When it comes to prospecting, they can be very competitive and direct, using all their capabilities. Because of this, they aren't necessarily the best listeners. Being objective, they don't take rejection or resistance personally; they just figure they have to get through their five "no's" before they're going to hear a "yes." Rapport can be a four-letter word for them because it can slow down the process and get in the way of business.

Many Trailblazers have a unique talent, which I believe stems from their motivational or manipulative gene. (Not really, but this talent does appear to be innate!) They can use others as a vehicle to get their jobs accomplished, typically without the others even knowing that's what's happening. A Trailblazer will call and invite you over to watch the game and get you to stop at the store and pick up the food and drinks. If he's really good, he can even get you to pay for them.

They look at selling as if it's a game of mental chess. They keep their eyes on the prize and are constantly looking for another way to close the business. Given that their presentations are so objective, their manner is often mistaken for a lack of sensitivity to customers' feelings. They can also miss many of these important selling clues. Another challenge for Trailblazers is getting motivated to make the sales pitch. They often make excuses that they need more time to prepare or they need more data.

When it comes to closing, they're exceptionally success-oriented and aggressive. Their analytical nature allows them to focus more on the facts, figures, data, and analysis. Another one of the Trailblazer's challenges is his intensity and drive: He doesn't want to sit around and wait for someone to make a decision.

Go-Getters' Selling Style

Go-Getters are often considered the consummate closer or salesperson. They have high levels of both dominance and sociability, and since the dominance is higher, they are results-oriented. Their high sociability gives them a great sense about people, their needs, wants, and desires. But they're *more* interested in the close. They're also highly driven and independent, two more factors that can strengthen their sales abilities.

Go-Getters are very suited to generating business, especially in new or tough markets. They're aggressive and can sometimes be considered too aggressive. They live for the challenge of finding new markets and opening new accounts. Because this is more fun and rewarding for them than maintaining existing relationships, they can neglect or even ignore the maintenance part of their business. When they communicate with existing clients, their intentions have more to do with up-selling than just visiting and listening to what their clients have to say. Go-Getters maintain a certain attitude in that if you want their time, you will have to compensate them for it. In other words, buy something.

They can be innovative in their methods and manner of selling if it brings them closer to their ultimate goal: the close. They deal well with pressure and can work on a wide range of projects at the same time. But

In a previous life, I worked for Cheshire, a Xerox Company, in Phoenix. I was selling a small binder that made a perfect bind, a product designed for the legal profession. I looked at the market and realized that I could either begin calling on law firms one at a time or find a better way to reach the market. Marketing individually seemed too tedious, so I bound about 100 samples, used a photo of an attractive model clad in underwear (briefs) on the cover page, and placed a caption that read, "Do your briefs get in a bind? If not, then perhaps we should be binding your briefs." I received a ton of phone inquiries, sold a bunch of equipment, and quickly became Cheshire's top sales representative in the Western region. This is an example of what I refer to as path-of-least-resistance marketing.

they also can be distracted, lose their focus, and procrastinate. They still get it done, though, and many of them work so well under pressure that they make it look easy. They can be among the best networkers because they tend to place people into two categories: people they know and people they've yet to meet. And the question foremost in their minds is, "What can I sell them?"

Their prospecting nature can be best described as extremely competitive and proactive. Rarely satisfied with what they have, they want the biggest territory and more and more opportunity. Go-Getters are very independent and always look for better or more productive ways to get to their markets.

Go-Getters have a high level of energy, which allows them to thrive on pressure, meet their quotas, and rise to the challenge of constantly prospecting. Their presentations are always goal-oriented because they set direction, maintain control, and push for results. Expect a fast-paced presentation with a number of trial closes. They're always closing, and their customers rarely realize they're being sold. Their presentations are all about the customers—not the presenter.

Go-Getters are strong closers, especially within a new business environment. They're usually good at reading body language and empathetic enough to understand the subtleties of a prospect's emotions, and they use that information to build a stronger relationship, thereby minimizing the customer's anxiety. Getting up and motivated can occasionally be a challenge, as they often make excuses that they need more time to prepare or they need more data.

Suggestions for a customer: Just buy!

Managers' Selling Style

Managers have a strong level of dominance and are more autonomous than sociable. They differ from Go-Getters in that they're more analytical and relaxed. Because of this, their selling style will be much different than those previously discussed.

Lacking a strong people-oriented approach and a strong sense of urgency, this profile is not well suited to new business development or tough markets. They're most comfortable selling in or to a technical community where their low-key approach gives them a selling advantage.

Strong-minded, they hate being told what to do, so it's fairly simple to manage or motivate them. Just give them their independence in exchange for complying with a number of rules or metrics. Their technical approach leads them to speak in a matter-of-fact, strictly business manner, which is sometimes too direct. They almost always approach their prospects with quantifiable benefits and favor business that, frankly, doesn't require relationships. Their natural selling style is transactional. They're loyal to their clients as well as their company. Because of their higher-than-average level of relaxation, they do well in a longer selling cycle and, in turn, can sometimes miss opportunities for a quick close.

When prospecting, they can be extremely competitive, always looking for opportunity. Listening may not be their forte. Those who overcome this typically do so by training themselves to repeat back what the prospect is saying or even write it down. This practice also gives Managers the opportunity to really think things through. Because of their independence, Managers have a tendency to be strong-willed even in the face of uncertainty or resistance. They aren't good at backing down. In some arenas that might be a drawback, but in sales it's nearly always an advantage as long as it doesn't come across as being rude or stubborn.

Because Managers are so analytical and objective in their approach, they deal well with rejection and rarely take it personally. If they do take it personally, no one will know it because they internalize their emotions. Systematic, they do a good job of maintaining their focus in a presentation. They follow a planned path, don't jump around, and stay on track. They do best in a prospecting environment where they can establish control and have a steady-paced approach to their prospecting activities.

When presenting, they're very goal oriented as they set their direction, maintain control of the sales-interview process, and work their presentation to achieve their goals. Because of their strong focus, they can miss or discount dissenting signals from their prospects or customers. On the other hand, this helps them to keep asking for the sale.

They tend to be both aggressive and systematic when closing. Remember, they're doggedly determined and persistent but do things in their own good time. Although this can be an asset in a long selling cycle, it can also prevent them from putting as much pressure on the situation as may be necessary.

The Network Infrastructure Corporation is a client of my company. Their COO, Frank Spaeth, has a Manager's personality. He's not only a great COO but also a great sales representative. He has the results orientation that comes with a high level of dominance, and because of his lower sociability level, he also has the technical orientation that allows him to speak the language of his technical clients. Just don't send Frank to a networking event and expect him to enjoy himself.

Motivators' Selling Style

Motivators have high levels of both dominance and sociability, but their sociability is greater. They're also very driven and independent, meaning they think well on their feet and display a higher-than-average level of energy, wanting to move things along quickly.

They're good at generating new business, and they're also good at dealing with some of the more mundane aspects of managing existing accounts. Thriving on pressure, they push to move sales along quickly, and they prefer a shorter selling cycle. In long-term sales, they have the drive to continuously move the sale along as long as they're hitting their marks and reaching the desired milestones. For example, they may want to set a second appointment before the end of the first appointment.

They're outgoing, extroverted, and innately perceptive and persuasive. They get their way through the use of warmth and friendliness. They enjoy the networking side of business and clearly prefer building relationships to taking a just-the-facts approach.

When prospecting, they can be highly competitive, but they may not deal well with prospects who don't take warmly to them. They can't understand why someone might not like them, and they don't handle rejection well at all. Their energetic side allows them to focus—seemingly easily—on many prospects at the same time. They have a need for constant action and movement, and it can become frustrating to them if things don't move along as quickly as they prefer. Being independent, they want to and are good at figuring things out on their own.

Their presentations are typically goal-oriented, and they are good at setting their own direction. They maintain a strong level of control in the sales-interview process. They're good at establishing a sense of urgency in the process but almost always do so in a warm fashion. They're the consummate rapport builders and use those skills (behaviors) to nullify the potential for rejection or to avoid situations where they might be confronted adversely. They're strong believers in the rightness of their arguments, but because of their sociability, they have the ability to be flexible enough to accommodate the needs of their customers and be open to others' points of view.

Motivators are success-oriented and can show considerable strength in asking for the order. They close often and early in the process. They also grow frustrated and bored with long delays. They understand the subtleties of a prospect's emotions and do a good job of reading their needs. Generally, they're persistent in closing. One of their few challenges is that not all Motivators are great with numbers. It is therefore important for them to make numbers their friends. Because of their lack of interest in details, paperwork can present a challenge. From an entrepreneurial perspective, they're great at the people side, which means that their corresponding opposite side isn't so great. It's people vs. numbers.

Authorities' Selling Style

Authorities have high levels of compliance and relaxation and are analytical and accepting. This makes them want to do things right. It may also mean that they find the selling process challenging. It's not unusual for Authorities to think that selling shouldn't be part of their responsibilities. It's an unproductive thought, since being in business for yourself makes selling an essential part of your responsibility for your company's success.

My chiropractor, Dr. Thomas Allen, has an Authority personality (Tier I), but his understanding of his position is that of a Go-Getter (Tier II). Not every day, but often enough to keep his business healthy and growing, he needs to sell his concepts, his professionalism, and his diagnoses. He's great at that chiropractic stuff, and his challenge is the selling side of the business. He does sell—he does a great job of it—but it also leaves him tired at the end of the day. For Dr. Allen, being emotionally tired or drained at the end of the day is a good thing—it tells him that he's doing the right thing (Tier III). It tells him that he is using his energy to accomplish something that is not natural for him. It's also important to know that this emotional drain is one of his natural challenges. Part of his wisdom was his partnering decision. His partner, Dr. Shay Shani, is a Trailblazer and provides the balance necessary to sustain growth. They have a unique mix of personalities and outcomes. On one hand, the Trailblazer Dr. Shani has a need to control, and on the other, Dr. Allen has a need to see that things are done right. Between the two of them, they have all of the bases covered. As you may recall, the Trailblazer and the Authority both have low levels of sociability. So how do they deal with the people side of their business? They have great employees so that regardless of their Tier I personalities, they always display warmth and structure, and they do it so very well.

Authorities work better when they're part of a supportive team or process, so new business development can be challenging. They're very good, however, with sales follow-up and implementation. They do well when they're able to sell in a nonassertive environment where they work with add-on sales, repeat orders, or in a warm market like a retail store or professional services.

They're very detail-oriented and thorough in their preparation but may find it difficult to stay on track if they meet resistance. They perform better with prospects who have decided to buy but need specific help with the complexity of the purchase or those who need help with their selection. Authorities have a relaxed and analytical nature and therefore do better with a longer selling cycle and stable relationships. They also excel with the technical application of the sale because they're good at understanding the complexities of the product or service. As long as they're dealing within the bounds of their expertise, they're fine. Outside those bounds, it's a whole different story as they want to learn more before they are totally comfortable proceeding.

When prospecting, they're more effective either with in-bound customers or in an office or retail environment. They can prospect outside, but do better if it's based on a warm lead, like following up on telemarketing leads or responses from a mailing. They're very systematic in their approach, and because they lack a tremendous level of drive, they do best in a more stable environment, such as route sales or distributorships where there are a tremendous number of entrepreneurial opportunities.

Authorities' style of presentation is consultative—they provide the prospect with choices or a range of opportunities from which to select. Remember, Authorities are Specialists and can give great presentations when they're talking about their areas of expertise. They're able to deal with topics of tremendous complexity and many specifications. They maintain a strong focus on the details, which can lead them to concentrate

> A Go-Getter client had a partnership with an Authority. They purchased and placed hundreds of small open-top freezers and located them in delis and snack shops in office buildings. They supplied the freezer for free—the deli just had to keep it stocked with the company's products. This didn't require much selling, and once the Go-Getter installed the freezers, it was easy for the Authority to go out and visit with the customers. The Go-Getter did the initial sale and installation, and the Authority did all of the follow-up and servicing once the deal was done. It was a perfect relationship in which each partner was able to use his strengths to their fullest ability.

more on the fine points than on the big picture. This is appropriate given that Specialists are better at the details than the strategy.

They almost always sell with an objective focus. They know the process of the presentation and may not be comfortable when the customer changes direction. They *can* deal with change—they just don't like it.

They're best at closing with a choice close or in an environment where the customer makes the buying decision. If they sense that there's too much resistance, they may defer the sale or the close until later. They don't display a high sense of urgency, allowing the customer to dictate the speed of the sale.

Collaborators' Selling Style

Collaborators are the high-sociability versions of Authorities. They're still Specialists and prefer doing things the right way, but they're more relaxed and accepting than Authorities.

They also work better in supportive roles. From an entrepreneurial perspective, they're great in retail, office, route-sales, and many franchise environments. They prefer building relationships to taking the all-business approach of those with lower levels of sociability. They have a good consultative style and shy away from the more transactional or confrontational styles of selling. They have the patience for a long selling cycle and the time it can take to build and nurture a relationship. Rome wasn't built in a day, after all, or a week, or a . . .

When prospecting, Collaborators are better served by working in warm markets such as in-bound leads, especially when the prospects need more information. Taking a proactive prospecting approach goes very much against their grain. Because of their sociable nature, they do well when they can build rapport and maintain relationships just by being themselves. Averse to risk-taking, they prepare for their calls and presentations. They can fall back on their sociability if and when they get into trouble. They do well with a scripted or repetitive response, and once they've been trained properly, they maintain what they learn.

They present in a manner that uses their relationships to their benefit. They prefer a warm consultative role in presentations where they are facilitating solutions with willing buyers. They're usually open and cooperative and base their communication on empathy and respect. They present in a systematic, laid-back manner and can be taken off track when they're selling to a strong Generalist who keeps interrupting and asking them to get to the bottom line.

Their closing style is to encourage a customer to make the buying decision. Collaborators will usually defer to the customer when met with resistance. Because of their sociability, they understand the subtleties of prospects' emotions and will usually focus more on their emotional needs than on the facts. Because of their patient nature, they deal well with longer selling cycles. From a management perspective, they may not always be comfortable closing and may therefore require frequent coaching and support to deal with the objections that can prevent a sale.

Diplomats' Selling Style

Diplomats have perhaps the best selling personality of all the Specialists. Like the other Specialists, they're compliant and accepting, but Diplomats also have more drive and sociability. These two factors help them to excel on the people side of the business and do so with a greater sense of urgency.

They're the royalty of retail. Actually, I should say they're the royalty of the "people" environment. In retail, distributorships, any kind of selling that involves recurring or ongoing relationships, they're your sales rep. They work well under pressure and can also put pressure on those around them, but they do it with warmth. They build consensus, collaborate with others, and are most comfortable when working with and through others. The Diplomat can be the master of the Specialist relationship builders.

They prospect best in warm markets, building business relationships with existing clients or responding to in-bound calls or customers. With the right training, motivation, and support, they can also do well when prospecting in retail-based environments or highly structured outside sales environments. Remember, they want to do things the right way. If you tell them what the right way is, they'll work toward that goal. Their restless, energetic approach spurs prospecting activity as long as they don't run into too much rejection or frustration. They prepare for their calls with a fairly high level of planning. Good at building rapport, they enjoy regular people contact and can become downright cranky if they don't have the level of social stimulation they require. Their risk is that they may want to be liked at the expense of getting the desired results.

When presenting to prospects, they deal well within their areas of expertise and are able to answer most questions based on their knowledge and preparation. They deliver an energetic, fast-paced presentation, imparting a sense of urgency in their message. They're open and agreeable, and this allows them to be good students and readers of others. Because they're such good communicators, they may not be the best listeners, especially with a technically-oriented prospect.

For Diplomats, closing comes more easily when it's initiated by the customer. They can have difficulty asking for the order, because they want to be liked: "If I ask for the order, I might put my relationship with the prospect at risk." They understand the emotions of others and are able to respond in an appropriate manner. They may not be natural closers but will probably be open to coaching. Because of their drive, they do best with a shorter selling cycle.

Remember the question "Was Jerry Maguire more of a closer or a professional visitor, and which of the seven personality types was he?"

Jerry was a professional visitor and a Diplomat. Remember at the beginning of the movie when he wakes up in the middle of the night and begins writing his manifesto? His concerns are two: taking care of the people (sociability) and not treating clients as slabs of meat. This shows a high level of compliance and sociability, as he was more concerned with creating a book to go by.

If you have high levels of sociability and compliance, you will more than likely have a lot of drive (this is where Jerry's energy came from) and be accommodating, agreeable, and cooperative. This adds up to difficulty in closing the deal, just like Jerry.

Selling Style Self-Assessment

Based on what I've read in this chapter, I feel that my selling style is most like:

Trailblazer   _____

Go-Getter   _____

Manager   _____

Motivator   _____

Authority   _____

Collaborator   _____

Diplomat   _____

I also have qualities similar to: _____

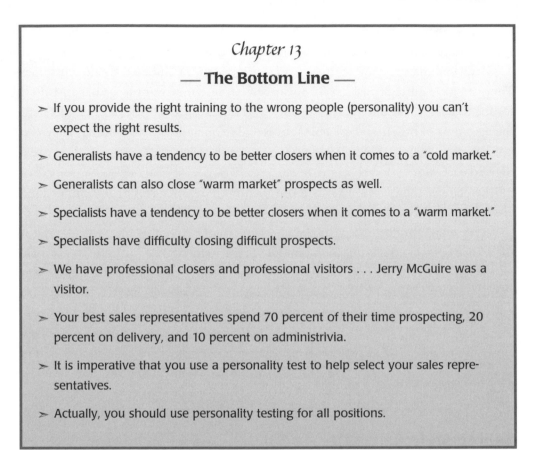

Chapter 13

— The Bottom Line —

➤ If you provide the right training to the wrong people (personality) you can't expect the right results.

➤ Generalists have a tendency to be better closers when it comes to a "cold market."

➤ Generalists can also close "warm market" prospects as well.

➤ Specialists have a tendency to be better closers when it comes to a "warm market."

➤ Specialists have difficulty closing difficult prospects.

➤ We have professional closers and professional visitors . . . Jerry McGuire was a visitor.

➤ Your best sales representatives spend 70 percent of their time prospecting, 20 percent on delivery, and 10 percent on administrivia.

➤ It is imperative that you use a personality test to help select your sales representatives.

➤ Actually, you should use personality testing for all positions.

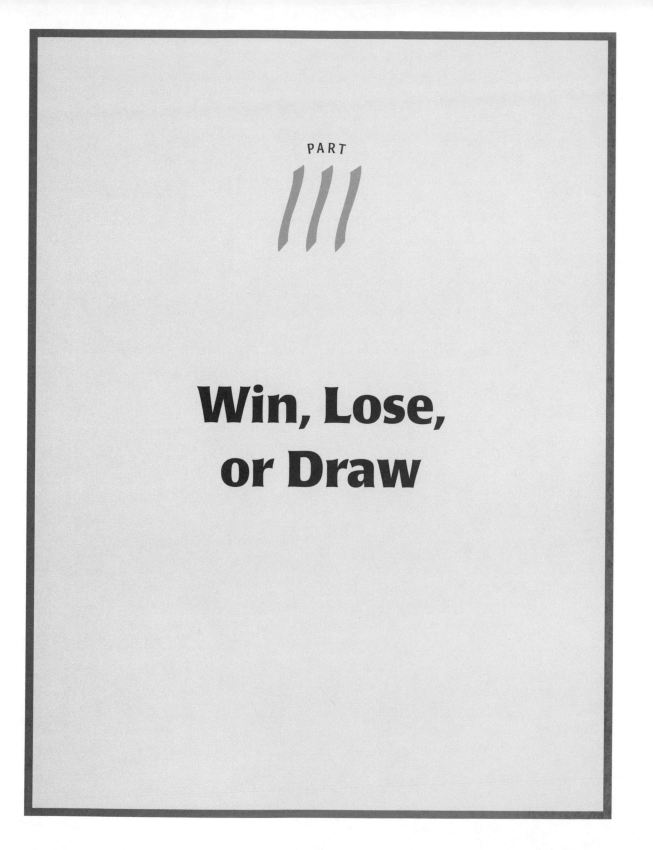

PART

III

Win, Lose, or Draw

14

What Makes Personalities Tick and What Ticks Them Off

MANY OF US LEARNED THE GOLDEN RULE IN SUNDAY SCHOOL—OR HEARD ABOUT it on CNN. "Do unto others as you would have them do unto you." That works great if people have similar personalities and are motivated by the same things. If the same things don't make people tick . . .

What you really want to live and work by is the rule, "Do unto others as they would have us do unto them." In other words, understand the motivational needs of each person you deal with. This chapter presents several ideas on what each personality type really needs to make it tick and what, if you don't honor their personalities, will tick them off.

But keep in mind, the lists here are only the tip of the proverbial iceberg. Ideally, you use these lists as a starting point and are then open to suggestions. Ask your employees or team members, "What can I do to really motivate you?" "What are the things that I do that tick you off?" Get the idea? By the way, when a Trailblazer tells you what ticks them off . . . Don't do it.

Trailblazers' Code of Conduct

Very dominant and more analytical than sociable, Trailblazers are driven and independent. They are all about results. They have very few friends, but ones they have are for life. Being liked is an expense they would prefer not risking; therefore, they show up for work for one reason—to win.

The following could tick off Trailblazers:

- *Controlling their activities too closely*. Do so, and they will go elsewhere.
- *Micromanaging*. Micromanagement makes them cranky.
- *Expecting them to report every little detail to you*. They want their independence, and they want to be measured on overall results.
- *Encroaching on what little authority you give them*. In their minds, one can never have enough authority.
- *Swaying them with emotional argument*. They equate selling with lying. No kidding.
- *Expecting them to be warm and fuzzy when working with others*. They work best by themselves.

On the other hand, the following can make Trailblazers tick:

- *Providing them with control, authority, autonomy, and independence*. They will fight you for it and reward you with results when they have it.
- *Providing them with challenges*. They enjoy the game. Business is a game to most Trailblazers. The money is often just a metric, Tier IV.
- *Providing them with the ability to delegate details*. They will control them anyway, so let them get it off their plates.
- *Providing them with rewards and the ability to get ahead*. They are all about results.
- *Communicating with them from a logical perspective*. They do not like being swayed by emotional argument. As soon as you start selling, they think something is wrong.

Go-Getters' Code of Conduct

Go-Getters have a high level of both dominance and sociability and are also driven and independent. Go-Getters have one thing over Trailblazers, and that is their ability to relate to others. Of course, Trailblazers probably look at that as a weakness. For the Go-Getter, it's actually a strength because they use it to their advantage.

The following could tick off Go-Getters:

- *Micromanaging.* They want and need their independence and will fight for it if they don't have it.

A number of years ago I was playing Chutes and Ladders with my daughter Rebecca. This is about the time she was learning to count and develop a forward-thinking ability. She was now able to determine what number she wanted the spinner to stop on so that she could go up the ladder. Being equally astute, she was also able to determine the number the spinner should stop on for me to go down the chute. Having determined both of these key concepts, she began stopping the game spinner so that it was in her favor. This might have been tolerable if I had been winning, but I was losing and I don't enjoy losing. I know, I know, the throngs of great parents are thinking, "How could you not want your daughter to win?" Well, I hadn't taken that course yet.

I needed intervention. I called out to my wife, "I can't play with Rebecca. She's cheating." To which Renee calmly replied, "Bill, Rebecca is 3. It is appropriate for her to cheat. You, on the other hand, are 45 and it is inappropriate for you to tattle." Rebecca is now 13; we recently celebrated her Bat Mitzvah in Mosada, Israel, which is adjacent to the Dead Sea. She plays a mean (wicked good if you live in New England) bass clarinet, is looking forward to high school, and will soon have her black belt in karate. Rebecca wanted her Bat Mitzvah in Israel in order to have a sense of her roots as opposed to having the traditional party at home. She has a Generalist personality and when she wants something from me she asks, "Dad, are you open for a suggestion?" And I listen.

- *Looking over their shoulders.* They want to be measured on overall results, and they get cranky if they feel micromanaged. Their attitude is "I was looking for a job when I found this one."
- *Keeping them out of the communication loop.* They have a high level of sociability, and they need that social stimulation to feel good about themselves.
- *Putting them in a position that requires a lot of repetition.* They can handle it and be good at it but only for a relatively short period of time.

The following can make Go-Getters tick:

- *Providing them the ability to set stimulating goals.* Don't be surprised if they have a tendency to go off on tangents.
- *Providing them with social stimulation.* Put them in an environment where they get to be with others.
- *Asking for and listening to their opinions.* They will give them to you anyway.
- *Allowing them to delegate the details.* They don't like them anyway.
- *Suggesting that they take on a team perspective.* Don't be too upset when they tell you that there is no "I" in TEAM.

Managers' Code of Conduct

Managers have a high level of dominance and a low level of sociability. They are more relaxed, analytical, and independent. The Managers are really pretty tough characters. They have the toughness of Trailblazers, but are much more patient. It is this factor that makes them loyal to their people. They really like to think things through, and this trait makes them appear stubborn.

The following could tick off Managers:

- *Doing everything your way.* They may have a different approach that could bring improvements.
- *Letting them get away with anything.* Hold them accountable. If you don't hold them accountable, they may lose respect for you.
- *Hesitating to speak your mind.* They many not seem open to the opinions of others, but if you ask the question, "Are you open for a suggestion?' they will actually listen.
- *Expecting them to become an instant friend.* They are relatively private people and are choosy as to whom they invite into their lives.
- *Complimenting them unnecessarily.* They are very private individuals and are not comfortable being swayed with superficialities.

- *Being put off if they come across as being a little less than diplomatic.* They are a little bit less than diplomatic.

The following can make Managers tick:

- *Urging them to delegate the details.* They can be very controlling. They know that they are tough on others, but they don't appear to care. Actually they do.
- *Allowing them to use their initiative and work independently.* They do their best work when they are working by themselves.
- *Welcoming their opinions and anticipating their willingness to be stubborn and take a stand.* (I threw that stubborn stuff to see if you are still reading. If you are a Manager, you may not have gotten it yet!)
- *Coaching them to adopt more of a team perspective.* Then get out of their way. I use the four-penny routine with Managers.
- *Minimizing deadlines/changes and explaining why you're changing something.* The Manager is quite the creature of habit, and they have difficulty embracing change.

Motivators' Code of Conduct

Motivators have a high level of both dominance and sociability, with their sociability greater than their dominance. They are also very driven and independent. They are great at most things that have to do with relationships and the results that can come from them.

The following could tick off Motivators:

- *Assigning them too many routine, repetitive tasks.* They don't deal well with a mundane environment. They enjoy change, and they will find a way of turning a stable environment into a more exciting one (for them).
- *Dampening their excitement and enthusiasm by keeping them on track.* Sometimes their tangents pay off with unexpected results.
- *Objecting if they let things go to the last minute.* They work very well under pressure. (You have no idea when this is being written. I have been making my wife Renee crazy for the last several months. I work best under pressure.)
- *Being too negative and insincere, or shutting them out.* Because of their high level of sociability, they need to remain positive and be in on things.
- *Micromanaging.* They enjoy their freedom. If they want their freedom, then make a deal with them. Give them freedom in exchange for their compliance on their metrics. Manage them by numbers.

The following can make Motivators tick:

- *Allowing for a fast changing environment.* They do some of their best work when they are allowed to go off on the occasional tangent.
- *Getting their buy-in as to setting deadlines.* Otherwise, it can be difficult to hold them accountable.
- *Building a strategy for them to stay in focus.* They know that they can be their own worst enemy, and they will usually be open for a suggestion or two.
- *Providing them with opportunities to interact with others.* Motivators enjoy working by, with, and through others and use their sociability as a tool to get things done.
- *Utilizing them to help resolve any people conflicts and to get others to open up.* The challenge here is that there is also the risk that the Motivator can have difficulty keeping it professional.

A Motivator in Action

Sometimes, I feel badly for my wife. Everyone in our family has a higher level of sociability than she does. She is an introvert surrounded by a sea of voices. My daughter Alex has the most sociability and has a Motivator personality. It serves her much better than it probably serves us, her parents. She is strong-willed and confident, knows what she wants, and is willing to speak her mind in order to get it. When Alex was living at home, her boyfriends were often invited to join us for dinner. Inevitably, she would somehow bring up the topic of our business, Accord Management Systems. She would even ask how much we charged for our services. (She was creating value.) Then, she would ask if we would be willing to let her boyfriend take a personality test. We always said yes, and to be honest, we felt better really knowing who she was going out with. We could also determine which ones we needed to worry about. Her high level of sociability and her ability to create a strong emotional argument is excellent. She is able to convince her professors, win over her friends, and build consensus in directing class and team projects. At the ripe old age of 21, she is fluent in three languages. Renee and I feel very comfortable that Alex will always be able to make her way.

Authorities' Code of Conduct

Authorities are true Specialists in that they have both low levels of dominance and sociability. They are very accepting and analytical. They also have high levels of both relaxation and compliance. They will do almost anything they can to stay out of trouble, avoid confrontation, and, above all, do things right. This is the personality you want for your surgeon. It is also that same personality as a traffic cop, school teacher, and an auto mechanic. Think about it the next time you are visiting with your doctor—that a great surgeon and incredible auto mechanic could share the same personality, despite their different skills, education, and experience. One probably drives a better car—the auto mechanic—and it's paid for.

The following could tick off Authorities:

- *Giving them vague instructions.* They do not deal well with ambiguity. They prefer specifics; after all their favorite question is "how." How do you want this done?
- *Making them responsible for difficult people.* They prefer harmony and will avoid the tough people decisions whenever possible.
- *Expecting them to make big decisions quickly or easily.* They base their decisions on their level of expertise. If they have it, they are cool with the decisions. If they don't, then they will want to take the time to learn more about the area under discussion.
- *Expecting results before they are ready.* This can make the Authority real cranky. Remember, the Authorities kind of ruminate. They take it and take it and take it, and then they may explode. It leaves everybody else wondering where the hell that came from.
- *Becoming overly frustrated or anxious if they are too caught up in the fine points.* That kind of attention to detail can sometimes prevent mistakes. It will still make a Generalist crazy, but it becomes normal frustration if others know it is supposed to be frustrating.

The following can make Authorities tick:

- *Reaching agreement with them on their specific goals, time lines, and expectations.* Otherwise, these can make Authorities really anxious. They take most things very seriously.
- *Giving them the credit they deserve.* But do your best to provide any recognition in a very professional manner, with few to no surprises.
- *Spending the time necessary to answer their questions about specific aspects of a project or task.* Remember they are real "how" people and will want to know

how something should be done. The rest of their thinking is: If they know how, then they will do it right. If they do it right, then they will avoid blame. The real challenge takes place when the Authority works for a Generalist and at the conclusion of a project the Generalist asks the Specialist, "Why did you do it that way?" Here comes the blame!

- *Being patient.* Do be patient. Do be patient largely because Generalists have little or no choice in the manner and Authorities hate being rushed anyway.
- *Encouraging them to set up their own routines and provide flexible time frames.* This is where the Authorities are really cool. They are usually very strong creatures of habit. They have three favorite restaurants, and they almost always order the same items. You always know what to expect.

Collaborators' Code of Conduct

Collaborators differ from Authorities mainly in their sociability. They are very warm and friendly, and much more outgoing than Authorities. Collaborators have the same basic attributes as Authorities except for their higher level of sociability. Therefore, you can go ditto for most Authorities' items plus these that are attributable to the sociability factor. The following could tick off Collaborators:

- *Shutting them out.* They feel they need to be a part of things.Notice I said "feel" not "think." They are the extroverts that feel.
- *Being insincere.* They can usually accept the good and the bad in people. However, that doesn't make it any easier for them to hold others accountable.
- *Putting pressure on them.* Do this only if it is absolutely necessary, and then give them as much notice as possible. Remember, they function best in a stable, calm, predictable environment
- *Leaving everything to the last minute.* They can handle some emergencies, especially if the task falls within their area of expertise. The challenge is that many Collaborators work with a Generalist and usually one that is driven and a natural procrastinator. This is where the Captain Chaos title for the Generalist comes from.

The following (primarily related to the sociability factor) can make Collaborators tick:

- *Including them as an integral part of your team.* They hate to be left out of things and can take it down right personally.

- *Actively soliciting their perspective in meetings and relying on their specialized focus.* Because of their sociability, they are comfortable talking in meetings, especially when it is about their areas of expertise.
- *Ensuring that they receive the credit they deserve.* This is important as they want their pats on the back.
- *Providing them with opportunities to interact with others and get their people fix.* If you are an introvert, then this will be a crazy-maker for you.
- *Making the most of their ability to communicate.* Seek their insights into people.

Diplomats' Code of Conduct

Diplomats are known to have it going on from an entrepreneurial perspective, even though they are accepting and compliant like the other Specialists. They also possess a high level of sociability and are driven. These two aspects allow them to do better in many relationship opportunities or environments.

The following could tick off Diplomats:

- *Assigning them too many routine, repetitive tasks.* They get bored quickly. They can handle the routine, but they can also put that pressure on others.
- *Becoming defensive if they constantly want to change things.* They do well under pressure and are comfortable with change.
- *Expecting results before they have finished the project.* Their thorough approach requires that they complete assignments fully. The good news is that asking them to hurry up works better with Diplomats than with any other Specialists.
- *Shutting them out.* They need to be in on things. They want to, and need to, be part of a team—your team.
- *Being insincere.* It hurts their feelings.

The following can make Diplomats tick:

- *Fostering a fast-changing environment and giving them a bit of rein.*
- *Involving them in setting deadlines and soliciting their agreement as to when a project or task will be done.*
- *Building a strategy for them to maintain their focus.*
- *Providing an overview of their role in relation to the whole.* They like this.
- *Providing them with opportunities to interact with others.* Remember they are usually pretty good at that teamwork stuff.

Code of Conduct Self-Assessment

Based on what I've read in this chapter, I feel that my code of conduct is most like:

Trailblazer _____

Go-Getter _____

Manager _____

Motivator _____

Authority _____

Collaborator _____

Diplomat _____

I also have qualities similar to: _____

Chapter 14

— The Bottom Line —

➤ The Golden Rule of "Do unto others as you would have them do unto you" should be changed to "Do unto others as they would have you do unto them." Treat others the way they prefer.

➤ Great leaders have an understanding of the motivational needs of others. Great leaders represent a very small percentage.

➤ Great leaders use personality assessments to objectively measure the personality of others so they know exactly how to treat them.

➤ High Dominant personalities prefer independence, control, authority, and autonomy.

➤ Those with high sociability enjoy social stimulation, recognition, and working with others.

➤ People with high levels of relaxation prefer a stable environment where they know what to expect and are rewarded for their loyalty.

➤ Highly compliant individuals like security, rules, policies, and a book to go by.

CHAPTER

Beating the Odds

An entrepreneurial client told me the following story. "In 1984, I lost it. Not my mental faculties but my financial wherewithal." Actually, he joked and said, "I'm not sure exactly what my wherewithal is, so let's say I was just about out of money." He had been working on a foreign project for an entire year. It was his moon shot—you know, the deal that makes a difference in your business world. (I personally believe that people should only spend 5 to 20 percent of their time working on their moon shots, but others make different choices.) He'd followed that business deal halfway around the world only to realize that it had been a mistake. He admitted, "It was a long, lonely flight home." He said the next morning he was sitting in bed feeling sorry for himself when he realized that he had a choice. He could accept this path of mediocrity that was on his doorstep, or he could get back in the proverbial saddle and get back to work. He chose the second option and has been going strong ever since.

Most entrepreneurial types not only have an innate urge to "get back to work," but many of them also have an inner drive to accumulate wealth and continue to increase their financial security. When I learned that 90 percent of our population retires at the age of 65 with less than $10,000 in the bank, I couldn't believe it. I acknowledge that everybody experiences challenges that affect their finances, but I also know that the outcome often has more to do with how they handle the situation than with the situation itself.

These major challenges seem to show up at least once every seven years or so. Just like the seven-year return of the locust, everyone has these experiences in life. The question is, what will you do when it happens next?

Turning Developmental Considerations into Strengths

I've worked with, coached, and provided direction for thousands of frustrated business executives, entrepreneurs, and wantapreneurs alike. The business executives usually have a strong sense of where they want to be; the good ones rarely have the patience that goes with scaling the corporate ladder. The entrepreneurs can be way too headstrong, and what they need is something to prevent them from sabotaging themselves. And as for the wantapreneurs, they need strong direction and a "book to go by." It's often easier to coach wantapreneurs than executives or entrepreneurs because they're looking for structure—any structure.

For example, at the end of World War I, the purpose of the Versailles Treaty was to punish the German people by requiring them to make reparations. The country was decimated; it was basically left without an infrastructure. As you may have noticed, the German people are a fairly by-the-book culture. Everything, for the most part, runs on time and is pretty structured. Well, at the end of World War I, they were left without a book to go by. So they embraced Adolf Hitler and the book *Mein Kampf*. The German people could have—perhaps would have—embraced almost any book at that time.

Self-awareness, cognitive capacity, goals, a road map to being your best, the desire to change—all sound like sound bites that could be found in many of today's best sellers. The difference between a sound bite and an accomplishment is actualization, being able to take direction and actualize it into achievable, measurable (Tier IV) results (Tier V).

Remember, for every behavioral strength there's a corresponding and diametrically opposed potential limitation. When I want to be politically correct, I refer to these potential limitations as developmental considerations. (Sounds nice, doesn't it?) These are the challenges that every personality type experiences. People can't help it—it's just a way of life. For example, consider the following potential limitations:

- If you're very dominant and self-confident, you may not be terribly open to suggestion.
- If you're accepting and a great team player, you may find it difficult to be highly results-oriented or to confront others.
- If you're highly sociable, have many friends, and work well with others, you may want to be liked at the expense of getting results.
- If you're highly analytical and great with numbers, your challenge may be dealing with others.
- If you have a high level of relaxation and are a strong creature of habit, your challenge could be dealing with change.
- If you have a lot of drive, you may get bored easily.
- If you have a high level of compliance and prefer having a lot of structure, you may find it difficult to work in an environment with little structure.
- If you're very independent and work well without strong guidance, your challenge may be working in positions requiring great attention to detail.

For example, Alexandra was a Specialist extraordinaire. More specifically, she was a Diplomat, one with very good taste. In fact she was a phenomenal chef. A graduate of a New York culinary school, she knew her way around a kitchen. She had tremendous flair and was great with people, but what she lacked was a flair for numbers, the strategic vision to really know what she could do with her talents. She lacked the self-confidence to open her own catering business.

After a couple years of experience in the catering business, though, Alex discovered a business opportunity that had her name on it. Well, actually it had someone else's name on it, but it felt like hers. She opened a location that offered cooking lessons, "cook it in advance" food preparation, and—her real dream—catering. Fast-forward four years, and Alex has a great business. She has an ample supply of customers and a very highly performing location. She is great with the people, great with the recipes, and great at selling once the potential customers come in. Her challenge was the Generalist side of the business. Remember the five-tier pyramid? Tier I was the core, the personality, the natural style, and Alex has a Diplomat's personality. As far as the behaviors (Tier II) required to get the job done, in Alex's case, it's the behaviors of the Go-Getter. Her actions (Tier III) consisted of the following:

- She wrote a business and marketing plan in conjunction with her SCORE consultant.
- She spoke weekly to women's clubs and provided samples.
- She offered cooking lessons as a part of silent auctions for the local schools and provided samples.
- She presented to local church and civic groups and provided samples.
- She advertised in the local newspapers and magazines and provided samples to their staffs.
- She passed out fliers to neighborhood businesses and provided samples.
- She offered her location for meetings for the local Chamber of Commerce and provided samples.
- She sent samples and invitations to people listed in her weekly newspaper as recently engaged, setting the stage for future wedding orders.
- She sent congratulation baskets of samples to new businesses.
- And she worked her behind off, night and day, every day for two years.

The bottom line is that Alex made and gave away a ton of samples, and today she has a very successful business. She did whatever it took, and today she has a salesperson, a staff, and more press than Napa Valley during the autumn crush. Most recently, Alex received a very nice offer to buy her business. It is not the exit strategy she is looking for. She wants to have her own line of retail products and to publish a catering book. Then she will consider offers. So, to date her results (Tier V) have been excellent. By the way, Alex measured her actions (Tier IV) every step of the way.

Alex's example shows what a Specialist is able to do with the right plan of action. The Generalist is certainly cut from a different cloth, but he achieves the same results. Take Hal Mitchell. Hal lived in the Midwest and became the reluctant owner a family candy business. Hal wasn't planning on taking over or even working in the family business, but when his father took ill, he dropped out of school and did just that. The company had been managed by a master candy maker, and it was Hal's job to make something of the business. While in college, Hal had held several part-time sales positions, and he was good, very good.

Hal's Achilles' heel was that he knew nothing about the candy business and his livelihood was in the hands of the hired help. He felt as if he were being held hostage and he was. He had the Tier I covered—he had a Go-Getter personality. He had most of the Tier II covered—he knew what he needed to do to be successful. And his action (Tier III) consisted of the following:

- He had no business plan but a sense of what he wanted to do.
- Soon after joining the company, he attended a candy school in Philadelphia and in a matter of several weeks was able to become a pretty decent candy maker. So that the current candy maker would not become suspicious, he told him that he had make-up tests to take so that that could complete the semester.
- He came in on weekends and practiced making candy.
- He began selling and opened a number of accounts at nearby truck stops. In his first year, he opened more than 100 accounts.
- He placed product announcement in a national hotel magazine.
- He began providing candy amenities to a number of hotels.
- He fired his master candy maker.
- He bought the equipment necessary to go from making candy by hand to a more automated system.
- He contracted with a private-label candy company to make his product, and he became a pure marketing organization.
- He sold his business, took care of his family, and later bought another business.

One Generalist, one Specialist, similar results.

Goal-Orientation and Motivation

To be a highly successful entrepreneur requires a high level of motivation. Here are some ways to improve your motivation:

- Give yourself a taste of success to develop faith in the worthiness of your goals. For example, if you'd like to start a career helping people in some way, volunteer somewhere to gain experience. If you want to write a novel, begin with a short story. Once you experience a "slice" of your goal, you'll be more driven to pursue it outright.
- Get a mentor. Do you know someone inspiring? Learn what you can from his experience.

- Consider that poorly chosen goals may be decreasing your motivation. Ponder questions such as: Are your goals realistic? Are they really what you care about, or do they represent other people's ambitions for you? Try to find a goal that's realistic and that motivates you.

- Are other things going on in your life that could be demotivating you? If you're stressed or dealing with major issues, it may be hard to even think about goals. Take care of these issues, and your drive should improve.

- Apply self-control and self-discipline. Practice delaying gratification and stifling impulsiveness.

- Take small steps if the big ones overwhelm you. If your goal, for example, is to "sell" a new idea at work, take care of all the details first. Gather information, do all the beginning steps, and things will take on a life of their own. Reward yourself when you complete different steps.

- Make contracts with yourself. Write down the reasons that you want to pursue a goal, and refer to it later when you feel discouraged.

- Learn to be your own coach. Practice positive self-talk, and give yourself a pat on the back.

- Post your goals somewhere prominent so you can see them every day.

Emotional Expression

Emotional expression is a critical aspect of emotional intelligence—a necessary component for successful entrepreneurs. Here are some ways to improve your ability to express emotions:

- Take small steps. Start expressing emotions that are the least intimidating, and you'll find that it's not as bad as you think. On the positive side, begin with genuine compliments, and then take it further to an expression of appreciation. When you need to communicate a negative feeling, try writing it if you feel too intimidated to say it. Like learning any new skill, it gets easier with practice.

- Choose what's most important. You obviously can't express every little thing you feel or throw all your strong emotions at someone. It's more effective (and healthier) to pace your expressions evenly. Don't wait for the floodgates to open because they can't hold up any longer.

- Learn to communicate effectively. An important factor in the effectiveness of expressing emotions is *how* we do it. Blowing up at someone, for example, is usually not the best way to communicate a feeling. Good communication skills are key. And being skills, they can be learned.

- Build self-confidence and self-esteem. The more confident you become, the easier it should be to express your feelings.
- Build meaningful, trusting relationships. Most people need someone they can talk to, someone to whom they can express their feelings without fear of rejection or ridicule.
- Consider the implications of not releasing your feelings: lack of intimacy with others, pent-up emotions, health problems, etc.
- Remember that communication involves a lot more than what's said. Your gestures, expressions, and tone of voice send signals that are just as strong as (or even stronger than) the words you choose.
- Practice distinguishing between what you're thinking and what you're feeling. They're not always one and the same, and you need to recognize this in order to clearly express where you're coming from.

Social Insight and Empathy

Being able to accurately assess people's opinions and emotions gives entrepreneurs an edge. Here are some ways to increase one's social insight and empathy:

Stranger than Fiction

Twenty years ago I ran the following ad in *The Wall Street Journal*: "Thirty-five-year old entrepreneur with strong corporate background seeks mentor who owns business, has no children to leave it to, and desires to retire and stay involved." To my surprise, I received about 20 calls, many of which were excellent opportunities. Unfortunately, I didn't feel passionate about any of them. They were all older business owners who had created high levels of net worth and had successfully put their children through college. Their children had become professionals and weren't interested in continuing the family business. There's a strong similarity between the responses I got and the responses of those reported in *The Millionaire Next Door*. It was the business owner's goal to provide an education sufficient to guarantee that the child wouldn't need to go into the family business. And many did not.

- Pay attention to how others are reacting and what they're communicating to you. Putting in the extra effort to really listen and observe can teach you a lot about human interaction and emotions.
- While you certainly can't fake empathy, you can increase your connection to other people by truly listening and trying to put yourself in their shoes.
- Build meaningful relationships that teach you about human nature.
- If you're not sure how someone is feeling, ask for clarification (if it's appropriate). A simple "How are you feeling?" or "Could you explain your perspective to me?" might do the trick.
- Put aside your own preoccupations to consider what might be going through other people's minds in different situations. Ask yourself how you'd feel in a similar situation. In every situation, there are several perspectives. Try to identify at least two or three ways to look at it. Put empathy into action. Get involved in helping people in some way (e.g., volunteering). The closer you get to a situation, the more you should realize the difficulties others might be facing.

To win, it becomes essential for the entrepreneur and the wantapreneur alike to understand how their own stupid switches affect them, how they turn themselves on and off. What are the things that cause you to react? What physical manifestations take place about three seconds before you blow your cool? Not sure? Ask your kids—they know. They might say, "Oh, Daddy gets those little lines between his eyes, and he starts to breathe really, really deeply." Learn this, and control your destiny.

Tripping the Stupid Switch

My wife came up with a solution about three years ago that made it possible for me to be told what to do (well, sometimes). Six magic words: "Are you open for a suggestion?" The nice thing about asking a person whether he's open for a suggestion is that it gives him the opportunity to turn his stupid switch off long enough to become responsive. If I'm still reactive, however, I might say, "What do you mean am I open for a suggestion?" Then it's time to ask the next question, which is, "If not now, when?"

In Their Own Words
What Entrepreneurs Said about Their Biggest Challenges

Q: *Was there a time where you were really challenged, lost everything and had to start over or were devastated?*

Yes   55%
No   45%

"There are two. One, when my father walked out on the business. He just quit and left me to pick up the pieces. I did. Second, I left the business because he came back and tried to tell me how to run it. After doubling the size, I felt that my way worked."

"About to go broke, I had to beg the bank for money, while asking them to let me forego principle payments. Wife studying for the bar so not working. I had to cut benefits at work. Employees revolted, thinking I was rich (I took home less than $45/week). Overcame it by doing what I had to, while keeping my eyes on the prize."

"I lost everything emotionally when my first husband, unable to cope with the success my newly formed business was having, left. It is a loss and a betrayal that left me hurting for a long time. I overcame it because I believe in love, I believe in the basic goodness of people, and I had a great circle of friends and family around me for support."

"Divorcing my first husband and moving out of the area to a 100 percent commission job—I had no choice but to make it—my three children needed me to succeed. I believe that each and every one of us has a memory somewhere deep inside us, for some of us it's right on the surface, and has to do with a time where we're competitive, where we were assertive, where we were tenacious, where we just said, 'I'm not going to take it and I'm going to fight for what is right!' And sometimes that could be the memory of a seven-year-old fighting with a sibling over the property rights for a doll. And you just said, 'This is my doll and I want it!' "

"After my second suicide attempt and failing, I asked for help from a power greater than myself. My prayer was answered, and I was told to give this gift away, for free."

"In 1990, within a six-month period, an employee embezzled $80,000; we lost our largest client due to a complete management shake-up (the president, vice-presidents, and all directors except one were terminated); our second-largest client (Japanese) closed its U.S. division due to the devaluation of the yen, and my partner left and moved out of state. I immediately downsized and sublet our space, but the landlord sued me for the remainder of the five-year lease, and I was forced into personal and corporate bankruptcy. I started over, fueled by three loyal clients, and gradually rebuilt."

"I'm on the verge at the moment—hitting the road and trying to make sales is the current action. Not willing to give up!"

"I suffered from tremendous self-doubt and depression a few years ago and knew I could not overcome it by myself. I sought the assistance of a therapist. It was the best thing I've ever done for our company and myself."

"While I was president of a trade association, my business began to lose tons of money. My CPA told me they didn't know if we were a 'going concern.' That scared the . . . out of me. I buckled down, and re-involved myself in everything, especially sales and marketing."

"Currently I am facing that challenge, and have many times in the past. The key is this: Understand what you do well, confront in your mind the worst possible outcome, take action on your thoughts and dreams, always move forward."

"Partners robbed me blind in two previous failed businesses. I licked my wounds, and started over with nothing."

"VCs tried to steal business—got bank to pull loan and bankrupt me—within three days clients gave me 700k to pay off. Negotiated 50 cents on a dollar payback."

Chapter 15
— The Bottom Line —

➤ Most entrepreneurial types not only have an innate urge to "get back to work," many have an inner drive to accumulate wealth and continue to increase their financial security.

➤ Most entrepreneurs go years without missing a day of work because of illness and yet their frustration is that they often times have employees that can't string 30 days of work together without missing one or two of them.

➤ Major challenges seem to show up at least once every seven years or so. The question is, What will you do when it happens next?

➤ For every behavioral strength, there's a corresponding and diametrically opposed potential limitation.

➤ Understanding five tier thinking brings you closer to achieving your goals.

➤ Beat the odds through a heightened level of self-awareness.

➤ Four penny technique increases our sociability. Start each day with four pennies in your right pocket. Your job is to the four positive conversations with four different employees each day (Tier III, actions). WIth each compliment we move a penny from one pocket to the other (Tier IV, metrics). This drives positive morale throughout the organization. Oh yeah. You can't end a compliment wit the word "but."

➤ There are a number of CEO or entrepreneur peer groups. For a list of organizations and links go to www.theentrepreneurnextdoor.com.

➤ Most entrepreneurs use their own form of a five-tier pyramid but they do so subconsciously. The key to the five-tier Performance Pyramid is doing so cognitively, consciously, and objectively.

16

How Entrepreneurs and Wantapreneurs Beat the Odds

with the Performance Pyramid

P EOPLE CAN CHANGE THEIR DESTINIES. THERE ARE THOUSANDS OF EXAMPLES WHERE INDI-viduals determine, then develop, and eventually possess the ability to compensate for their personalities, or enhance their personalities. In essence, they change their behaviors to such an extent that they are able to accomplish the results necessary to achieve their goals. It is really a tremendous job that these individuals do. Everyone can do this to various degrees, most just don't give it much thought.

Imagine you're at the airport and about to enter the security screening area. Do you think some people need to change their personalities to successfully navigate the perils of their attitude? Many Generalists become accommodating, agreeable, cooperative, and patient in the security area. They don't necessarily want to but without making those changes, they don't get to where they want to be. Or consider family vacations. In this situation people must be more sociable, more patient, and more agreeable. What about trade shows? If you are more introverted, remember the last time you attended a trade show or an industry networking event. These are only short-term examples, of course. Imagine what has to happen in order to manifest those changes longer term. The rest of this chapter consists of examples of people who made behavioral changes (Tier II and IV) to take their game to the next level.

Trailblazers

Gordon Logan, CEO of Sport Clips, is a Trailblazer. He started Sport Clips, a franchise specializing in haircuts for men and boys that recently opened its 325th store. A few years ago Gordon observed that no hair care chain or franchise was specifically targeting men and boys' haircuts, and that traditional barber shops were closing at a rapidly increasing rate. It was here that the idea began. Gordon's strength is his ability to strategize, understand, and create process and systems. His challenge is the letting go, delegating to others. The way Gordon deals with this is by his creation of systems. If he manages by numbers and metrics, then he can manage by and through these. It makes his job of holding others more accountable—he does it by the numbers—easier. What Gordon has been able to do is create a phenomenally loyal group of employees and management teams. He cares about the well-being of those within his organization, employees and franchisees (or as Sport Clips calls them, Team Leaders) alike.

Go-Getters

John Hasenauer is a Go-Getter and the founder and CEO of iHomeowners, an e-commerce company located in Calabasas, California. John's personality provides him with an advantage because he is able to handle both the strategic and people sides of his business. An INC 500 recipient and an extremely driven individual, the continuing challenge of growing his company is a constant motivator for John. But his drive has gotten the best of him on more than one occasion. His drive allows him to think and move at light speed; the corresponding challenge is that this same drive frustrates him because his people rarely move as fast as he prefers. The old John, when working with his subordinates, would come in, take over, and begin to provide direction. This also sabotaged his direct reports. He has changed his style not because it was easy but because it was necessary. This last year John received an unsolicited offer to purchase his company; he turned it down because he knows he will be able to get more in another year or two. John is willing to take the risk. Stay tuned, and periodically check out the web site www.theentrepreneurnextdoor.com. It will let you know what happens.

Managers

Michael is a great example of a Manager with the innate ability to see the big picture but often times gets tripped up on the people side of his business. As a professional CEO of a Southern California electronics firm, Michael has been at the forefront of its technology and offerings since he took over the reins some ten years ago. Michael's greatest challenge derives from his level of relaxation. His relaxation correlates to a higher level of loyalty to his employees. His challenge is that he has difficulty letting go of employees. In other words, he has allowed his loyalty to get in his way of holding others accountable. Michael has a CEO coach who in essence has painted a picture of the behaviors necessary for Michael to display in order to be a great CEO. He uses metrics and an newly hired executive vice president to hold others accountable. His EVP is the buffer between Michael and his people, and it is the EVP's responsibility to make the difficult people decisions.

Motivators

Bev is a Motivator who is also a professional speaker and owns a training and development company. She is the rainmaker who has made her dream of business success a reality. The author of several books and the employer of more than 20 independent contractors who provide her tools to international clients, her challenge is and always will be her ability to hold others accountable, to make the difficult people decisions. In order to grow to the level she has, Bev has surrounded herself with a very strong and dominant management team. This allows Bev the opportunity to do what she does best, present and write. Bev is still the rainmaker; she just has help with the confrontational side of her business.

Authorities

As you know, I am a member of TEC, The Executive Committee. The person that starts up a new group is called a TEC Chair. TEC Chairs are supposed to have

Go-Getter personalities. I know this because my company assists TEC in its selection. Every now and then I present to a TEC group with, much to my surprise, a Chair who has an Authority personality. Why in the world they would want to do that job is beyond me, but they do, and they do a good job. So a lesson I've learned in 15 years in this business is that there will always be people who surprise you, even amaze you, and they do so because of what they are able to accomplish in spite of themselves. There will always be those anomalies that are able to manifest success contrary to what others might expect based on their personalities.

Collaborators

My father, Lou Wagner, was a Collaborator. He had a number of gifts, but his greatest were his ability to deal with people, the level of loyalty he maintained with them, and his desire to do things right. He was a natural-born entrepreneur; country western music promoter; owner of a record store, TV store, appliance store, and jewelry store; and Muzak franchisee. He actually opened the first color TV store in Peoria, Illinois. What my father was able to figure out was how to use those in his life to get what he wanted, and he used these relationships to build other relationships and opportunities. He was ahead of his time, most of the time. My entire life was spent being exposed to one type of business or another. It was my father who modeled the relationship sale. I have learned well.

Diplomats

Gary Siegle is an acquaintance. At one time, he owned a California Closets franchise. He built his business based on his relationships with others. His challenge was the difficulty he had in holding others accountable. He did it. He didn't like it, but he did it. Later, Gary sold his franchise, searched his soul, and decided his passion was for speaking. As a former English professor, Gary began to develop a presentation he could speak on. He calls himself The Grammar Coach. It wasn't easy, but he has been working on it for the past five years, and today is a successful speaker. To begin his speaking practice, Gary needed to increase his level of dominance and let go of his compliance. He was able to do it. It was just a challenge.

Change is inevitable. It can be difficult, but it is inevitable. But not for everyone. Those who are able to change, adapt, and grow will be able to make the needed changes in their behaviors, then adapt and manifest these behaviors into actions, and finally, just like the examples here, be able to reach their goals. You too can accomplish your goals. It just requires heavy lifting.

Personality Style Self-Assessment

Based on what I've read in this chapter and the rest of this book, I feel that my personality style (Tier I) is most like:

List your top 3, and number them 1, 2, and 3.

	This Chapter	The Majority of Chapters
Trailblazer	_____	_____
Go-Getter	_____	_____
Manager	_____	_____
Motivator	_____	_____
Authority	_____	_____
Collaborator	_____	_____
Diplomat	_____	_____

I also have qualities similar to: _____

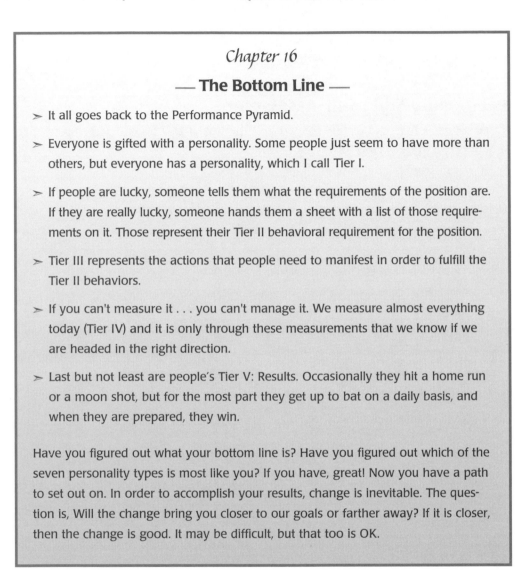

Chapter 16

— The Bottom Line —

➤ It all goes back to the Performance Pyramid.

➤ Everyone is gifted with a personality. Some people just seem to have more than others, but everyone has a personality, which I call Tier I.

➤ If people are lucky, someone tells them what the requirements of the position are. If they are really lucky, someone hands them a sheet with a list of those requirements on it. Those represent their Tier II behavioral requirement for the position.

➤ Tier III represents the actions that people need to manifest in order to fulfill the Tier II behaviors.

➤ If you can't measure it . . . you can't manage it. We measure almost everything today (Tier IV) and it is only through these measurements that we know if we are headed in the right direction.

➤ Last but not least are people's Tier V: Results. Occasionally they hit a home run or a moon shot, but for the most part they get up to bat on a daily basis, and when they are prepared, they win.

Have you figured out what your bottom line is? Have you figured out which of the seven personality types is most like you? If you have, great! Now you have a path to set out on. In order to accomplish your results, change is inevitable. The question is, Will the change bring you closer to our goals or farther away? If it is closer, then the change is good. It may be difficult, but that too is OK.

17

The Goldilocks Theory

Creating an Organization That's Just Right

GOLDILOCKS WENT FOR A WALK ONE DAY AND PRETTY SOON, AND SHE CAME UPON A house. She knocked, and when no one answered, she went in. At the table in the kitchen, there were three bowls of porridge. Given that Goldilocks was very hungry, she tasted one of the bowls of porridge, but it was too hot. The second bowl she tasted was too cold. But the third bowl was just right, and she happily ate it. In the living room, the first chair was too small, the second was too big, and the third was just right. But when she sat in it, it broke to pieces. Finally, being tired, she decided to take a nap. She went upstairs and the first bed was too hard, the second was too soft, but the third was

255

just right. Was this really a fairy tale, or was it a fable that had more organizational development implications?

Imagine that Goldilocks was an entrepreneur looking to assemble the perfect team. Some applicants were too strong, some were not strong enough, and some were just right. Or, what about looking for that perfect opportunity? Some were too expensive, some were too mundane, and some were just right. Short of a fairy tale and the guaranteed happy ending, how can we tell which employee or opportunity is just right?

The essence of this work is measuring those qualities that are typically the most important to measure. Unfortunately, they are also the most neglected and difficult to measure.

My company, Accord Management Systems Inc. is the consultancy that my wife, Renee, and I co-founded some 15 years ago. I have a great team; Goldilocks would be proud. But if you can't get it right in our business using our tools, then something is wrong. These past several years have generated a number of interesting projects. They typically included a scoping exercise, where we identified challenges, recommended solutions, implemented our ideas, and measured our results. Here are a few of these challenges, their solutions, and their results.

Situation and Challenge I

A master franchisee in the quick lube industry owned 14 locations. After attending one of our informational seminars, he knew that he did not have the right people on the proverbial bus. Actually, he knew this already because of his operational results. He had lower bay technicians who forgot to replace oil pan plugs correctly. He had cashiers who felt that selling was a form of lying. He had managers whose nature caused too many employees to quit. The owner of the franchise had a Manager personality, and in spite of this, his company ran upwards of 1,000 cars per day.

Accord Management Systems measured the behavioral requirements of each and every position. We found that the behavioral requirement of a lower bay technician was an Authority personality. Upper bay technicians could either be Authorities or Collaborators. Their sociability would come in handy as they sometimes covered the register when the cashier was on break. The cashier should be a Diplomat, and the assistant manager should be a Go-Getter or a Motivator. These last two would be best because of their levels of sociability, which were imperative in terms of selling

FIGURE 17.1: **Master Franchise Case Study—Employee Job-Fit**

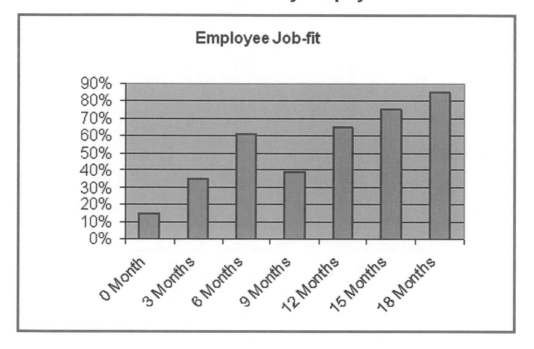

and retaining customers. That was what Goldilocks had in mind. In reality, the personalities of store managers and cashiers were for the most part grumpy bears who couldn't sell or manage very well. In fact, when we started working with this company only about 15 percent of their employees possessed the right personalities (Tier I) for their positions (Tier II). Goldilocks wasn't a happy camper but the existing employees knew what kind of oil to use, the thickness of brake pads, and the warranty on wiper blades.

Figure 17.1 shows how we were able to move forward in job-fit. You will notice that there was a setback in the acquisition of the right talent between the sixth and ninth month. This was due to the fact that management promoted a number of better employees to training and quality assurance positions. The company also implemented a 90-day probationary policy for new hires, and there were a number of new hires that despite their apparent fit weren't performing well enough. They were terminated.

Once the new teams were in place, the management team also added the right training and expectations. The expectations also included the right metrics (Tier IV) so that each store knew how it was doing every day, week, and month. They embraced the theory that if you can't measure it, you can't manage it, and they did both

FIGURE 17.2: **Master Franchisee Case Study**

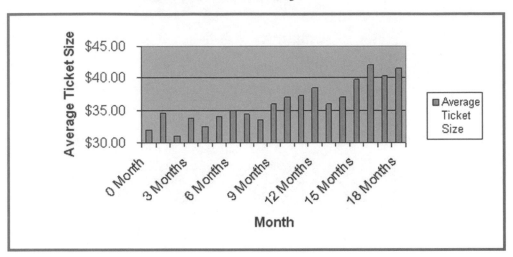

Figure 17.2 shows how sales increased as employee job fit improved. That's right. The company wrote an average of 1,000 tickets per day and by the end of the 18-month case study, it was able to increase average ticket size by over $6 per ticket. That adds up to additional annual revenues of $2,160,000. For the most part, that occurred without increasing the largest line item, employee costs. This is a proof statement. If you measure the behavioral requirements of each and every position and hire against those benchmarks, you will be able to determine what each seat on the bus requires and place the right people in the right seats. These are results (Tier V).

Situation and Challenge II

A client, a buying group of home improvement materials, was transitioning from a buying group to a franchise. They had thousands of members. Each was highly independent. Store signs tended to be personal, like Bob's Flooring. Its challenge was to have the signs read "THE NAME OF FRANCHISE" in big letters with "Bob's Flooring" in smaller lettering, thereby creating a stronger brand. We created a Franchise Engagement Survey, which included about 70 questions and several demographics. The demographics included "tenure," "plans on moving and when," and "plans to remodel and when." We discovered that 32 percent of their members were planning on either moving or remodeling within the next three years. The owners of the company had not been aware of this but saw it as a definite opportunity. They created a branding initiative in the form of a new sign that was paid for by the franchisor. The franchisee got a new sign paid for by someone else, and the franshisor got the consistency it wanted. Had it not asked the right questions, it would have missed a tremendous opportunity. To see an example of engagement surveys, go to www.the entrepreneurnextdoor.com and click on engagement survey.

Situation and Challenge III

A Midwest manufacturer was concerned about its level of employee engagement. Employee engagement is a measure of employee satisfaction. Engaged employees are three times more productive than are disengaged employees. We designed an engagement survey that measured the employees' engagement (feelings) about how they perceived they were being treated by their supervisors, management, and senior management. We measured 14 major areas that encompassed more than 65 questions and responses. We discovered that the manufacturer had an aging workforce. This in itself wasn't either a surprise or a problem. The problem was that 27 percent of this aging workforce was planning on retiring five years sooner than the manufacturer had anticipated. This new information allowed the manufacturer the opportunity to begin looking at those within the company who had the right personalities to move up within the organization. In essence, it allowed the company get the right people on the bus and to provide them with the right training. It also allowed it to be proactive and create solutions before the problems became noticeable.

Situation and Challenge IV

A franchisor dealing in early childhood education was frustrated as its franchisees were performing at different levels. The franchisees all paid the same franchisee fee; all had virtually identical build outs; all had the same training. So what was the problem? We surveyed the personalities of its 250 franchisees. We segmented these surveys based on performance. We also created a franchise engagement survey that included about 70 questions designed to determine franchisee level of engagement. Did they like what they were doing and the decision they made to buy into this opportunity?

We discovered that there was a direct relationship between the engagement of the franchisee, the personality of the franchisee, and the royalties generated by the

FIGURE 17.3: **Engagement and Personality Survey of Leading Franchisor**

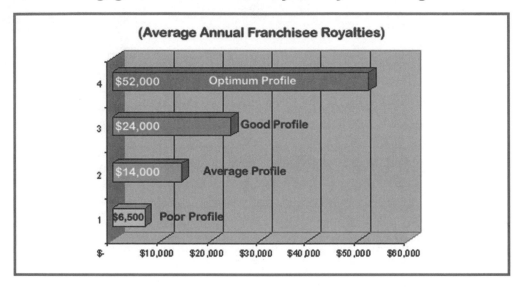

FIGURE 17.4: **Personalities Involved with Each Accomplishment**

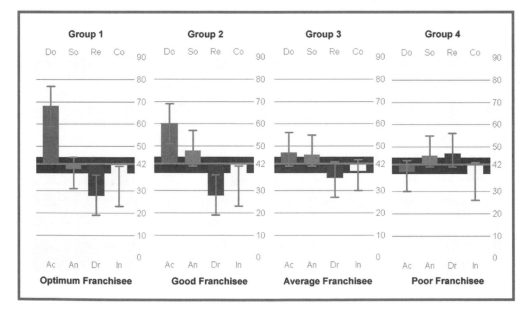

franchisee. See Figure 17.3 and 17.4. The optimum profile was that of Trailblazers with a slightly higher level of sociability. They generated $52,000 in annual royalties.

This means that they generated more than $600,000 in annual revenues, of which the franchisee got to keep 92 percent, or $552,000. But what if the franchisee did not have a Trailblazer personality? They made less. To solve this, the franchisor created a training program for all its franchisees that showed them the behaviors (Tier II) and the actions (Tier III) necessary to be more successful. Ultimately, many of these franchisees delivered better results (Tier V).

The Program

The position of franchisee was a combination of teacher, store manager, and store-owner. The franshisor determined what the right Tier II: Behaviors were for the position. They are listed below with the personality factor listed in italics:

1. Very competitive, ambitious, and goal-oriented *(Dominance)*
2. Wants responsibility for and authority over others *(Dominance)*
3. Enjoys overcoming objections/resistance and achieving goals in the face of obstacles *(Dominance)*
4. Restless, driving, and energetic *(Drive)*
5. Sense of urgency to get things done quickly *(Drive)*
6. Works well under pressure and deadlines *(Drive)*
7. Independent and persistent *(Independence)*
8. Wants to take charge and show initiative *(Independence)*
9. A balance between a people and a work orientation *(Sociability)*
10. Works well with people yet does not require a lot of social or people stimulation *(Sociability)*

The training program determined a number of Tier III: Actions that when acted upon would eventually lead to better Tier V: Results. The actions were:

1. Call on local schools and day care facilities and discuss the franchise educational programs and how they supported the curriculum of the teachers.
2. The franchisee offered and sponsored a number of programs that were community-oriented in order to get her name into the market.
3. The franchisor purchased mailing lists that indicated residents within a three-mile radius. This list was sorted to only include those homes with children.
4. The franchisee spoke almost weekly to various civic groups about the centers programming. At each stop she offered a free day pass.
5. The franchisee developed a birthday program and marketed it through schools, day care facilities, and church groups.

The franchisees were able to increase their student count within 120 days of successful implementation of the above actions. Not all of the franchisees choose to participate.

Situation and Challenge V

A client, a telemarketing organization, had watched its sales plummet over the previous six months. Its interview process for prospective new employees began with its human resources manager conducting an initial screening interview. From there, a second and final interview was conducted by the telemarketing manager.

Dominance in Action

One of the best ways to observe someone's high dominance is when he's in action. When you're watching sports, do you ever find your body moving as if you're trying to help the athlete move or run? You move to the right to make a tackle. You hold your breath when a golfer's shot is curving the wrong way. I've seen this most recently at the bowling alley. My son Josh and I were bowling, and I noticed that the other bowlers were leaning, moving, dancing, and prancing in a feeble attempt to affect the motion of the ball. I don't think this works.

What does work is using your personality in its most effective manner. Josh is all of 11 years old and only weighs about 60 pounds sopping wet, but he has the personality of an athlete twice his size. He loves to play football and lacrosse and has his first degree red belt in karate. (He should have his black belt within the next 12 months.)

Lacrosse is a really a neat sport because you have players moving really fast as they go in and out, bobbing and weaving with the intent of scoring a goal. Josh is aggressive, driven, refuses to give up, and loves to both play and win. He is fortunate because he has always had great coaches (not me, I'm the cheering section). But as I watch Josh's team, it's obvious that a number of the kids don't enjoy competing at the same level. This is the difference in our natural styles (Tier I). When the coach guides the players and tells them that they need to dial it up a notch, this represents Tier II: Behaviors, and when the coach says shoot or pass this is an example of Tier III: Actions. Scoring is a form of Tier IV: Metrics needed to win (Tier V: Results).

We discovered that the personality required for the new employees was a Diplomat. The telemarketing manager had a Go-Getter personality, but the kicker was that the HR manager was an Authority.

The company actually needed an HR manager who was a Diplomat or a Collaborator. It wanted someone with sociability, and it got someone who was very analytical and believed that selling was an extension of lying. Because of this, when an applicant had a higher level of sociability and began selling himself, the HR manager immediately began to dislike the applicant. The only applicants who made it to the second interview were those who were introverts. The telemarketing manager was doing the best he could with what he was able to hire; unfortunately, it wasn't good enough. Once the company was able to determine the challenge presented by the introverted HR manager and began to utilize personality testing, it was able to turn around its operation within 30 days. That is the power of being able to measure the operation (Tier IV).

Situation and Challenge VI

A client was trying to determine which personality type would be best for the position of store manager—a Generalist or a Specialist. It looked at the performance levels of these two personality types. After looking at hundreds of data points, the client found that the sales generated by Generalists over the first six months in their positions was 32 percent greater that the results generated by Specialists.

Now What?

I invite you to go to www.theentrepreneurnextdoor .com, and click on "SURVEY ME." You'll be asked a few questions about what you've read. That will let us know that you've bought a copy of this book. You will be invited to take a behavioral survey (test) that will provide

We have tested and tested and tested. We have surveyed and surveyed. And each and every time the results were what we expected. We've learned about the people side of the business. We've learned that we can predict what's going to happen. And if we can predict it—guess what— we can change it, make it better, or just celebrate in our wisdom. Actually, we aren't that wise, but we have learned. We learned that if you first measure the behavioral requirement of the position and then hire with that benchmark in mind, the odds of that person performing the way you want are pretty good. We can tell you 90 percent of the time who can't do a job; the other 10 percent, you are going to have to figure it out on your own. It's not that tough when you have removed the wrong 90 percent.

you with additional insights into yourself and the business decisions you'll make in the future.

The web site is constantly updated, and once you've taken your first survey, you'll be invited to take others. I know you'll find this to be of both interest and value. You may register for our newsletter, and you'll receive updates, discounts on products or services, and, perhaps most importantly, literally thousands of dollars of value. My company is still negotiating with an international organization that works with franchisees to see what additional benefits it will provide you, my readers. So stay tuned. Remember in Chapter 2, I talked about Plumeus? It has agreed to allow you the opportunity to take an Entrepreneurial Test. This will help you determine what you want to be when you grow up.

Why do we do this? Fair question. We do this because someday you'll own a business and need a company to help you get the people side of the business right, and—voila—you'll contact us at www.accordsyst.com. It's somewhat self-serving but with value added.

During the five years that I've been a member of the CEO organization The Executive Committee, 15 of us have gotten together every month to, as I put it, "lie to each other about how well we're doing." Our mornings consists of a speaker covering a particular topic, and our afternoons are spent discussing our most pressing issues, 90 percent of which are people issues. When a member raises an issue, he takes about 10 minutes to discuss it and what he expects to gain from our discussion. At this point, the rest of us ask questions aimed at sharing our insights, ideas, and potential solutions. My advantage is my training and understanding of the concepts discussed in this book. It's like playing a game: "I can solve this problem in five questions. No, I can solve this problem in four questions." Get the idea? Because of my training, I ask more behaviorally-oriented questions. When we digest this information with an overall understanding of the team in question, we can determine a plan of action. The answer to almost every question you may have about positions, employees, or yourself are available in the preceding pages.

Your next steps are:

1. Determine who you are (Tier I). Are you a Generalist or a Specialist? If a Specialist, are you a Diplomat, a Collaborator, or an Authority? Then study your favorite subject, yourself. Generalists get to do this, too; you just don't need to be told because you don't listen anyway.

2. Determine the qualities of the position you are in or want. What you are looking for are the behaviors the position requires (Tier II). Does the job require

you to be more aggressive or accommodating? It's essential that you determine what the job requires. The next step is to look at the gap between who you are and who you need to be. That represents the hard work before you.

3. Determine the actions that will support your endeavor (Tier III). This becomes a specific action plan that involves, to say the least, action. If you are buying or investing in a business, see how much of Tier II and Tier III it provides you. If it does not provide much, then you might want to consider looking elsewhere. Tier III involves marketing, meeting, and doing the things that move you toward your goal.

4. Make sure you are measuring the right items otherwise how will you know if you are growing in the right direction (Tier IV).

5. Reap the results (Tier V).

And as we know, it's all about the results. I wish you well.

In Their Own Words
What Entrepreneurs Said about the Corporate Environment

Q: *If you have previously worked in a corporate environment, what do you feel you learned or gained from this experience?*

"Understanding corporate politics and how it influences corporate buying, (2) understanding the market that I am now selling into, (3) managing people."

"Politics; management experience; how to sell to corporations based on knowing their problems."

"That people achieve positions and income that are based on things other than performance."

"How to grow an organization to a point of future stability, how to treat employees, breadth of business functions."

"Structure and systems."

"The buck stops here. That you have to be constantly aware of the big picture or it gets away from you. People—especially clients—are also fair weather friends!"

"I learned how to work hard. It was a family business, so I was always worried that others would think I had it easy because my grandfather started the biz."

"I learned to win big at a game I hated."

"The value of learning to work harmoniously with other people."

"Corporate politics can inhibit the growth of a company."

What Entrepreneurs Said Sets Their Company Apart

Q: *What do you feel makes your company extraordinary or sets it apart from the competition?*

"The people and the value that we create for the customer."

"A true focus on the client's needs and related benefits. We will do whatever it takes to provide customer satisfaction. It is not about us—selfless people."

"We want to be a great company. That is my challenge to the people who work here, and I think they've accepted it."

"We accept nothing less than excellence from ourselves and our clients."

"Adding a value for my customers' business."

"The best customer service and professionalism."

"I don't think our company is extraordinary. But, I hope we will be someday."

"We have proven ourselves to be a company that does not operate under a short-term philosophy. We think as a long-term partner not just a supplier of commercial engines and engine parts. We possess a relentless dedication to quality and a tireless commitment to providing customer service and support."

"Employees, focus on customers being number one, team-oriented, innovative, aggressive."

"Corporate culture. Everyone talks about it. No one understands it. In the technology business I'm in, attracting and retaining the best and brightest is nearly impossible. I have found a way to make it easy. My approach defies everything you read and hear about, but in a time when others pay headhunters high fees for technical talent, I turn people away."

"Our people. They care deeply about what they do!"

"We never say NO."

"Soul and passion. We believe what we do is a necessary service to better the balance and value of people's lives."

"The people, the vision, the systems, the talent, and quality of work produced."

"Be a leader and let others manage."

"My staff."

What Entrepreneurs Said about Their Greatest Business Challenges

Q: *What is the most difficult or challenging responsibility you have as a CEO?*

"My current situation is the need to hire good people, to motivate, and retain them. This is the hardest challenge I've ever faced, and I have a newfound respect for those who are naturally adept at working with people and motivating them."

"Learning to be a good leader and manager, financial fuel to keep up with growth plans."

"Working with my brother and father, having to confront them due to my strong belief that they were not and could not properly direct the company's future growth. There was a strong lack of trust in our futures through their style of management."

"PEOPLE! I've always been internally motivated and assumed that others were as well. Keeping my people's eyes on the target is truly more challenging than I ever expected."

"Finding replacements for the good people who have left. And training these new people."

"Knowing who the right people are to hire."

"Overcoming brief periods of self-doubt. I am really an insecure person. To compensate for my insecurity, I must overcompensate through doing what others are not willing to do, do it more often, and do it today rather than tomorrow."

"To let people know my current business can be successful. My wholesale business started out with 26 investors. I didn't run the company from the start, but owned the property. Everyone I spoke to told me the business will not last—the competition will have me for breakfast. But, the investors only saw $$$ signs. Less than six months after I opened, I lost $300,000, fired the president, etc. Investors blamed me since I formed the company and ran the company for free for six months. I bought all the stocks after one year. Greatest challenge now is to let the investors know it was a good company, but they hired the wrong people to run it."

"Putting together a cohesive team."

"Co-leading with my husband."

"Communicating and aligning the entire company to achieve our goals."

"Managing people; knowing what to do is only half the battle, getting people to do it is the rest."

"Tools—those things people normally get in college. Leading, recognizing trends, creating a flat work environment that actually works."

"Today, the challenge is to meet my spouse's emotional needs."

"Having no one to bounce ideas off of or who will provide a different perspective to my ideas."

"Dealing with people if they don't live up to our expectations."

"Allowing others to lead."

"Developing leadership and good management skills in people without much experience."

Creating an organization that is just right is far from easy. The key, as you have just read, is often times understanding what needs to be done (Tier II) and doing it (Tier III).

What Entrepreneurs Said They Have to Accomplish Before Retiring

Q: *What do you feel you must accomplish before you can retire?*

"Give back and help younger entrepreneurs as well as special not-for-profit group(s)."

"Build the company so that all who have put time, effort, sweat, and tears into the process can be proud of working for the company, i.e., financial and great environment."

"Financial freedom to have a strong annual income plus some extra money for investments and 'playing around with new ideas.' Let's face it, entrepreneurs never really retire."

"The business must be built to the point where it is self-sufficient, with people and systems in place to keep it evolving and growing on its own. I would then spin off my own separate division to do what I'd rather do."

"Find something as exciting as business to keep my hyperactive mind busy and most importantly out of trouble."

"Retire? Not me!"

"I'm probably already there, but I want to insure TOTAL financial freedom for me, spouse and kids (and maybe their kids)."

"I really don't see myself fully retiring before I am in my late 60s. I have to make sure that my money needs are taken care of beyond conservative projections."

"Reach the 100 goals I set when I was 25 years old."

"No such thing as complete retirement. One more company."

"Become a self-made philanthropic individual who made it without having to step on someone on the way to the top."

"Sell the business when it has enough value to warrant enough cash in the buyout to sustain my personal lifestyle objectives for life."

"I have sold three companies successfully to employees. I am currently selling a fourth company (the first to struggle). This leaves one to go, and the new owner-to-be (current sales manager) and I are talking."

Bibliography

Books

Buckingham, Marcus, and Curt Coffman. *First, Break All the Rules: What the World's Greatest Managers Do Differently.* New York: Simon & Schuster, 1999.

Buckingham, Marcus, and Donald O. Clifton. *Now Discover Your Strengths.* New York: Free Press, 2001.

Coffman, Curt, and Gabriel Gonzales-Molina, Ph.D. *Follow This Path: How the World's Greatest Organizations Drive Growth by Unleashing Human Potential.* New York: Warner Business Books, 2002.

Collins, Jim. *Good to Great.* New York: Harper Collins, 2001.

Gerber, Michael. *The E-Myth Revisited: Why Most Small Businesses Don't Work and What to Do about It.* New York: Harperbusiness, 1995.

Hansen, Mark Victor, and Robert G. Allen. *The One Minute Millionaire: The Enlightened Way to Wealth.* New York: Harmony Books/Crown Publishing Group, 2002.

Janda, Louis Ph.D. *Career Tests: 25 Revealing Self-Tests to Help You Find and Succeed at the Perfect Career.* Boston: Adams Media Corporation, 2004.

Kiyosaki, Robert. *Rich Dad, Poor Dad: What the Rich Teach Their Kids About Money That the Poor and Middle Class Don't.* New York: Warner Books, 2000.

Mackay, Harvey. *Pushing the Envelope: All the Way to the Top.* New York: Ballantine Books, 1999.

Stanley, Thomas. *The Millionaire Mind.* New York: Andrew McMeel Publishing, 2000.

Stanley, Thomas, and William Danko. *The Millionaire Next Door, The Surprising Secrets of America's Weatlhy.* New York: Pocket Books, 1999.

Sulloway, Frank J. *Born to Rebel: Birth Order, Family Dynamcs, and Creative Lives.* New York: Pantheon Books, 1996.

Article

Timmons, Jeffrey "New Venture Creation," in Larry W. Cox and S. Michael Camp, *Survey of Innovative Practices,* (Irwin McGraw-Hill, 1999, p.3).

About the Author

*F*OR NEARLY 20 YEARS, BILL WAGNER HAS BEEN AT THE FOREFRONT OF ENTREPRENEUR-ial practice and research.

He has devoted nearly all of his adult life to understanding entrepreneurs and entrepreneurship—first as a student, then as an entrepreneur, and now as a teacher.

Wagner is the co-founder and CEO of Accord Management Systems, Inc., a firm dedicated to helping executives draw logical conclusions about themselves and the people within their organizations. Working hand-in-hand with entrepreneur-focused organizations such as The Executive Committee (TEC), the Young Entrepreneur's Organization (YEO), and the International Franchise Association (IFA), Wagner is able to stay on the cutting edge of research and knowledge on entrepreneurship.

He is an expert in due diligence, mergers and acquisitions, organizational alignment, succession planning, and tactical applications such as selection, leadership development, motivation, and team building. He helps audiences and clients understand why issues exist, what to do about them, and how to fix them. Wagner calls himself an "insultant" rather than a mere consultant, and believes the difference is in the message. He rocks the boat and tells the truth, helping clients become their own organizational therapists. He focuses on questioning answers rather than answering questions.

Unlike other organizational specialists, Wagner focuses exclusively on using behavioral tools from a strategic, rather than a tactical, perspective. As a result, he is one of the most in-demand authorities on the subject today. Each year, Wagner presents to thousands of CEOs at more than 100 seminars and workshops across the country. Well over 90 percent of those who hear him speak are entrepreneurs, CEOs, or senior level executives. Widely published, his articles and interviews have appeared in such publications as *Inc.* magazine, *California CEO* magazine, *Workforce* magazine, *Wells Fargo's Business Advisor, Handbook of Business Strategy, Lodging and Hospitality, Federal Credit Union, Los Angeles Business Journal, Franchise World, The Wall Street Journal, Entrepreneur,* and *YEO's Axis* magazine.

Prior to founding Accord Management Systems, Wagner held corporate positions at Xerox, Frito-Lay, and Protection One Alarms. A graduate of Bradley University, he resides in Westlake Village, California, with his wife and co-founder of Accord Management Systems Inc., Renee, and their three children, Alex, Rebecca, and Josh.

Glossary

BRAIN DOMINANCE. The preference for right- or left-brained thinking and for conceptual or experiential thinking. (The Herrmann Brain Dominance Institute of Lake Lure, North Carolina, is a leader in this field.)

COMPLIANCE FACTOR. The measurement of the compliance factor within a personality. Are you more compliant, conservative, risk-adverse, and wanting to do things the right way, or are you more independent, strong-willed, and opinionated? The former is an example of a high level of compliance, and the latter is an example of a lower level of compliance.

DOMINANCE FACTOR. The measurement of the dominance factor within a personality. Are you more dominant, aggressive, and assertive or more accommodating, agreeable, and cooperative? The former represents a high level of dominance, and the latter represents a lower level of dominance.

EMOTIONAL INTELLIGENCE. The learned ability to understand, use, and express human emotions in a healthy and skilled manner. (We work closely with the Pluemus Company, leaders in the field of test development in this area.)

ENTREPRENEUR. French for one who undertakes. A person who assumes the organization, management, and risks of a business enterprise (*The Columbia Encyclopedia, 5th Edition*, 1993, 1221).

GENERALIST. An individual who possesses the personality characteristics of an entrepreneur. He prefers and is better at the big-picture, more strategic side of the business. He also has more dominance than compliance in his personality.

HIRED GUN. A professional manager, one who is typically hired to support the entrepreneur. The manager that is tasked with accomplishing the tactical end of the business or enforcing the desires of the entrepreneur.

INTRAPRENEUR. A person who has an entreprenurial spirit, but is still working in a corporate environment.

RELAXATION FACTOR. The measurement of the relaxation factor within a personality. Are you more relaxed, methodical, calm, and patient, or are you more driving, intense, and impatient? The former is an example of a high level of relaxation and the latter is an example of a lower level of relaxation. This measures the pace at which people work.

RISK-TAKER. The genetic predisposition toward taking risk and participating in risky activities.

SERIAL ENTREPRENEUR. A person who has started a number of business ventures. A person who may be challenged when it comes to focusing on a single issue, one who may be easily distracted but accomplishes and has a tremendous belief in himself.

SOCIABILITY FACTOR. The measurement of the sociability factor within a personality. Are you more sociable, warm, and friendly, or are you more analytical, private, and reserved? The former represents a high level of sociability, and the latter represents a lower level of sociability. It has to do with style of communication.

SPECIALIST. An individual who possesses the personality characteristics of a wantapreneur. Specialists are the experts of the world, great with detail and the tactics of the business. They have more compliance than dominance in their personality.

TEC. The Executive Committee, now Vistage International.

WANTAPRENEUR. An individual who does not possess the typical personality traits of an entrepreneur yet still desires to work in his own business. To achieve entrepreneurial success, he may have to compensate for his developmental considerations.

YEO. Young Entrepreneurs Organization, now Entrepreneurs Organization (EO).

Index

A

Author, about the, 273–274
Authority
    action items for, 115–117
    beating the odds, 251–252
    code of conduct, 233–234
    leadership style, 195–196
    learning style, 174–175
    motivation, 145–148
    personality graph, illustration of, figure 5.5,
        81–82
    personality traits of, 81–82
    selling style, 219–221
    strengths and weaknesses, 114–117
    traits of, 81–82

B

Beating the odds
    how different personality types go about,
        249–254
    making personality changes for,
        237–247

Bibliography, 271–272
Brain dominance assessments, 24–27
Branding initiative through new signage,
    258–259
Business success, 1–18
Butthead, "our," 185

C

Car choice, 10
Challenger disaster, 206
Challenges, entrepreneurs tell about their
    biggest, 244–246
Chiropractor, personalities comprising practice
    of, 219
Choice and destiny, 6–9
Clintonesque defined, 77
Closing, 213
Collaborators
    action items for, 119–120
    beating the odds, 252
    code of conduct, 234–235
    leadership style, 196–198

leadership style, illustration of "Point Easy," figure 11.4, 197

learning style, 175–176

motivation, 148–150

personality graph, illustration of, figure 5.6, 83

personality traits of, 82–84

Point Easy concept for, 197–198

selling style, 221–222

strengths and weaknesses, 118–120

traits of, 82–84

Compliance factor, 68

Consensus building, 205–207

Corporate environment, what entrepreneurs say about the, 265

Creating an organization that's just right, 255–270

D

Dating or vacation personality, illustration of, figure 6.1, 97

Defining moments, what entrepreneurs said about their, 101–105

Delegation and authority, 188

Diplomats

action items for, 121–122

beating the odds, 252–253

code of conduct, 235–236

leadership style, 198–199

learning style, 176–177

motivation, 150–152

personality graph, illustration of, figure 5.7, 85

selling style, 222–223

strengths and weaknesses, 120–122

traits of, 84–85

DNA of entrepreneurial success, 93–100

Dominance

factor, 64–65

in action, 262

Drive, 131–153

E

Education, 157–160, 203–209

and experience, 157–167

grades, illustration of, figure 9.2, 159

graduation rates, illustration of, figure 9.1, 158

time spent on personal development and, illustration of, figure 12.1, 204

Emotional insight into self, 32–33

Emotional intelligence (EQ)

and role it plays in business, 31–32

expression as critical aspect of, 242–243

how to increase, 34

knowledge and behavior aspects of, 32–34

measuring, 27

sample entrepreneur survey result, illustration of, figure 2.3, 31–32

skills and characteristics, 27–31

Emotions, ability to express, 33

Empathy, 33–34

Engagement survey

and training program solution for early childhood center franchisees, 259–262

franchise, 258–259

midwest manufacturer, 259

of leading franchisor, illustration of, figure 17.3, 260

Entrepreneur

illustration of ideal, figure 2.2, 26

next door, who is it?, 5–6

Entrepreneurial

elements, illustration of, figure 2.1, 25

profile, illustration of, figure 3.1, 42–49

profile, putting the results into perspective, 49–61

Entrepreneurship, personality factors and, 85–91

Experience
    age when first started business, illustration of, figure 9.3, 161
    background, 162–163
    job fit, 163–165
    occupation of entrepreneur's father, illustration of, figure 9.4, 163
    the best salespeople, illustration of, figure 9.5, 164
    what entrepreneurs said about surprise business challenges, 166–167
    what entrepreneurs say they've learned from their, 165–166

F

Family business, educated "out' of, 243
Friction between departments, 207

G

Glossary, 275–277
Go-Getter
    action items for, 108–110
    and Authority partnership, 220
    beating the odds, 250–251
    code of conduct, 229–230
    leadership style, 191–192
    learning style, 171–172
    motivation, 138–139
    personality graph, illustration of, figure 5.2, 76
    strengths and weaknesses, 108–110
    selling style, 215–216
    traits of, 75–77
Goal orientation or motivation, 33, 241–242
Goldilocks theory, the, 255–270
Greatest business challenges, what entrepreneurs say, 267–269

H

Headliners, 4
Herman Brain Dominance Institute (HBDI), 24–27

entrepreneurial elements measured by, 25
ideal entrepreneur, measured by, 26–27
How to succeed in business the first time, 1–18
Humor, 95

I

Ideal entrepreneur, illustration of, figure 2.2, 26
In their own words, what entrepreneurs say about
    advice, 207–208
    corporate environments, 265
    defining moments in their personal lives, 133–135
    leadership, 188–189
    starting a business, 34–38, 68–70
    surprise business challenges, 166–167
    their biggest challenges, 244–246
    their greatest business challenges, 267–269
    what sets their company apart, 266
    what they must accomplish before retirement, 269–270
    what they've learned from their experience, 165–166

J

Jerry Maguire, "show me the money," 213

K

Knowledge is power, 203–209

L

Leaders
    and specific personality styles, 190–199
    effectiveness of in your organization, 180–184
    effectiveness of in your organization, illustration of, figure 11.3, 183
    single most important experience in preparing to be entrepreneurial, 188–189

Leadership
  and management, 179–201
  examining from a personality perspec-
    tive, 17
  how specific personality styles lead,
    190–199
  skills, growing, 184–188
Learning, 169–177
Lessons learned, 133
Long-term personality, 99

M

Male and female entrepreneurs
  comparing traits of, 86–91
  deviation in the McQuaig system, illus-
    tration of, figure 5.10, 89
  distribution of word survey profiles, illus-
    tration of, figure 5.8, 87
  female *vs.* male entrepreneur graphs,
    illustration of, figure 5.9, 87
  YEO chart of personality types illustra-
    tion of, figure 5.11, 90
Managers
  action items for, 110–112
  beating the odds, 251
  code of conduct, 230–231
  leadership style, 192–194
  learning style, 172–173
  motivation, 139–142
  personality graph, illustration of, figure
    5.3, 78
  selling style, 216–217
  strengths and weaknesses, 110–112
  traits of, 77–79
Marketing
  definition of, 211
  example of path-of-least-resistance, 215
Master franchise case study
  employee job fit, 256–258
  employee job fit, illustration of, figure
    17.1, 257

Master franchisee case study, average ticket
  size, illustration of, figure 17.2, 258
McQuaig System, the, 23
Measuring people *vs.* organizations, 19–21
Millionaire Next Door, the
  as book's genesis, 5–6
  prodigious savers vs. entrepreneurs,
    10–11
Motivators
  actions items for, 113–114
  beating the odds, 251
  code of conduct, 231–233
  in action, 232
  leadership style, 194–195
  learning style, 173–174
  motivation, 142–144
  personality graph, illustration of, figure
    5.4, 80
  selling style, 218–219
  strengths and weaknesses, 112–114
  traits of, 79–81
Mottoes, entrepreneur's favorite business, 22

N

Now what?, 263–264

P

People factors, 180–184
  illustration of, figure 11.2, 180
Performance Pyramid
  climbing the, 11–18
  illustration of, figure 1.1, 11
  tier I, entrepreneurial personality ele-
    ments, illustration of, figure 1.3, 14
  tier I, personality factors, 12–14
  tier I, personality factors, illustration of,
    figure 1.2, 13
  tier II, job behaviors, 14–15
  tier III, actions, 15–16
  tier IV, metrics, 16
  tier V, results, 17

Personal Action Plan
    illustration of, developmental areas, figures 7.2, 7.4, 125–126, 128–129
    illustration of, strengths, figures 7.1, 7.3, 123–125, 127–128
Personality
    as paving way to success, 19–40
    behavioral studies, 22–23
    benefits of understanding, 94–96
    changes, short-term, 96–99
    changes, short-term illustrated in dating or vacation, 96–99
    factors and entrepreneurship, 85–91
    find the long-term, 99
    studies as model of predictability, strategic understanding and tool for succession, 186
    testing, history of, 21–23
    the four factors, 64–68
    types, 73–91
    why?, 21–23
Poor performance, putting up with, 183–184
Prospecting, 213

R

References, checking, 21
Relaxation factor, 66–67
Retirement, what entrepreneurs say they must accomplish before, 269–270
Risk, different definitions of, 9

S

Sales, 211–223
    terms/insider jargon, 212–213
Self sabotage, avoiding, 27
Self-knowledge as greatest knowledge, 9–11
Selling, 211–223
Situation and challenge
    I, 256–258
    II, 258–259
    III, 259

IV, 259–262
V, 262
VI, 263
Sociability factor, 65–66
Social insight, 33–34
    and empathy, 243–244
Sound advice, what entrepreneurs said about, 207–208
Steps for you the reader to take after taking survey on www.entrepreneurnext door.com, 263–264
Store manager position, examining performance levels of two personality types in making hiring decisions, 363
Success
    DNA of entrepreneurial, 93–100
    or failure, determinants of, 23–24
    your personality can pave the way to, 19–40
Surprise business challenges, 179–180
    illustration of, figure 11.1, 180

T

Telemarketing organization, personality testing to correct hiring practices of HR manager with Authoritarian personality, 262
Tools, tests, surveys and assessments, 24–31
Trailblazer
    action items for, 107
    beating the odds, 250
    carving out a niche, 106
    code of conduct, 228
    leadership style, 190–191
    learning style, 170–171
    motivation, 135–137
    on the wrestling team, 24
    personality graph, illustration of, figure 5.1, 74
    selling style, 214–215
    strengths and weaknesses, 105–107

traits of, 74–75

Triumphs and tragedies, 101–129

Turning developmental considerations into
strengths, 238–241

V

Vacation time and type, 10–11

W

Web site, reader survey at www.entrepreneur
nextdoor.com, 263

What entrepreneurs say sets their company
apart, 266

What makes different personality types tick
and what ticks them off, 227–236

Who are *you?*, 41–61